The Women of Helfta

The Women of Helfta

Scholars and Mystics

Mary Jeremy Finnegan, O.P.

The University of Georgia Press

Athens and London

© 1991 by the University of Georgia Press
Athens, Georgia 30602
All rights reserved
Designed by Mary Mendell
Set in Trump Medieval
Typeset by Tseng Information Systems, Inc.
Printed and bound by Thomson-Shore
The paper in this book meets the guidelines for permanence and
durability of the Committee on Production Guidelines for Book
Longevity of the Council on Library Resources.
Printed in the United States of America
95 94 93 92 91   5 4 3 2 1
Library of Congress Cataloging in Publication Data
Finnegan, Mary Jeremy, 1907–
The women of Helfta : scholars and mystics / Mary Jeremy Finnegan.
p. cm.
Rev. ed. of: Scholars and mystics. 1962.
Includes bibliographical references.
ISBN 0-8203-1291-6 (alk. paper)
1. Gertrude, the Great, Saint, 1256–1302. 2. Mechthild, of
Magdeburg, ca. 1212–ca. 1282. 3. Mechthild, of Hackeborn, 1241 or
42–1299? 4. Helfta (Convent : Eisleben, Germany) 5. Nuns—
Germany (West)—Eisleben—Biography. 6. Mystics—Germany
(West)—Eisleben—Biography. 7. Eisleben (Germany)—Church
history. 8. Eisleben (Germany)—Biography.
I. Finnegan, Mary Jeremy, 1907–   Scholars and mystics. II. Title.
BX4667.F55 1991   271'.97—dc20
                                                    [B] 90-39089 CIP
British Library Cataloging in Publication Data available

An earlier edition of this work was published under the title
Scholars and Mystics (Henry Regnery, 1962).

For my Sisters

Contents

Preface *ix*

List of Abbreviations *xi*

1 Helfta *1*

2 The Women of Helfta *11*

3 "The Nightingale of Christ" *26*

4 The *Book of Special Grace* *44*

5 From the Land of Unlikeness: Gertrude the Great *62*

6 The Writings of Gertrude *81*

7 Gertrude in Her Community *98*

8 Aspects of Gertrude's Spirituality *113*

9 Veneration of the Sacred Heart *131*

10 The Death of Gertrude *144*

Notes *151*

Bibliography *161*

Index *169*

Preface

UCH of the current interest in medieval women mystics has focused on the three mystics of the Saxon monastery of Helfta: Gertrude the Great (1256–1301/2), Mechtild of Hackeborn (1241/2–1298), and Mechtild of Magdeburg (1207?–1282). The writings of these women provide not only a firsthand account of mystical experience but a revelation of character and personality. Moreover, they portray in graphic detail the thirteenth-century milieu in which the community, while contending with difficulties and challenges, maintained an atmosphere where art and learning, courtesy and holiness flourished during one of the stormiest periods of German history. A remarkable abbess, Gertrude of Hackeborn (not to be confused with Gertrude the Great, a member of the community), is responsible for the spiritual and intellectual eminence of the monastery.

"Every monastery has its own history, and many sweeping statements about medieval monasticism are based on inadequate knowledge."[1] Fortunately, information about Helfta is available: charters and other legal documents testify to the relations of the community with benefactors as well as to actual and projected foundations. Of even greater interest is the image of the community supplied by the writings from Helfta: the *Legatus divinae pietatis* (The Messenger of God's Loving Kindness), written in part by Gertrude of Helfta and in part by an anonymous contemporary "compilatrix" who lived in the same convent; Gertrude's *Exercitia* (Spiritual Exercises); the *Liber specialis gratiae* (Book of Special Grace), which treats of Mechtild of Hackeborn, written by Gertrude and several other nuns; and Mechtild of Magdeburg's *Das fliessende Licht der Gottheit* (The Flowing Light of Divinity).

These writings furnish a composite picture not only of the three mystics but of the community in which they were active and influential members. At Helfta a familial atmosphere witnessed to "the grace of a common life."[2] The monastery school attracted not only pupils and their parents but also many visitors who came to seek counsel from the nuns. Dominican friars from Halle came to instruct and preach to the community. Some of these friars also sought spiritual direction from Gertrude of Helfta and Mechtild of Hackeborn. At times the numerous guests became burdensome to both nuns; Gertrude once took to her bed "to escape the tumult of visitors."[3] In spite of such distractions and the threat of hostile invasions, it appears that the stability of monastic life, sustained by common prayer and contemplation, accounts for the basically serene atmosphere of Helfta.

The *Legatus divinae pietatis* and the *Liber specialis gratiae* provide a corrective to some stereotypes of medieval women. Although physical fragility and illness are acknowledged and accepted, there is no hint of intellectual inferiority or subordinate status. An identity crisis was not among their afflictions.

The present work, an extensive revision of *Scholars and Mystics* (Chicago: Regnery, 1962), utilizes recent critical texts and contemporary scholarship. I am indebted to Gertrud Jaron Lewis, Mary Clemente Davlin, O.P., and Massimila Wilczynski for most generous assistance. Sister Florence Marie Gerdes, C.S.J., Helen Florence North, and Margaret Kocher, O.P. have kindly shared their expertise. Jerome Heyman, O.P., the staff of the Rosary College Library, and in particular, Corinne Stich, have provided help in securing materials. I owe special thanks to Mary Arlowe, Director of Academic Computing, whose skill and patience are equal to all demands.

Abbreviations

DS Dictionnaire de spiritualité, ascétique et mystique, doctrine et histoire. 14 vols. and fascicle. Paris: Beauchesne, 1937–. References are to volume and column.

DTC Dictionnaire de théologie catholique. 15 vols. Paris: Letouzey, 1909–50. References are to volume and column.

Ex. Gertrude d'Helfta. *Les Exercices.* Vol. 1 of *Oeuvres Spirituelles.* Edited by Jacques Hourlier and Albert Schmitt. Sources chrétiennes 127. Paris: Editions du Cerf, 1967. References are to exercise number and line.

Leg. Gertrude d'Helfta. *Le Héraut* [Legatus divinae pietatis]. Vol. 2 of *Oeuvres Spirituelles.* Edited by Pierre Doyère. Sources chrétiennes 139. Paris: Editions du Cerf, 1968. References are to book, chapter, and section.

Licht Mechtild of Magdeburg. *Das fliessende Licht der Gottheit.* Translated and edited by Margot Schmidt. Einsiedeln: Benziger, 1956. References are to book and section.

Livre Mechtild of Hackeborn. *Le Livre de la Grâce Spéciale: Révélations de Sainte Mechtilde Vierge de l'Ordre de St. Benoit.* Translated by nuns of Wisques, from the Latin edition of Solesmes. Tours: Mame, 1928. References are to book, chapter, and page.

NCE *New Catholic Encyclopedia.* New York: McGraw-Hill, 1967.

Par. Dante Alighieri. *Dante's Paradiso.* Italian text with English translation and comment by John Sinclair. New York: Oxford University Press, 1961. References are to canto.

PL *Patrologia cursus completus: series latina.* Edited by J.-P. Migne. 221 vols. Paris, 1841–64. References are to volume and column.

Purg.   Dante Alighieri. *Dante's Purgatorio.* Italian text with English translation and comment by John D. Sinclair. New York: Oxford University Press, 1961. References are to canto.

Rev.   *Revelationes Gertrudianae ac Mechtildianae.* Vol. 1, *Exercitia; Legatus divinae pietatis.* Vol. 2, *Liber specialis gratiae; Documenta.* Edited by monks of Solesmes [Louis Paquelin]. Poitiers-Paris, 1875, 1877. References are to volume and page.

1 Helfta

THE monastery of St. Mary at Helfta in northern Saxony was at once representative and outstanding among thirteenth-century religious houses. Called "the crown of German cloisters" and set in a place of great natural beauty, it was not only a center of literary and artistic culture but a school of spirituality as well.[1] During its flowering, three mystics lived at Helfta: Gertrude the Great; her friend and mentor, Mechtild of Hackeborn; and the former Beguine, Mechtild of Magdeburg. Founded in 1229 within the castle precincts of Mansfeld and later transferred to Rodarsdorf, the community had finally settled at Helfta near Eisleben. Here it acquired its reputation for learning and culture. This period of renown began in 1251 with the election of the Abbess Gertrude of Hackeborn and ended in approximately 1302 with the death of her namesake, Gertrude the Great, last and most famous of the three mystics of Helfta.

The subsequent history of the community is a troubled one. The invasion of Helfta by Albert of Brunswick in 1342 brought about another change of location when the community was transferred to Eisleben, or "new" Helfta.[2] Since 1959 the ruins of the convent church at "old" Helfta have been protected as historical monuments.

From its beginnings the community was distinguished by the religious fervor of its lay benefactors as well as of its members. Two anecdotes illustrate the reputation of its founders, Elisabeth of Schwartzburg and her husband, Burchard, count of Mansfeld. On one occasion after the death of her husband, the countess went on a pilgrimage to Marburg to visit the tomb of her patron saint, Elisabeth of Hungary. Among the throngs crowding at the grave was a poor man carrying an afflicted child who apparently had been born without eyes. Not knowing who the countess was, he asked her to take the child to the grave while he went to the market. Elisabeth did so, praying that through the saint's intercession the child might be cured. As she prayed, she meditated penitently on the contrast between the saint's life and her own, reproaching herself for misusing her eyes to enjoy useless sights. Suddenly she heard a crackling sound "as of parchment tearing" and to her amazement saw that the skin had opened, revealing bright gray eyes. Until the end of her life, the account concludes, the child born blind had perfect vision (*Rev.* 2:717–19).

The nuns at Helfta also honored Elisabeth's husband, Count Burchard of Mansfeld, as founder and benefactor. At the annual mass offered on the anniversary of his death, Mechtild visualized him wearing a robe with the images of all the former members of the community and all who would later join it. His crown had a corresponding number of gold fleurons. On another anniversary she envisioned him in richly bejeweled garments, embroidered with the names of all his virtues. "Where did you acquire such a variety?" she asked. "Not by my own works," he replied, "but by the goodness of God and the merits of the congregation I loved so dearly." He explained to Mechtild that it was on the entry to heaven of her sister, "the magnificent and royal Abbess Gertrude," that he had been so attired (*Livre* 5.10.323; 7.20.401).

This Abbess Gertrude was the second superior of the community. In 1229 her predecessor, Cunegund of Halberstadt, "devout and Godfearing," had come with seven "grey" (i.e., Cistercian) nuns to Mansfeld, the home of the founders, Count Burchard and Elisabeth (*Rev.* 1:v). During these times of baronial wars, however, proximity to a castle was a danger rather than a protection. When Burchard died shortly after the arrival of the nuns, his widow suggested that the community move to nearby Rodarsdorf. She herself accompanied the sisters and remained with them until her death in 1240. In 1251 Cunegund was succeeded by Gertrude of Hackeborn, who, though only nineteen, had been unanimously elected. Seven years later in 1258, a shortage of water necessitated the community's second removal. The site of the new establishment was Helfta, on land given by the brothers of the abbess. The ground was gently sloping and fertile. Woods, fields, and orchards were threaded by spring-fed streams flowing into the lake of Seeburg. A company of ecclesiastics and nobles assisted at the solemn entry of the community into its new home. The guests included the two counts of Mansfeld and Querfurt, sons-in-law of Burchard; Rupert, the archbishop of Mansfeld; and Vulrad, archbishop of Halberstadt. Vulrad offered the mass and presided at the reception of several young women into the community. Among those received were Sophia and Elisabeth, granddaughters of the founders; both figure in the later history of the monastery (*Rev.* 1:vii).

Despite the patronage of noble families, life was difficult at Helfta. The rigors of the daily routine were compounded by the pressure of debts, losses by theft, and exposure to assault. These trials were intensified during the Great Interregnum, a period of anarchy and turmoil from the death of Frederick II in 1250 to the election of Rudolph of Hapsburg in 1273. The quarrels of the feudal lords continued even after the election. Many of the nuns were related to the barons, but such family ties afforded no protection; on the contrary, they subjected the community to involvement in local feuds. One of these disputes resulted in an attack against Helfta in 1284 by Gebhardt of Mansfeld, whose sister and cousin were members of the community. With a band of followers he invaded the cloister, ate meat there on Good Friday, and behaved with such violence that he was excommunicated by Pope Martin IV. Gebhardt died suddenly the next year, and at the request of his widow, Irmingarde of Schwartzburg, he was eventually buried within the monastery in the mortuary chapel built by his father. His sister Sophia was elected abbess in 1291. Three years later his son, who had bequeathed the monastery twenty-nine acres of wooded ground, was accompanied to his grave by all the nuns in solemn procession (*Rev.* 1:xiv).

Throughout such vicissitudes the Abbess Gertrude not only governed her monastery with calm fortitude but, as Josef Stierli declares, "brought it to the highest level of feminine culture known to the Middle Ages."[3] It is understandable that her death in 1291 was a calamity. The account of her last hours is filled with expressions of sorrow and affection. With loving minuteness her namesake, the younger Gertrude, writes that she had governed her monastery "for forty years and eleven days" when she was attacked by her last illness (*Leg.* 5.1.1).[4]

The successor of the Abbess Gertrude was Sophia of Mansfeld. During her incumbency the war between Adolph of Nassau and his rivals devastated Thuringia. A detail in the life of Mechtild of Hackeborn shows how the members of the community were involved in the disorders of the time. A lady who feared for her husband, knowing that his enemies were planning to ambush him and keep him captive until their prisoners were released, begged Mechtild to pray for him. She did so and received a consoling answer which reassured the lady. When she again asked prayers for her husband's protection from his numerous enemies, Mechtild told her, "He will go through much more adversity and peril, but the Savior will preserve him from captivity and serious injury" (*Livre* 5.30.354).

The nuns were themselves exposed to trials, some at the hands of clergy. The interdict of 1296 is an example. (This ecclesiastical penalty excludes an individual or community from participation in certain church functions.) The interdict was imposed on the nuns at Helfta during the fifth year of Sophia of Mansfeld's term as abbess. The exact reason is not known. Mechtild says that while the see of Halberstadt was vacant, the canons of the cathedral placed an interdict upon the community, "greatly afflicting it on account of certain pecuniary matters" (*Livre* 1.27.94, cf. *Leg.* 3.16.1). This would imply that the financial problems of the convent became more numerous. The writings of Gertrude and Mechtild record the grief of the nuns at the silencing of organ and chant, the deprivation of mass and the sacraments.

In 1298, because of poor health, the Abbess Sophia resigned her office and an interregnum of five years followed, after which Jutta of Halberstadt was elected (*Rev.* 1:xiv). During this interregnum the community lost its most outstanding member, Gertrude the Great, who died in 1301/2 at the age of forty-five.

In 1342 Albert of Brunswick invaded Helfta with a large army. He had been elected to the episcopacy of Halberstadt, but the Holy See did not confirm his election. Instead, the Pope suggested as suitable alternates Giselbert of Holzsac, first, and then Albert of Mansfeld. When the latter was confirmed by the Holy See as bishop of Halberstadt, his sister Luitgard was abbess at Helfta. The would-be bishop, Albert of Brunswick, stormed the convent and with his own hand set fire to it, while his men broke into the cloister to destroy vestments, books, ornaments, and everything else they could find. Louis Paquelin prints a Latin transcription of verses lamenting the calamity of the disputed election and the destruction of the monastery. Four years later, in 1346, Burchard IV of Mansfeld, father of the Abbess Luitgard, transferred the community to Eisleben, its fourth and last site. The exodus occurred on the feast of St. Severin, when the mass *Da pacem* is sung (*Rev.* 1:xxv).[5]

Little is known of the nuns of Helfta from their transfer to Eisleben until 1451 when Sophia of Stolberg, the abbess, compiled some notes on the history of her community. In them she mentions that she drew her information "from our chronicle and from our own certain knowledge." Unfortunately, the cloister record is lost, and according to Heinrich Grössler, her notes cannot be accepted as wholly reliable.[6]

Approximately fifty years later, about 1500, a reform of the rule was introduced under the auspices of the Abbess Catherine of Watzdorff. It was this abbess whom Luther castigated in a pamphlet, published in 1524, calling her "a second Jezebel." His pamphlet tells of the "miraculous escape" of a young nun, Florentina, who fled from the convent to Wittenberg to join the Lutherans. The fury of the peasants against the monastery at the time of their revolt in 1525 is thought to have been inspired by this work. They attacked and pillaged New Helfta, throwing the books and manuscripts of the monastery into beer vats. The Abbess Catherine fled to Old Helfta where she died soon afterward. According to Louis Paquelin, the Solesmes editor of the writings of Gertrude the Great and Mechtild of Hackeborn (*Revelationes Gertrudianae ac Mechtildianae*), it is not known whether Catherine had a successor; Grössler however names two: Anna of Watzdorff and Walberg Reubert. With the intrusion of a heretical prelate in 1546, the religious community of Gertrude and Mechtild became extinct (*Rev.* 1:xxxii).[7]

More than three hundred years later, on 17 November 1868, the feast day of St. Gertrude the Great, the buildings of New Helfta were purchased for the foundation of the Benedictine monastery of Trud Helfta, named for the saint. Mother St. Michael (Elisabeth Falger), the prioress, together with a group of nuns from the convent of Osnabruck, took possession of the property. The Catholic residents of Eisleben had assisted in the restoration of the monastery, but all the citizens gave the nuns a cordial welcome. Severe hardships awaited the community, however. Soon after the establishment in Eisleben, the prioress, Mother St. Michael, was stricken by paralysis and died on 13 July 1873 (*Rev.* 1:xxxvi). A year later the May Laws of 1874 brought new trials. These enactments were part of the Kulturkampf, the contention between the German imperial government and the Catholic church over religious training and ecclesiastical appointments. The May Laws deprived the community of their property, and it was not till 1890 that the site could be repurchased for the construction of a church dedicated to St. Gertrude. According to Father Walter, the acting curate of the parish of Eisleben-Helfta, relics of St. Gertrude may be buried under the foundation of this church in the Klosterplatz of Eisleben. Dean Westerman, the builder, had a large structure razed but found no trace of the saint's body. It is not known whether the nuns who left Helfta brought the relics with them. The actual site of the cemetery at Helfta is unknown. In 1916 some of the buildings at Old Helfta were still standing. What had been the convent church, however, had been made into a granary, the roof and vaulting removed and many of the lancet windows blocked up. Today Sunday mass is offered in an evangelical church for the Catholics who live in the area.[8]

Helfta's "golden age" began with the election of the Abbess Gertrude of Hackeborn in 1251. During her long term of office the community attained a high degree of culture and spirituality. As noted earlier, the original foundation was made by Cistercian nuns in 1229. The General Chapter of 1228 had forbidden the foundation and direction of communities of nuns. It did not, however, object to the adoption of the Cistercian rule and customs by unaffiliated convents. It appears that Helfta must have been essentially autonomous. Evidently this independence accounts for the free adoption of Cistercian customs.[9] Both Gertrude of Helfta and Mechtild of Hackeborn refer to Benedict as "holy father," the title given to a founder.

The nuns at Helfta were unquestionably influenced by the Friars Preachers. The proximity of the Dominican convents of Halle and Magdeburg makes it more than likely that they were the usual preachers at Helfta. Under papal order and later, in 1256, by ruling of the Chapter of Florence, the friars were required to act as the spiritual directors not only of Dominican nuns but of the members of the other orders as well. Greatly outnumbered by their charges and impeded in their studies by this obligation, the Dominicans made many efforts to be relieved of this duty. They were briefly successful in 1252 when Innocent III granted their request, but two years later he withdrew his permission. The Chapter of Florence also confirmed this obligation. Moreover, Herman of Minden, Provincial of the Friars Preachers from 1286 to 1290, recommended that learned friars be chosen as the directors of well-educated nuns. Heinrich Denifle sees an important connection between the rise of mysticism in Germany and the papal order enjoining the Friars Preachers to assume the spiritual direction of women.[10] According to Jeanne Ancelet-Hustache, "The Friars Preachers knew how to direct these intelligent women and to develop their inclination to contemplation." She asserts that through the Friars' instruction, the nuns were introduced to the interpretation of the Scriptures and to the writings of the Fathers and Doctors of the Church.[11]

The sermons heard by the nuns at Helfta must have been basically Thomistic in content since the General Chapter of 1278 had imposed the teachings of Thomas Aquinas on all Dominicans. Mechtild of Hackeborn's tribute to Thomas and Albert the Great suggests a thorough familiarity with both; neither had yet been canonized (*Livre* 5.9.322–23). It was probably a Dominican who preached the sermon that inspired Gertrude to ask for the wound of divine love. This episode will be recounted in a later chapter.

Many passages in the writings of Gertrude and Mechtild reflect the daily life of the hard-working community. In a household which numbered more than one hundred members the amount of manual work was considerable. A passage in Mechtild's *Liber* expresses the attitude toward such labor: "No virtue will be judged meritorious unless ennobled by the exercise of manual labors" (*Livre* 2.38.182). All the nuns undertook such work as spinning and ordinary household duties. The abbess was often the first at work. Realistic scenes of homely domestic activity pervade the writings from Helfta. Many such images occur in Gertrude's comparisons. These "similitudes," as she calls them, will be discussed in a later chapter.

In the busy life of the monastery even the hours spent in the chapel were seldom undisturbed. Mechtild speaks compassionately of the overburdened portress, who was frequently summoned from mass to attend to guests. She told her, as from Christ, "Every step taken in obedience is like a coin put into my hand, increasing her sum of merits" (*Livre* 3.45.243). Care of the sick was a duty of frequent occurrence in the large community; Gertrude is said to have overtaxed her strength in her devotion to the sick. Apparently the nuns received some professional care; she refers several times to the skill of doctors in restoring health through potions. Bloodletting was a regular practice, usually taking place in the spring (*Leg.* 3.65.3).

The importance of music in the monastic life at Helfta is evident.

Mechtild's *Liber* contains numerous references to melody, both earthly and heavenly. In the Rule of St. Benedict many chapters deal with the proper performance of the daily choral recitation of the psalms, hymns, and readings that constitute the Divine Office, the *opus Dei*. In addition to this religious exercise, it was the custom at Helfta as at Cluny to recite additional psalms which greatly prolonged the Office. These *psalmi familiares* were said in choir at the beginning or end of each canonical hour. Evidently at Helfta certain of these special psalms were assigned to one nun who said them outside the hours of Office either by herself or with several others. The Offices of the Trinity, of the Virgin Mary, and of the saints were recited as private devotions. Among the hymns mentioned in Gertrude's writings are *Jesu nostra redemptio, Rex Christi factor omnium, O Crux ave, Gloria laus, Veni Creator, Quem terra pontus aethera*, and several stanzas of *Jesu dulcis memoria*. When she speaks of the *Ave stella maris*, she is probably referring to the hymn now known as the *Ave Maris Stella*. It was the custom to "farce" certain psalms by adding prayers after each verse. This was done with the *Benedicite* when the community was fearing an armed attack. For the souls of the dead the nuns recited the Great Psalter, which is also a "farced" arrangement of the psalms with long prayers after each one. Gertrude once asked why this Psalter was advantageous to the souls of the dead, for it seemed to her that the exceedingly long prayers caused more weariness than devotion. She was given to understand that Christ's intense desire for the deliverance of these souls led him to release great numbers of them from Purgatory when the Great Psalter was recited (*Leg.* 5.18.1–2).[12]

There is little evidence of any notable lack of fervor among the nuns at Helfta. Mechtild speaks of slothfulness in attending a solemn service (*Livre* 3.14.206). Gertrude once fell asleep at mass and was awakened by the bell at the elevation of the host (*Leg.* 3.15.1). The association of the nuns with noble families—relatives of the sisters and their pupils—may have led to some excessive interest in "worldly affairs." Gertrude and Mechtild show minute knowledge of social customs and ceremonies. Although the usual mediocrities probably impaired the dedication of the community, the general impression of Helfta is that of an orderly conventual household.

Although common prayers and the necessary activities of the monastery occupied several hours of each day, the community at Helfta also spent much time in study and teaching. That both Gertrude and Mechtild were teachers is clear from many passages in their writings. Gertrude calls her friend "an incomparable teacher" (*Livre* 5.30.352).

Since the time of Boniface and his disciple Lioba, abbess of Bischofsheim in Mainz, more than five centuries earlier, a strong tradition of education for women had developed in Germany. Of Lioba it is recorded that during her midday rest she would correct the mispronunciations of the novices who read the Latin Scriptures to her. She would never permit the nuns to stay up late because "lack of sleep dulls the mind, especially for study."[13] German women notable for intellectual achievement include the tenth-century canoness, Hrosvitha of Gandersheim, whose didactic dramas are patterned on the comedies of Terence. The twelfth-century Alsatian abbess, Herrad of Hohenbourg, compiled the *Hortus Deliciarum*, an encyclopedia of the Christian faith, including articles on astronomy, natural history, and philosophy. The accompanying illustrations, either by Herrad herself or made under her supervision, are, according to George Sarton, "a real encyclopedia of Christian iconography."[14] The best-known of these learned German nuns is Hildegard of Bingen, mystic and writer, famed as a pioneer in science, a poet, dramatist, and musician. Her *Scivias* describes twenty-six visions illustrating the relations of God and humankind through creation, redemption, and the Church.

Priests and monks could study, but many laymen, engaged in the numerous armed conflicts of the time, were deprived of the opportunity. The education of cloistered nuns was comparable to that of the clergy and in some instances superior. Bound by rule to choral prayer and spiritual reading, they had to be skilled in chant and have some knowledge of Latin. Hildegard carried on an extensive correspondence with ecclesiastics. Citations in monastic literature show familiarity with the authors of classical antiquity. Hrosvitha calls herself a pupil of Terence.

The sound education provided by the monastic schools helped to raise the level of intellectual life outside the convent since many girls who did not become nuns were educated by them. According to Franz Specht, novices were ordinarily instructed in the courses of the trivium—grammar, rhetoric, and logic. It was not unusual for them to advance to the quadrivium—arithmetic, geometry, astronomy, and music.[15] Gertrude, Mechtild, and their unnamed amanuenses are competent in grammar and rhetoric. It is clear that theology was included in the curriculum; the orthodoxy of Gertrude's writings is unquestioned.

In addition to study and teaching, the copying of manuscripts occupied some of the nuns. According to G. H. Putnam, "It is difficult to estimate the extent of the services rendered by feminine hands to learning and to history throughout the Middle Ages. They brought to the work a dexterity, an elegance of attainment, and an assiduity which the monks themselves could not attain, and some of the most beautiful specimens of calligraphy which have been preserved from the Middle Ages are the work of nuns."[16] The eleventh-century nun Diemude (or Diemudis) of Weissenbrun in Bavaria, scribe and calligrapher, copied a large number of books, including five missals, two Bibles, many homilies, and extracts from the Fathers of the Church.[17] Abbo of Fleury associates the work of the copyist with prayer and fasting as a means of mortification.[18] A weary scribe at St. Gall wrote: *Tres digiti scribunt, totum corpus laborat* (three fingers write and the whole body labors).[19] The best use of the hands, says Mechtild of Hackeborn, is to raise them in prayer or to write (*Livre* 3.48.245). The younger Gertrude was perhaps the most scholarly member of the community at Helfta, but the nun who wrote her biography (book 1 of the *Legatus*) is evidently a scholar as well—she quotes Bede, Augustine, Jerome, Bernard, Gregory, and Hugh (Richard) of St. Victor.

It should not be forgotten that the nuns carried on the steady pursuit of learning and sanctity despite the distractions inseparable from conducting a school, the pressure of acute financial difficulties, and periods of grave danger when marauding barons threatened the monastery. It is largely owing to the calm stability of the nuns under the leadership of their second abbess, Gertrude of Hackeborn, that Helfta reached and maintained its intellectual and spiritual eminence.

2 The Women of Helfta

ERTRUDE of Hackeborn, abbess and countess, ruled the community for forty years. She had been elected in 1251 while the nuns were still at Rodarsdorf. After the move to Helfta, she continued to govern the community until her death in 1291. During her long abbacy she was able to impress her ideals on a community numbering more than one hundred members (*Leg.* 5.1.2). The character and personality of the abbess inspired so much confidence that many of the distinguished families of the region sent their daughters to her to be educated. Important names—Mansfeld, Querfurt, and Stolberg—appear in surviving documents. The abbess herself and her sister Mechtild belonged to a prominent family, the barons of Hackeborn and lords of Wippra. The site of the family estate near Halberstadt is still known by its ancient name although the line became extinct in the fifteenth century (*Rev.* 1:vi).[1]

In addition to the abbess and her sister, other members of the family joined the community. In a panegyric of the Abbess Gertrude it is said that her affectionate kindness toward all the sisters was so great that an observer could hardly discover which sisters were related to her. She showed the same affection to the children in the monastery school, and they loved her dearly. Her sister Mechtild writes, "She was gentle and indulgent with the little ones, holy and discreet with the young, wise and kind with the old" (*Livre* 6.1.361, 363). At the same time, the Abbess Gertrude maintained a high level of intellectual achievement among her charges. Free from any morbid distrust of learning, she was known to say that if the study of letters should be neglected, soon the Scriptures would no longer be understood and monastic life would begin to decay (*Livre* 6.1.362). This conviction reflects the belief of St. Gregory: "The devils know well that the knowledge of profane literature helps us to understand sacred scripture."[2] The abbess spared no effort to obtain books and insisted that all the nuns, particularly the younger and less knowledgeable, be diligent in their studies. She shared Bernard of Clairvaux's ideal: "God forbid that we should think the bride has been admonished on the grounds of ignorance of God, for she has been gifted not merely with great knowledge of him who is both her Bridegroom and God, but with his friendship and familiar intercourse."[3]

The abbess was also a prudent manager, utilizing to the full the resources of Helfta. Many benefactions were recorded during her long term of office.[4] Her solicitude extended to a second convent that she founded at Hedersleben, where in 1253, only two years after her election, she sent twelve nuns from Rodarsdorf. A gift of land from her brothers, Louis and Albert, had made this foundation possible. The charter of the new convent states that the provost Otto, the Abbess Gertrude, and the chapter of the community pledge themselves willingly to readmit "our beloved sisters" if at any time the pressure of poverty or the destruction of the property at Hedersleben should make such a return desirable. The troubled times in which the document was drawn up—it is dated 1262, nine years after the new foundation—make such a precaution understandable.[5]

Because of the similarity of names, the abbess has sometimes been mistakenly identified with the younger nun, Gertrude the Great, a member of her community. For many years the Roman breviary perpetuated the error in the commemoration of the feast of St. Gertrude. The saint's birthplace, which is actually unknown, was also incorrectly given as Eisleben in the second nocturn of her feast. This confusion of the saint with her abbess recalls the sardonic French expression "to lie like a second nocturn." In recent editions of the Roman breviary the error is corrected. Gerard Manley Hopkins, misled by the 1865 English translation of Gertrude's *Legatus*, writes in "The Wreck of the Deutschland": "Gertrude, lily, and Luther, are two of a town."[6] The confusion between the saint and her abbess has caused some writers to refer to the nun Gertrude of Helfta as a countess and some artists to depict her with the abbatial crozier.

The Abbess Gertrude maintained her concern for the nuns even in her last illness. She insisted on being carried to the bedside of another sister who was also ill, and though so weak that she was unable to speak, showed her affection and sympathy by gestures (*Leg.* 5.1.16). Since she had always been as active as her increasing corpulence would permit, she was distressed because she could no longer work with her hands. She appealed to Gertrude, who told her, "The King in his kindness never expects his chosen one to work on her own adornments, when, overwhelmed by his endearments, she takes his hand. What most pleases him is that in all circumstances she be ready to do his will" (*Leg.* 5.1.7).

When her illness interfered with the duties of her office, she wished to resign, but after consulting her namesake Gertrude, she was told that God had left her the partial use of her faculties in order that she might still govern her daughters, even to the extent of correcting those who did wrong. It grieved her to see the sisters tiring themselves in her care when there was no hope of her recovery. Gertrude told her as from Christ, "Let her rejoice that I make use of her to increase their merits, for I regard as done for myself all the services she receives and all the love shown to her by even a single word" (*Leg.* 5.1.8, 9, 11).

The abbess died in 1291 after a five-month illness—"minor apoplexy," according to the *Legatus*. After her death the younger Gertrude visualized her in glory, holding a lily and other flowers in one hand and with the other leading the spirits of all the members of the community who had preceded her in death (*Leg.* 5.1.32). Her sister Mechtild also saw the spirits of the community, both sisters and lay brothers (*conversi*), circling the abbess in a joyful dance and singing *O mater nostra*. It seemed that Christ showed compassion for the bereaved nuns as the abbess offered him their tears in a golden chalice. This tribute was a reward for her vigilance and discretion in governing (*Livre* 6.9.376). In fact, the nuns' grief was largely caused by fear that after her death, religious observance would be less perfect (*Leg.* 5.1.28, 29).

In Mechtild's *Liber* it is said that her sister, the Abbess Gertrude of Hackeborn, was one of two abbesses—Cunegund of Halberstadt, her predecessor, was the other—who received a particular reward because none of those in their charge had been lost (*Livre* 5.10.323).

Of more enduring fame than their abbess are the three mystics of Helfta—Gertrude the Great, Mechtild of Hackeborn, and Mechtild of Magdeburg. Although not canonized, Mechtild of Magdeburg has through her writings contributed to the reputation of the convent that became her final home. Her book, *Das fliessende Licht der Gottheit* (The Flowing Light of the Godhead), is important to students of mysticism and of medieval literature. Many others are attracted by Mechtild's personality as well as by her vigorous and lyrical style.

Born about 1207 in the archbishopric of Magdeburg, Mechtild was, she says, the best loved of her family, members of the ruling class (*Licht* 4.2).[7] She mentions the rich apparel of friends and relatives (*Licht* 7.27). When she was twelve, she received a "greeting" from the Holy Spirit, which was repeated daily for thirty-one years. This experience filled her with sorrow, love, and the desire to be treated with contempt. At the age of twenty-three she left her family in order to give herself to God without distraction. For forty years she lived as a Beguine in the city of Magdeburg.[8]

The word Beguine is derived from the name of Lambert le Bègue, a priest of Liège, who counseled women to live in community and minister to the sick and the poor. These women were not cloistered nor were they obliged to bring a dowry. In the thirteenth century Beguines were numerous—there were thousands of them in Germany alone, where the Dominicans took a special interest in them.

Although Mechtild was not without friends and admirers, her writings evoked opposition, and about 1270, worn out by age and illness, she left Magdeburg for Helfta. Because the name Mechtild occurs in the list of abbesses in the Cistercian convent of St. Agnes near Magdeburg, Fridegar Mone, writing in 1867, surmised that Mechtild might have been abbess there in 1273.[9] Lucy Menzies accepts this conjecture.[10] Other scholars have been doubtful, pointing out that the name Mechtild was so common that its occurrence in the Cistercian records may be coincidental.[11] Moreover, according to Neumann, Mechtild of Magdeburg was at Helfta from about 1270 until her death in 1282.[12]

An episode reported in the *Legatus* tells of an unnamed visitor "of great authority in matters of divine revelation" who came to Helfta because of its reputation in order to find spiritual assistance. There she conversed first with the young Gertrude and then with Mechtild of Hackeborn, sister of the abbess. Gertrude's manner was so humble that the visitor, who had come from a distance, was disappointed. She was far more impressed by her conversation with Mechtild, but realized by a spiritual intuition that Gertrude was more highly favored by God. Paquelin, editor of the Solesmes edition of the *Legatus,* suggested that the unnamed visitor might have been Mechtild of Magdeburg before her transfer to Helfta.

Pierre Doyère however, considers it unlikely because her definitive entry to Helfta took place in 1270 when Gertrude the younger was only fourteen with her first mystical experience eleven years in the future. He believes that the incident probably occurred after the death of Mechtild of Magdeburg about 1282 (*Leg.* 1.3.2, n. 1).

Before leaving Magdeburg for Helfta, Mechtild had lived for forty years in contact with many levels of society. While ministering to the poor and the sick she practiced numerous austerities. "All during my youth I warred against my body with mighty blows—sighs, tears, confessions, fasts, vigils, disciplines, and constant prayer.... These were the weapons of my soul, and with them I vigorously conquered my body. Then for twenty years I was weary, ill, and weak, first from repentance and sorrow, then from holy desire and spiritual striving. Much bodily illness followed" (*Licht* 4.2). Throughout her life Mechtild suffered from illness.

A lifelong source of support and understanding was her association with the Dominican friars who had come to Magdeburg in 1224. Her confessor, Henry of Halle, lector of Neu-Ruppin, had been a pupil of Albert the Great. Many passages in Mechtild's writings praise Dominic and his followers. Chapters on the six virtues of the saint, on how God loves the Order of Preachers (for sixteen reasons), on the continuation of the Order till the end of the world, and on the merits of individual Dominicans, reflect a strong attachment to the friars. Her brother Baldwin, who later became subprior at Halle, was probably accepted into the Order through her influence. She writes, "St. Dominic I love above all saints." "Dominic, my dear father! I have a small share in thee for which I have longed many a day" (*Licht* 4.20; 2.24). This last sentence gives some basis for the belief that Mechtild was a Dominican tertiary, a member of the third order. The Dominicans at Halle were active in disseminating the teachings of Albert the Great and Thomas Aquinas. Since the friars were the confessors at Helfta, one of them, most likely her confessor, Henry of Halle, was probably responsible for recommending her transfer to Helfta.

The years of mental and physical suffering preceding the old Beguine's removal to Helfta had left her frail and unwell. The nuns, who no doubt knew her by reputation, welcomed her. Soon after her arrival she underwent a serious illness that resulted in blindness. "Not long after I came to the convent I suffered a painful illness so that my attendants grieved over me" (*Licht* 7.4). She was distressed at the thought of her uselessness: "Lord, what shall I do in this convent?" she asked. "You shall enlighten and teach and stay here in great honor," she heard (*Licht* 7.8). Carola Sharp cites this passage as evidence of Mechtild's integration into the community at Helfta.[13] Mechtild considered herself unlearned: "My German is faulty and Latin I do not know" (*Licht* 2.3). She was abashed when the nuns sought her counsel: "Everything that you ask me for, you will find a thousandfold in your books" (*Licht* 7.21).

After her stormy years at Magdeburg, Mechtild found healing and consolation at Helfta despite her sense of uselessness. Her gratitude breaks forth in a series of exclamations:

> Thus speaks a beggarwoman: Lord, I thank you that since in your love you have taken from me all earthly riches, you now clothe and feed me through the goodness of others.... Lord, I thank you that since you have taken from me the sight of my eyes, you serve me through the eyes of others. Lord, I thank you that since you have taken from me the strength of my hands ... and the strength of my heart, you now serve me with the hands and hearts of others. Lord, I pray you for them. Reward them on earth with your divine love that they may serve you with prayer and every virtue until they come to a blessed end. (*Licht* 7.64)

While still at Magdeburg, Mechtild had been aware of the corruption and turbulence of the times. She prayed for all regions oppressed by unjust rulers, and for "all princes in Germany and elsewhere ... that they may undertake no sinful warfare" (*Licht* 6.37). When she came to Helfta she found the community deeply concerned about the dangerous situation. "I was commanded to pray most earnestly because of the trouble there now is in Saxony and Thuringia" (*Licht* 7.28). Among the wars that brought most distress to the region toward the end of the thirteenth century was the conflict between Albert of Austria and Adolph of Nassau. Villages were pillaged and churches sacked. Many passages in the writings from Helfta refer to these disorders.

There was suffering within Helfta also, and Mechtild shared in the trials of the community: "My heart is full of pity for the troubles of this community." Evidently one of the ordeals was the dissemination of slanderous reports about the nuns. "I spoke in the night in the desert of my heart to our Lord: 'Lord, how does this prison please you?' Then our Lord spoke: 'I myself am imprisoned in it.... In my perfect innocence I was beaten with them. They should not grieve about what they hear'" (*Licht* 7.53).

Despite these trials, Mechtild found friends to console her in her old age and decrepitude. Both Gertrude and Mechtild of Hackeborn speak of her admiringly, and the words of the refugee from Magdeburg testify to her appreciation as her days were drawing to a close: "I take leave of all my dear friends. I thank God and them that they have helped me in my need. Were I to be here longer I should always be ashamed of the wickedness they see in me" (*Licht* 6.28).

Mechtild died in 1282. During her last illness, Gertrude, who was at her deathbed, was distressed to see that the old sister's mind was wandering and that, as had happened at Magdeburg, some members of the community were skeptical of her revelations. For this reason she prayed that after Mechtild's death miracles might occur to silence her critics. She was given to understand that signs and portents are not needed to achieve Christ's victories (*Leg.* 5.7.2).

Mechtild of Hackeborn's *Liber* records that she saw a vision of a festival in heaven with virgins dancing around Christ. They sang "new songs" in praise of the congregation of Helfta. "Sister M." as Mechtild of Magdeburg is designated throughout the writings of Mechtild and Gertrude, appeared with these virgins, illuminated by a ray of light from the heart of Christ, signifying the gift of divine love (*Livre* 4.8.259; see also 5.3.310–11).

While still living as a Beguine in Magdeburg, Mechtild had been compelled to write an account of her experiences. It was in 1250, when she was forty-three years old, that she told her confessor, Henry of Halle, about her mystical encounters: "Then I, poor thing, went trembling in humble shame to my confessor, told him about these matters, and asked for his counsel. He said I should go on joyfully and confidently. . . . Then he ordered me to do what makes me often weep for shame when I see my utter unworthiness: that is, that I, a powerless woman, should write this book from the heart and mouth of God" (*Licht* 4.2). Again she declares, "I can say only a little word, no more than a honeybee can carry away on its feet from a full flask. . . . I am afraid before God if I keep silent, and I fear ignorant persons if I write" (*Licht* 3.1).

At the same time, Mechtild was convinced that she had a mission. She understood as from Christ the words: "I send this book as a messenger to all spiritual people, who are the pillars of the Church, the good and the bad, for if the pillars fall, the building cannot stand" (*Licht* 5.34). To fulfill this mission, she was obliged to write of the secret ways of God with her soul. She had also to face the hostility aroused by her exposure of the ill-conduct of her contemporaries, specifically the citizens of Magdeburg, lay persons, clergy, and members of religious orders.

In unveiling the relations of God with her soul, Mechtild uses the language of court and chivalry in many lyrical passages, of which the following is among the best known:

> I cannot dance, O Lord, unless you lead me.
> If I leap high joyfully, you yourself must first leap and sing—
> Then I too shall leap with love,
> From love to knowledge,
> From knowledge to fulfillment,
> From fulfillment to beyond all human senses.

A youth, who is Christ, answers, "Madam, in this dance of praise, you have done well" (*Licht* 1.44). A modern historian of dance, Lincoln Kirstein, refers to Mechtild of Magdeburg as "a holy German lady who danced, a mystic sister." He quotes the foregoing account of her dance of praise.[14] All three mystics of Helfta describe dances of saints, angels, the Virgin Mary, and Christ.

Mechtild celebrates the wisdom of love as well as its ecstasy. "It is the nature of love first to overflow in sweetness, then to become rich in knowledge, and finally to long eagerly for reprobation" (*Licht* 6.20). This teaching becomes specific in her description of the spiritual garments of the bride of Christ. Her working clothes are made of fasts, vigils, disciplines, confessions, sighs, tears, prayers, fears, and firm control of mind and body. Her wedding garments are temptations, maladies, daily sorrows, and all the other sufferings found abundantly in sinful Christendom (*Licht* 7.65).

An allegorical passage describing a poor maid (Mechtild herself) in a great church expresses the supreme joy of union with God. The poor maid, ashamed of her miserable garments, suddenly sees that she is robed in a purple cloak woven of love. She is wearing a golden crown inscribed with the words:

> His eyes in my eyes
> His heart in my heart
> His soul in my soul
> Enclosed and at peace.
> (*Licht* 2.4)

The compulsion that drove Mechtild to communicate such mystical experiences also led her to rebuke her neighbors. It is evident that she had a wide acquaintance among all levels of society, whom she accuses of hypocrisy, self-indulgence, vanity, and avarice. She does not exempt her fellow Beguines, whom she sees guilty of taking communion as a matter of routine: "O you foolish Beguines! What makes you so presumptuous that you do not tremble before our almighty Judge when you so often receive God's body in blind routine? Though I am the least among you, I am ashamed, I blush and shudder" (*Licht* 3.15). It grieved her to the heart that "spiritual people" are so imperfect. "When it pleases God to look so lovingly on a favored soul that a little spark from his divine Heart flies to that cold soul and sets it on fire, the human heart begins to burn.... Our Lord wishes to make that earthly person heavenly so that others might follow, love, and know God in him. But the human mind and understanding say 'No. I can be of great use in active works.' So say these same cloistered folk who are so extremely wise" (*Licht* 6.13).

Even the Dominicans, whom she frequently praises, do not escape her strictures. They have declined from their first fervor and now lack zeal in preaching and hearing confessions. She also reproaches the Franciscans, whom with the Dominicans she had honored as sons of God. "Alas! how much of what they faithfully followed has passed away!" (*Licht* 5.24).

Such were the admonitions that exposed Mechtild to resentment. Much of the harshest condemnation came from the clergy, whose sins she considered most blameworthy. "The soul reminded our Lord of his earlier words: You told me more than six years ago that spiritual people would treat me with contempt. They do so, determinedly and often with sly malice" (*Licht* 3.16). She had desired to experience rejection and scorn. Now she asks: "Ah dear Lord, how long must I stay here on earth in this body like a post or a target at which people throw stones or shoot, and have long besmirched my honor?" (*Licht* 6.38).

Such attacks did not deter her from admonishing persons in authority. Her counsels to superiors show shrewd practicality as well as zeal:

> You shall also go to the kitchen and see to it
> that the provisions for the brothers of the house are good enough,
> that your thriftiness and the cook's laziness
> may not rob our Lord
> of sweet song in choir,
> for a hungry monk never sings well

and a hungry man cannot study deeply.
Thus might God often lose the best
because of the least.
(Licht 6.1)[15]

Mechtild was well aware of the antagonism she inspired. She says, "I was warned about the book and told by some people that if it is not buried it should be burned" *(Licht* 2.26). Notwithstanding these threats, she continued her writing over a period of fifteen years. In her desolation after such attacks she wrote "Ah, Lord! seeing you have taken from me all that I had from you, give me by your grace the gift every dog has by nature, that I may be faithful to you in my spiritual ordeals without any complaint" *(Licht* 2.25).

While still a Beguine at Magdeburg, Mechtild had completed the first six books of *Das fliessende Licht.* Later at Helfta, she dictated the seventh book to the nuns. The original manuscript, written in Middle Low German, is lost. Henry of Halle collected and arranged the pages but evidently not in chronological sequence. According to Neumann, at least two Dominicans at Halle made a Latin translation of the first six books soon after Mechtild's death [ca. 1282]. In 1344, a secular priest, Henry of Nördlingen, made a High German translation of the *Licht,* which he sent to Margaret Ebner at the Dominican convent of Medingen. The only complete codex containing all seven books is in the library of the monastery of Einsiedeln.[16]

As the many criticisms indicate, the work was well known at Magdeburg. Even her friend and confessor, Henry of Halle, was, she says, "surprised" by her "bold language" *(Licht* 5.12). She sometimes uses masculine pronouns when speaking of herself. Examples of her vigorous style are numerous. She writes "Your [Christ's] enemies have thrust me out of sight like a reeking corpse" *(Licht* 5.21). Seeing herself in a vision standing beside the Virgin Mary, she exclaims "—that a miserable crow should stand by a dove!" *(Licht* 2.4). In the long "Complaint of the loving soul" she asks,

> Should my flesh decay, my blood dry up,
> my bones freeze, my veins shrink,
> my heart melt away in your love. . . .
> my soul cry out with the roar of a hungry lion,
> how will it be with me then?
> Where then will you be?
> Beloved, tell me that!
>
> *(Licht* 2.25)

Mechtild employs a variety of forms: lyric, dialogue, prose narrative, and prayer. Images of courtly life and ceremony are frequent, particularly in the early books. Personifications of love, desire, Christianity, virtues, and the senses occur in several allegorical sections; metaphorical garments are often associated with such passages. Images of nature—birds, animals, clouds, flowers—are numerous. A combination of natural and theological imagery occurs in the following passage:

> [Christ speaks] I bend down to you
> >The highest branch of my holy Trinity
> >From which you pluck
> >The green and white and red apples
> >Of my gentle humanity.
> >>(*Licht* 2.25)

The three colors are those of liturgical vestments. Symbolic color and images are combined in the description of the bride's attire: "She has a garment of purple silk; that is hope, adorned with truth and crowned by song. . . . She wears a hat of peacock's feathers; that denotes good fame on earth and high honor in Heaven" (*Licht* 1.46).

The Flowing Light of the Godhead, the title chosen by Mechtild herself, expresses the dominant image in her writing. This image refers not only to light, but also to water, wine, honey, blood—all liquids, as symbols of the motion, transference, and communication of divine love and grace.[17] A passage presumably by Henry of Halle appears in the last chapter of the sixth book: "What is written in this book flowed out of the living Godhead into the heart of Sister Mechtild. It is here faithfully recorded as God gave it from his heart and as she wrote it with her own hand. Deo gratias" (*Licht* 6.43).

A recent study explores Mechtild's efforts to find the "likenesses that mirror the archetypal relationship of the Divine to the human." Her anguished acknowledgments of the inadequacy of human words to mirror the ineffable are ultimately resolved when she hears interiorly an assurance that the humanity of Christ is "a comprehensible image of [the] eternal divinity."[18] As will be seen, Gertrude's similitudes, while also dealing with the relationship of God with the human person, are in a quite different mode.

Among Mechtild's contemporaries many sought her counsel. The scope of her ministry is shown by the titles of some chapters—e.g., "How to Bear Suffering Gladly for God," "Of the Rule of a Canon; how he should comport himself," "Sister Mechtild Writes to her brother B[aldwin] of the Order of Preachers." This letter ends, "Dear Friend, be united to God and rejoice in his will!" (*Licht* 6.42). Some of her writing is aphoristic: "Human beings are by nature faint-hearted" (*Licht* 3.1). "Training costs noble maidens much pain. They must discipline themselves in every way and often tremble before their mentor" (*Licht* 3.5). "God has enough of everything except intimacy with the soul; of that he can never have enough" (*Licht* 4.12)—and the corollary—"If you want to have love, you must let yourself be loved" (*Licht* 2.23).

Mechtild knew that her writings would be of lasting value. She wrote: "Any honest woman or good man who would have liked to speak with me and after my death cannot do so, should read this little book" (*Licht* 6.1). The admiring scribe adds in the Prologue "nine times." Mechtild was correct in believing that after her death her book would live. More than a hundred years after she left her parents' home for Magdeburg, Henry of Nördlingen wrote to Margaret and Christina Ebner: "I send you a book called *The Flowing Light of the Godhead*. I am led to do this by the living light of the radiant love of Christ, for to me, this book in delightful and vigorous German, is the most moving love poem I have ever read in our tongue."[19]

Among other gifted nuns, members of the community at Helfta, were three descendants of the founders: "Sophia Senior"—so called to distinguish her from her cousin of the same name—who transcribed many books; her sister Elisabeth, a painter and illuminator; and their cousin Sophia, who was later abbess.[20] Associated with these women were others whose names are not recorded: the nun or nuns who wrote the *Legatus divinae pietatis* (Herald of Divine Love), books 1, 3, 4, and 5, from Gertrude of Helfta's dictation or from their notes; the ones who assisted her in compiling the account of Mechtild of Hackeborn, the *Liber specialis gratiae* (Book of Special Grace); and various members of the community whose words, actions, and deaths are reported in the *Legatus* and the *Liber*. Both books afford intimate glimpses of the varied personalities in the community. Gertrude remarks that one nun had taken great pleasure in a bedspread embroidered in gold (*Leg.* 5.8.1). The nineteenth-century translator is convinced that a nun could not have owned such an article and that her peccadillo must have occurred before she entered the convent.[21] It is possible that after she became a nun she might have spoken complacently of her former possessions.

Both Gertrude and Mechtild report in some detail the last words and acts of several persons, including lay associates as well as nuns. Gertrude tells of a young nun who died twelve days after the death of the Abbess Gertrude. Her friendliness, innocence, and fervor had endeared her to the community, and the suddenness of their loss was hard to bear. She had prayed that she might enter heaven without delay, but as she was young "and in time of youth one is seldom free from slight negligences," she was purified from her faults by experiencing great fear of the devil in her last illness. Gertrude was confident that her patience in sickness and this ordeal of fear had made the young nun ready to see God (*Leg.* 5.2.1). The *Legatus* also records the deaths of two sisters, members of a noble family, who died within thirty days of each other. Gertrude believed that the younger sister received a particular reward from God because of her devotion to the eucharist (*Leg.* 5.5.1, 6). This indicates that there were at least three pairs of sisters at Helfta: the Abbess Gertrude and her sister Mechtild; Sophia and Elisabeth, descendants of the founders; and these two, who are designated simply as M. and E.

Gertrude tells also of another nun, notable for her patience and fervor, who though seriously ill, had been unwilling to make her confession because she had no grave sins. When the priest came, she pretended to be asleep. Later, as her condition worsened, she asked for a priest but was unable to complete her confession. Gertrude believed that after her death Christ received this nun lovingly, consoling her for her disquiet on seeing another sister who was ill being given more care than she herself was receiving. The community had mistakenly supposed that the latter was not in immediate danger. After her death, which occurred a month before her companion's, she prayed for her to Christ, saying, "Give her all that you have given me, for I can think of nothing better" (*Leg.* 5.9.1, 2). This is one of many instances recorded in both the *Legatus* and the *Liber* in which the mystics of Helfta are aware of the state of the dead. After the death of the Abbess Gertrude, Mechtild envisioned her hand in hand with their sister Luitgarde, who had died in childhood (*Livre* 1.24.85).

Gertrude's *Legatus* provides a sidelight on her relations with this nun. As she envisioned the spirit of her departed companion looking at her affectionately, Gertrude said, "You always loved me, yet you seemed unwilling to take my advice during your illness." Acknowledging the truth of Gertrude's words, the nun replied, "Now your prayers for me have more efficacy since you offer them purely from charity and for the love of God" (*Leg.* 5.9.7).

Though many nuns, the Abbess Gertrude among them, lived to an advanced age, a number of the deaths recorded in the *Legatus* and in Mechtild's *Liber* are those of young sisters. Gertrude's description of the death of one of her young companions reveals the intimacy of community relations. The dying nun was in her last agony when she bade farewell to the sisters and promised to pray for them all. As her sufferings increased, she said, "O Lord, you know all my secrets; you know how much I wanted to spend my strength in serving you faithfully until I became old and infirm. But since I see that you wish me to go to you, all my desire is changed into longing to see you. This sweetens the bitterness of death." After a moment, she asked to have the passion read to her, and pointed out the place where the reader should begin: "Then Jesus, lifting up his eyes to heaven . . ." (Jn 17:1) "for," she added, "if you begin with 'Before the festal day,' (Jn 13:1) there will not be time to finish." At the words, "And bowing down his head, he gave up the spirit" (Jn 19:30), she asked for the crucifix, and having kissed the wounds, died peacefully. Since the community had known this nun from her childhood, she may, like Gertrude, have come to Helfta as a pupil in the monastery school (*Leg.* 5.10.1, 2).

Male members of the community included a provost, a number of farm workers, and some lay brothers. These last, *fratres conversi*, performed various types of work under the direction of the abbess. Once when Gertrude heard the bell calling the workmen to their meal she became aware that it pleased God when his people sought their necessary refreshment (*Leg.* 4.14.8). When one of these brothers was dying, Gertrude had been much occupied. After his death she reproached herself for having neglected him, since he had been more faithful and devoted than the other brothers. He had shown kindness in many ways, giving alms to the poor, little gifts to children, and fruit to the sick (*Leg.* 5.11.1). A certain brother Herman had also served the community faithfully. He had, however, been much attached to his own will so that when he did anyone a favor it was on his own terms. He had also been somewhat slow to forgive injuries, and for a long time would give the offender a severe look when they met. Nevertheless, he had won such affection by his faithful service that the nuns prayed fervently for his recovery and shed tears when he died (*Leg.* 5.12). Another brother, designated simply as "F," was obliged to expiate in the next world his fault of working to obtain various articles without the superior's permission and then hiding them (*Leg.* 5.15). Gertrude also believed that a brother "Th[omas]," thanks to the merits of the community, received after death a greater reward for his work at Helfta than had come to him for even longer service elsewhere (*Leg.* 5.14).

3 "The Nightingale of Christ"

WHEN Mechtild of Hackeborn was born in 1241, she was so frail that it was feared she might die unbaptized. Her nurses carried her posthaste to a priest who was about to say mass. After baptizing her, he said, "Why are you afraid? This child is not going to die. She will become a holy nun in whom God will work many wonders, and she will live till she is old" (*Livre, préambule,* 5).

Mechtild's entry into the monastery was as precipitous as her baptism. The family home was near Rodarsdorf where the community was then situated. One day when Mechtild was seven, her mother brought her to visit her sixteen-year-old sister Gertrude, the future abbess of the community. To the mother's dismay, the child went to each sister in turn, begging to stay. When the nuns joined their pleas to hers, the mother finally yielded and went home without her. As many of the children in the convent school were her own age or younger, Mechtild did not lack companions. Her education progressed under the direction of her sister, who became abbess in 1251. The nuns moved from Rodarsdorf to Helfta in 1258 when Mechtild was about seventeen. She had already been received into the community, and her formal consecration followed in due course.

Mechtild taught the children in the abbey school and may have been in charge of all the studies there with the title of *Lehrmeisterin*. The name of the nun who held this office is recorded as Mechtild of Wippra. As noted earlier, the barons of Hackeborn were also lords of Wippra, and a member of the family might use either or both names. Philipp Strauch has pointed out that Mechtild of

Hackeborn died in 1299 [others say 1298], while a Mechtild of Wippra was living in 1303.¹ This seems conclusive evidence against their identification. Mechtild of Wippra may have been a cousin or niece of the Abbess Gertrude. The frequency of the names Mechtild, Gertrude, Sophia, and Elisabeth causes many problems for researchers. Whatever her title, it is clear that Mechtild of Hackeborn was a teacher. Like her friend, the young Gertrude, she often uses comparisons drawn from academic life. Both nuns call Christ "the best of teachers." Mechtild's *Liber specialis gratiae* records a formal commission to her as teacher. It seemed to her that Christ said: "I entrust to you the simple and innocent children symbolized by the lamb; you are to teach them, preparing them to know and to love me" (*Livre* 4.60.306).

It is as singer and choir mistress that Mechtild is most often designated. The title *Domna Cantrix* (Lady Chantress) identifies her throughout the *Liber*. Gifted with a remarkable singing voice, she served the community as chantress and director of the choir. She instructed the novices in the ceremonies of the choral office and assisted them in memorizing the long liturgical texts. David Knowles has pointed out the necessity for memorization: "Until the fourteenth century the choir was in darkness save for candles on the lectern, except on great feasts; it was, therefore, essential that the monks should know by heart not only the whole psalter with the customary canticles and hymns, but the versicles also, the anthems, and the whole of the 'common' office of saints."[2] For forty years Mechtild led the chant of the nuns, intoning the psalms of the Divine Office and supervising the choir. "The nightingale of Christ," as Gertrude calls her, she repeatedly refers to him as *cantor cantorum*.

In the primary sources for the life of Mechtild, the writings from Helfta, Mechtild is not called mistress of novices. Nevertheless, as directress of the choir and official chantress, her position would have brought her into close contact with the novices. Several passages in the *Liber* contain instructions for them.

Although for many years Mechtild had experienced mystical communications, she had told no one until she believed herself divinely enjoined to do so. Her confidant was not her sister, the Abbess Gertrude, but the younger Gertrude to whom she herself had given spiritual direction. Even to her she did not tell everything but only what she believed would give honor to God and help to others. These confidences were sometimes interrupted, particularly during her frequent illnesses. Often she would come to a stop, unable to find words for her experiences. At times her voice was so low that she could hardly be heard. More than once she was in anguish for fear that it might be her own imagination rather than the voice of God that she heard interiorly. Not until she was fifty was the record of her experiences written. This was by order of the Abbess Sophia, successor to the Abbess Gertrude, and the consent of "a prelate," perhaps the bishop of Halberstadt. Popularly known as *Revelations of St. Mechtild*, the book is the *Liber specialis gratiae* (Book of Special Grace). Mechtild was in her last illness when the book was begun by Gertrude and another nun. On learning that it was being written, she was distressed, and only a mystical intuition reconciled her (*Livre* 2.43.187–88; 5.31.357–58).

Mechtild's death at fifty-seven in 1298 brought great sorrow to the community and particularly to her closest friend. Gertrude's account of the death of "our chantress of blessed memory" relates that Christ, *cantor cantorum*, intoned the words, "*Venite, benedicti patris mei, precipite regnum*" (Come, blessed of my father [Mt 25:34]) for his "nightingale." During her agony, Mechtild repeatedly murmured, "Good Jesus, good Jesus." As the nuns approached to ask her prayers, although she could hardly speak, she immediately answered each, "yes" or "gladly" (*Leg.* 5.4.9, 18; *Livre* 7.11.391). Because of Gertrude's own illness during Mechtild's last hours, she had not been able to pray for her friend as often as she wished. After Mechtild's death she offered prayers in honor of the five wounds of Christ to atone for this neglect. She was consoled as she visualized flowers springing from the wounds and sensed her friend's voice acknowledging her remembrance. Thereafter, Gertrude invoked Mechtild with confidence based on a conviction of her friend's holiness and, in particular, of her patience during her long illness. "Never was there anyone like her in our monastery," she writes. "Alas, I fear there will never be another" (*Leg.* 5.4.23; *Livre* 5.30.352).

As sister of the abbess, as official chantress, and member of a well-known family that had for three generations been patrons of the community, Mechtild of Hackeborn was a prominent person. According to Gertrude's testimony, she remained profoundly humble. "The word of command does not become me," she said (*Livre* 1.23.82). Her respect for superiors was undiminished by the fact that her sister held the highest office in the community. At the service of everyone in the house, Mechtild was so generally useful that it seemed, says Gertrude, "that God wished none of his gifts to her to escape notice." To her spiritual endowments were added natural gifts: "knowledge, intelligence, mastery of humane letters, a beautiful voice—all that rendered her able to serve the monastery in every way" (*Livre, préambule,* 5). Set apart by so many gifts, Mechtild nevertheless remained one of the sisters. Like her sister, the Abbess Gertrude, she was *"communis"* (sociable), one of the community.

Strict with herself, Mechtild was always approachable. The *Liber* refers to her familiar contact with laypersons as well as with priests and friars. Her friends were aware of her occasional absentmindedness. Once when dining with guests, she declined meat, but when one of the visitors quietly placed before her a piece of meat, she ate it at once, serenely unconscious of her action. St. Bernard, it is said, went to a meal "as if to torment."[3] Mechtild's neighbors might have shared his attitude when she was so absorbed in contemplation that she was unaware of the noisome condition of the egg she was eating. Her companions were less enraptured (*Livre* 5.30.352).

Like her friend, the younger Gertrude, Mechtild lived the common life as fully as her health permitted, seeing in every detail a source of divine grace. On the feast of John the Evangelist when the bell rang for Matins in the early morning, she envisaged angels with flaming torches escorting the sisters to the sanctuary. Those who had risen from their beds with love and joy (*ex amore hilariter*) were more blessed than others motivated by fear (*Livre* 1.6.20). At other times, when the nuns performed the penance of taking the discipline, it seemed to her that the sound of the strokes made melody in heaven: "the holy angels dance; the demons run away; souls are delivered from suffering, and the chains of sin are broken" (*Livre* 2.27.167).

Mechtild's insistent prayer for her companions was that God might always sustain them in his service, multiply his blessings on them, make them grow in virtue, and prosper in every good work (*Livre* 4.6.256). When experiencing an assurance that Christ would fulfill all her desires, she envisioned herself leading him to each sister in turn that he might bless her. His gift to each was "the breath of his spirit" (*Livre* 3.20.217). Finding in Mechtild a model as well as a teacher, says Gertrude, the nuns flocked to her, listening to her with all the attention they would give a preacher (*Livre* 5.30.352). One of the themes inspired by her mystical encounters was the diagnosis of spiritual maladies: "Some souls are afraid to entrust themselves to [Christ's] tenderness, and in their fright try to flee from [his] face; they have a trembling paralysis. Some are flighty and inconstant; thoughts run helter-skelter through their minds; a single word is enough to make them impatient or angry. Others have a sleeping paralysis; they do everything languidly and halfheartedly." Mechtild taught that meditation on the passion of Christ is the remedy for these ailments (*Livre* 4.37.287).

Associated with such meditation was veneration of the face of Christ. One of the most famous relics at Rome, attracting thousands of pilgrims, was a cloth which was believed to bear the image of the face of Jesus. According to legend, a woman named Veronica met Christ on the way to Calvary and offered him her veil to wipe the blood from his face. When he returned it, the veil bore the imprint of his features. Pilgrims came from many countries to venerate the relic, particularly during 1300, the jubilee year. On that occasion, a monk from York was crushed to death by the throngs surrounding the image.[4] Julian of Norwich in the second of her "showings" reveals her familiarity with the relic. In her vision of the face of Christ she says, "It made me think of the holy Vernicle at Rome, which he imprinted with his own blessed face, when he was in his cruel Passion, voluntarily going to his death, and of his often changing color, the brownness and blackness [of the blood], his face sorrowful and wasted."[5]

Although a prioress and her companion are among Chaucer's Canterbury pilgrims, nuns were not permitted to go on pilgrimage and several councils forbade them to do so. In 1318 Archbishop Melton of York ordered that if any nun made a vow to go on pilgrimage, she should say instead as many psalters as it would have taken days to perform the pilgrimage.[6] Mechtild made a similar suggestion in preparation for the second Sunday after Epiphany when the image of the Holy Face was venerated at Rome. She urged the nuns to make a spiritual pilgrimage by reciting as many Our Fathers as there are miles between Helfta and Rome. She also composed a prayer in honor of the face of Christ, one of many which she dictated, "so many that if they were gathered into one volume, it would be larger than the psalter" (*Livre* 1.10.31; 5.30.352–53).

Gertrude and the unnamed nun who with her compiled the *Liber* believed that Mechtild's spiritual gifts were "not so much for herself as for us and for those who will come after us" (*Livre* 5.30.351). Mechtild herself shared this view. When she told others of the mystical communications she received, as a rule she did not attribute them to Christ or the Virgin Mary. The following examples are representative of her counsels:

> If any obstacle arises in our service of God, whether from the attitude of others, from external circumstances, from our own desires, memories, or from any other cause—whatever the impediment, we should take it as a messenger from God, sending it back to him, so to speak, with praise and thanksgiving. (*Livre* 3.15.208)

> Three things very pleasing to God are: first, never to abandon one's neighbor in need, and to excuse shortcomings and sins as much as possible; second, in troubles to take refuge only in God, entrusting to him alone everything that disquiets the heart; third, to walk with him in truth. (*Livre* 4.7.257)

> When it is time to eat or sleep, say: "Lord, in union with the love with which you created this useful thing for me, and yourself made use of it when you were on earth, I take it for your eternal praise and for my bodily need." (*Livre* 3.27.225)

> We should be lovingly grateful not only for the spiritual blessings God gives us, but for all bodily necessities such as food and clothing, receiving them with a sincerely thankful heart and considering ourselves unworthy of them. (*Livre* 4.6.256)

> Works which give no human satisfaction may nevertheless be very pleasing to God. (*Livre* 3.9.203)

> What best pleases God in members of religious orders is purity of heart, holy desires, gentle kindness in conversation, and works of charity. (*Livre* 1.27.93)

> You can never be in so large a crowd that you are not alone with me [Christ] if you turn to me with your whole heart. (*Livre* 3.10.203)

In an extended precept, Mechtild tells how one may attain to God by consecration of the bodily senses. She understood these counsels as coming from Christ: "Seek me through your five senses, just as a host awaiting the arrival of a very dear friend looks through the doors and windows to see if the expected guest is coming. The faithful soul ought to watch for me unceasingly through the senses which are the windows of the spirit. If he sees beautiful or lovable things, let him think how beautiful, lovable, and good is the one who made them. When he hears an enchanting melody or an excellent discourse, let him say to himself: 'O how sweet will be the voice that will one day call me!' And when he hears conversation or something read aloud, let him seek his beloved in it" (*Livre* 3.44.242).

Mechtild was not unaware of her sisters' faults, often accusing herself of the same ones. She mentions sleepiness and sloth ("slugerie and slewth" in *The Booke of Gostlye Grace*), particularly during community prayers. In keeping with her conviction that Christ's merits can compensate for all human failings, she offered his labors during his youth in reparation for them (*Livre* 3.14.206–7).[7]

The secret of the gentle kindliness which attracted so many persons to Mechtild may be learned from one of the counsels she herself received at the Introit of the mass, *Ego cogito*, "I think thoughts of peace and not of affliction. If you wish to be my very dear daughter and to be like me, imitate me in these ways. Just as I think thoughts of peace and not of affliction, you should always try to have a quiet heart and peaceful thoughts, never contending with anyone, but yielding humbly and patiently. Just as I listen graciously to all who ask, you must be kind and generous to everyone. Try to bring everyone out of captivity, that is, to bring help and consolation to those in trouble and temptation" (*Livre* 3.39.238). Mechtild's relations with her companions did not end with their deaths. Once she recognized among the nuns in the choir a friend who had recently died. "Tell me," Mechtild asked, "is everything in the next life just as I told you it would be?" "Yes," was the answer, "it is all as you said. Now I have received my hundredfold." The account concludes with an image recalling the scenes in Dante's *Paradiso:* "then, circling the celestial dwelling, she returned to the Lord" (*Livre* 1.1.10).

Not only the community but also friars and laypersons desired Mechtild's counsel and friendship. That they came great distances in unsettled times when travel was unsafe gives some indication of her influence. Her knowledge of the life and customs of the nobility would have made her familiar with the needs of some of these suppliants. Many passages in the *Liber* show her acquaintance with the manners of the aristocracy. It is likely that her relatives were among the visitors to the monastery. As she wondered whether Christ had maintained communication with his kinsfolk after the return from Egypt to Nazareth, she recalled the text: "They [Mary and Joseph] sought him among their relatives and friends" (Lk 2:44; *Livre* 1.5.20). A number of passages in the *Liber* show the extent of Mechtild's influence outside her own community. She prayed for "an ill-tempered person" (*Livre* 5.53.297) and for another "who thought himself wiser than his superior." Despite his fault this person, she believed, merited a special award after his death because he had served mass devoutly (*Livre* 4.15.265–66). Some of the Friars Preachers consulted her when they were harassed by temptations. She encouraged one by a forceful comparison: "Those temptations cannot hurt you any more than gnats can destroy a mountain" (*Livre* 4.40.290). Her visitors realized the singularity of Mechtild's gifts. According to her biographers, "When the holy inebriation overcame her, even guests and strangers became aware of the heavenly intoxication she had so long kept hidden" (*Livre* 2.26.165). She was able to read the thoughts of many persons who asked her prayers.

The monastic letter is a recognized genre in medieval literature.[8] Mechtild sometimes corresponded with those who consulted her. The *Liber* contains a letter addressed "Dearly beloved daughter in Christ." Representative of Mechtild's counsels, it combines instruction and encouragement, opening with the assertion, "The lover of your soul is holding your hand in his right hand." She assures her correspondent that Christ's virtues can supply for her deficiencies—a characteristic theme in Mechtild's spirituality. She develops this theme by associating each of Christ's fingers with a virtue: by figuratively joining one's fingers to his, one may find a remedy for spiritual ills. "Join your finger to his by confessing your infidelity toward this gentle and faithful lover." She employs military terms with the vigor and assurance natural to one living in turbulent times and familiar with St. Paul's metaphors of spiritual armor (Eph 6:11–17): "If thieving wicked thoughts try to take you by surprise, run to the arsenal and there clothe yourself with the ever-shining armor of your Savior's passion and death" (*Livre* 4.59.301–5). Other passages remind her friend that nothing is to be preferred to the love of Christ.[9] If she gives him her heart in joy and confidence, he will give her his. Even if deprived of consolation, she must continue to praise him. "Ask the Lord of hosts to give you his own strength to conquer temptations" (*Livre* 4.59.304).

After receiving a particular blessing, Mechtild often prayed that one of her companions might receive the same grace. Gertrude was her confidant, but passages in the *Liber* indicate that she had at least four close friends. Such statements as "A nun . . . with whom she had lived in close intimacy," "all those who had surrounded her with devotion or affection," and in particular, a vision of four lilies symbolizing "the virgins who had made an offering to God in her praise," show the atmosphere of familial relationships in the monastery (*Livre* 1.1.10; 7.13.393; 5.25.347). After Mechtild's death two of her friends in thanksgiving for the blessings she had received undertook to recite an anthem for each day of her life (*Livre* 5.25.345–46). Another friend arranged to have a mass said for each year of Mechtild's life (*Livre* 5.25.346–47). It was probably Gertrude who asked her to obtain for her friends whatever virtue each was lacking. "In the light of eternal truth," was the answer, "I now see clearly that all my love for those who were dear to me in life is no more than a drop in the ocean in comparison with the love of the Sacred Heart for them. I see also why God permits persons to keep certain faults which humiliate and discipline them but make them advance every day in the way of salvation. I would not wish to change by one iota what the Lord's wisdom and mercy has planned for each one" (*Livre* 7.12.393).

Mechtild's spiritual life was rooted in the liturgy, particularly in the chants and hymns of the *Opus Dei*, the Divine Office. Her mysticism "is steeped in the Opus Dei," says the editor of *The Booke of Gostlye Grace.*[10] The French translators of the *Liber specialis gratiae* speak of the intelligent piety that she brought to the melodies of solemn prayer (*Livre*, p. vi). Jean Leclercq has noted that in the Cistercians' preface to their reformed antiphonary, ideas of musical technique were adapted to spiritual considerations.[11] Many passages in the *Liber* illustrate Mechtild's adaptations. For her, music was not only a bridge between heaven and earth, it was the meeting place for all members of the Mystical Body. When she intoned an anthem, she seemed to hear the angels continue it with the community; when a virgin entered heaven, her steps sounded melodiously; she declared that the voice of Christ will be the eternal reward of those who close their ears to useless and harmful words (*Livre* 1.12.37; 2.36.180; 4.21.270). One night "when she could not sleep for sorrow," she heard the angels singing, "Cast your care upon the Lord and he will sustain you" (Ps 54:23; *Livre* 1.15.46). During the chanting of the daily Office and at mass, her devotion was so apparent that the other nuns were moved to similar fervor. Many of her mystical experiences occurred while she recited the psalms. As she obeyed the rubric which directs that the chantress should bow her head after intoning an antiphon, she heard interiorly the words of Christ, "You are bowing under the outpouring of grace and expressing praise and thanksgiving" (*Livre* 2.1.134). She guided the nuns in the performance of the Office: at the beginning of each liturgical hour they were to bow in homage to the humility which made the Son of God descend from heaven in becoming man. At the conclusion of each hour they were to give thanks for all that Christ did and suffered, especially in whatever action in his life was commemorated by that hour of the Office (*Livre* 3.30.229–30).

Once during Advent, Mechtild envisioned Christ standing in the middle of the choir, while from his face "more radiant than a thousand suns" came rays which illuminated all the sisters (*Livre* 1.4.12). Again, when she was praying for the community, she heard the Virgin Mary intone the hymn, "*Jesu corona virginum,*" and from the air the voices of saints and angels continuing with the line, "*Te laudamus in saeculum*" (*Livre* 1.12.38–39). As she bowed when reciting the *Gloria Patri*, she once saw the Virgin Mary opposite her bowing likewise (*Livre* 1.39.122). In her complete absorption in prayer, Mechtild would sometimes extend or raise her hands, completely unconscious of what she was doing (*Livre* 5.30.354).

References to music pervade the *Liber specialis gratiae*. Mechtild's exceptionally beautiful singing, the expression of her own fervor and the inspiration of her companions, was not without its cost. According to the *Liber*, sometimes in her fatigue and exhaustion it seemed to her that she could no longer breathe, yet she continued to sing with such ardor that she would not have stopped even if the effort were to cost her life. Sometimes the realization of divine love overcame her and she had to be assisted from the choir. At other times her conviction of Christ's presence sustained and enabled her to continue the chant. She seemed then to be singing "in and with God" (*Livre* 3.7.200). Both Gertrude and Mechtild refer to the responsory, "*Regnum Mundi,*" which was sung at the ceremony of reception of the habit, at a nun's funeral, and at other times. On the day of her burial, the nuns heard Mechtild's voice joining theirs as they sang it: "I have despised the kingdom of the world and all earthly splendor for the love of my Lord Jesus Christ, whom I have seen, whom I have loved, in whom I believed, whom I have loved exceedingly" (*Livre* 7.18.399). About five weeks after the death of the *Domna Cantrix*, Gertrude envisioned her in company with Christ "directing the chant according to her custom" and saying, "When I chanted with you in the choir, I desired to raise your thoughts to God as the notes ascended, and to draw down his grace upon you with the descending notes. That is what I am still doing" (*Livre* 7.19.400).

Because for Mechtild, music was the chief means of praising God, she was in anguish whenever it was perverted or misused. During the carnival season before Lent when she heard the people singing lascivious songs, she was so grieved (*zelo Dei et compassionis effectu nimium inardescens*) that to make reparation she strewed broken glass and sharp instruments on her bed. As a result, she was for a long time unable to sit or lie down. This is the most severe penance recorded in her life (*Livre* 5.30.353). It seems that neither she nor Gertrude practiced severe bodily penances, and it would be rash to assume that this one is typical of the regimen at Helfta. Perhaps some of the songs that Mechtild heard were similar to the *Carmina Burana*. The collection is from the thirteenth century, but many of the songs are from an earlier period. Although some are exceedingly beautiful, the singers of others are described by Peter of Blois as "*illicitos amores canere et se corruptorem virginum iactitare*" (singing of unlawful loves and boasting of the corruption of virgins). According to a modern critic, certain of the songs are "of an unmatched obscenity."[12]

It was not only by her music that Mechtild served her community. As Gertrude testifies, she also helped her sister, the Abbess Gertrude, with wisdom and efficiency in both spiritual and external affairs. To all the nuns, particularly those who were suffering, she was a trusted counselor. In this she was obeying what she believed to be Christ's injunction, "Strive to help and console those who are sorrowful or despised" (*Livre* 4.60.306). According to the *Liber*, "Everyone who approached her came away comforted or enlightened." Gertrude, who also had many persons seeking her advice, remarks, "Everyone loved her and wanted to be with her, and in the end this was a great burden" (*Livre*, préambule, 5). Nuns who suffered from scruples, who found it hard to obey their superiors, who were overwhelmed by their duties, all fled to Mechtild for advice and encouragement. Worn out by her services, Mechtild once feared that she had gone too far in helping someone. As she suffered this anxiety, she visualized Christ holding the garments of the person she had been helping, and preparing to mend them himself. "Do not be afraid," she heard him say; "everything you do for her you do for me" (*Livre* 4.49.295). As she prayed for a woman burdened with heavy manual labor, Mechtild envisioned her kneeling in prayer before Christ while he poured on her uplifted hands a healing balm. She understood this gesture as signifying the gift of his own works to sanctify hers and to supply what was lacking in them (*Livre* 4.34.285). When Mechtild had no opportunity to confess her sins before receiving communion, she experienced a consoling insight: if a powerful king is coming to lodge, one cleans the house immediately. But if he is so near that there is no time to throw out the dirt, one hides it in a corner till later. So if one has the sincere desire to confess her sins and never commit them again, they are erased from God's sight and he no longer remembers them. They must, however, be renounced later by confession (*Livre* 2.14.144). This is one of many domestic images in the writings of both Mechtild and Gertrude.

During mass in the summer, seeing some sisters sleepy and distracted, Mechtild exclaimed, "O Lord, how weak and miserable human beings are, since even during the sacred mysteries they cannot keep awake!" Then it occurred to her that it would not be hard to keep awake if one thought of the joys of heaven or the pains of hell. "But if one cannot?" she questioned Christ. "Whoever has a beloved friend," was the reply, "grieves at being deprived of his presence. If one realizes that I am an infinitely loving and faithful friend ready to share with whoever comes to me those secrets that fully satisfy her desire, she would be eager to find all her delight in me. She would certainly not sleep if she knew the heartfelt joy, the strength of those who possess me, the liberty that I give" (*Livre* 3.20.216).

Mechtild habitually prayed for those who were suffering. Once she visualized the nuns laying their pains and burdens like green leaves on the cross of Christ. He accepted them all and carried them patiently and joyfully while all the sisters helped him (*Livre* 1.18.56). This appears to be a visual interpretation of Psalm 54:23: "Cast your burden on the Lord and he will sustain you." To a sister who was discouraged she brought the message: "Why is she troubled? I created her for myself; I have given myself to her for the fulfillment of all her desires. I am her father by creation, her mother by redemption, her brother in the sharing of my kingdom, her sister by dear companionship" (*Livre* 4.50.296). Such images of multiple relationships with the divinity are common in the writings of the mystics. They see the union of the soul with God as subsuming and transcending all human relationships.

More than once, as she watched the community go to the altar to receive the eucharist, Mechtild saw each sister holding a lamp which brilliantly illuminated her face. These lamps symbolized the sisters' hearts burning with the love of God. Catherine of Siena uses a similar comparison in a letter to her young niece, Nanna (*Livre* 1.4.13).[13] Many of Mechtild's counsels are directed to the novices. As in scriptural times the prophets prefaced their admonitions with "Thus says the Lord," so Mechtild transmitted to the novices the divine counsels as she perceived them: "Let them [the novices] pray often and devoutly, read and hear Scripture willingly, apply themselves to study, obey the rule carefully, preserve humility above all things without comparing themselves to others, and never look down on anyone. If they pray as I wish, I [Christ] shall teach them my divine will and everything they need to know. While they read, I shall make them taste my sweetness; I shall sanctify them while they work; for their obedience to the rule I shall give them my compassion, my strength, and my help. In their humility I shall find my repose" (*Livre* 4.16.266–67). To someone who asked what God desired her to do, Mechtild replied, "Behave like a young bride without beauty, wealth, or rank who has been chosen for love alone and raised to royal honors. Naturally, such a bride will be particularly grateful, faithful, and loving. So one should be endlessly grateful because I [Christ] have chosen her before the creation of the world, ransomed her dearly at the price of my blood, and destined her for special love and familiarity with me" (*Livre* 4.32.282–83).

The keynote of Mechtild's spirituality is the praise of God; of this, her service as chantress is the most obvious expression (*Livre* 7.16.396–98). In addition to this evidence, the account of her mystical experiences as recorded by Gertrude and the unnamed nun or nuns who compiled the *Liber specialis gratiae* provides much information, particularly about her relations with the community. Both she and Gertrude, together with the Abbess Gertrude, encouraged scrupulous or hesitant nuns to receive the sacrament. Mechtild also urged them to be generous in praying for others. "One should be as liberal as a queen at the king's table," she would say. "He is pleased when we confidently expect great things from him" (*Livre* 4.32.284). Teresa of Avila shared this conviction: "It would be insulting a great emperor to ask him for a farthing."[14] Ida Görres, quoting from the documents of beatification and canonization of Thérèse of Lisieux, writes: "The Lord's words to St. Mechtild touched her deeply: 'I tell you it gives me great joy when men expect great things of me.'"[15] Again, Mechtild says, "He never wearies even if we entreat him a thousand times a day" (*Livre* 4.23.273).

This confidence led her to participate as fully as possible in all the community observances. On Easter morning she walked in the customary procession despite her weakness, even though she had to be led by the sisters and use a staff. As she did so, she visualized Christ beside her, carrying a crimson banner (*Livre* 1.19.63). At another time, the staff was given a symbolic interpretation: as Mechtild was grieving over her faults, Christ appeared and gave her a staff which represented his human nature. She was surprised to see that it had no knob at the top. "I shall put my own hand there to sustain you," she was told. "From now on, whenever I give you consolation in your sadness, know that my hand is supporting you; but when you feel no consolation, know that I have withdrawn it. Then you must cling to me with a faithful heart" (*Livre* 2.13.144). "What do you do, Lord, when I pray or recite psalms?" she once asked. "I listen," was the answer. "When you work, I rest, and the more zealously you work, the sweeter is my rest in you . . . when you sleep, I watch and guard you" (*Livre* 3.16.211). This is one of many passages illustrating Mechtild's penchant for asking questions according to her custom (*Livre* 1.31.106). One question, addressed to her "best of teachers," concerned his greatest suffering during his passion. She learned that it was the dislocation of all his members when he was stretched on the cross. This agony is mentioned more than once in the *Liber*. In another passage it is reported that she heard Christ say, "Remember also my lifelong thirst" (*Livre* 2.17.148; 3.6.198). As she desired to know how Christ praised his father, she heard interiorly the answer, "Now and always by the one word, *Fiat*" (*Livre* 2.20.154).

To a modern reader her questions to the Virgin Mary seem quaint. The *Liber* records a dialogue occurring during the Christmas season: "My Lady, why were you without a bed and other necessary things?" As she pondered, the answer came to her mind, "Nothing was necessary. I bore my innocent child without pain." "But when your relatives and friends came to visit you, what could you offer them, poor Lady, even though you were Queen of heaven?" Again she understood the answer, "They had no need of my provisions; on the contrary, they brought me what I needed" (*Livre* 1.5.19).

One of Mechtild's questions is on a topic of special interest to the medieval mind: were the souls of Solomon, Samson, Trajan, and Origen saved? Although Paul lists Solomon among the heroes of faith (Heb 11:32), the text in 3 Kings (11:9) reads "His mind was turned away from the Lord." Gregory writes, "Solomon . . . who received the gift of wisdom . . . was not to persevere."[16] According to Augustine, "Solomon made a good beginning but a bad ending."[17] Mechtild of Magdeburg uses her characteristic imagery to assert, "Solomon's words illuminate, but not his works, for he himself is darkened" (*Licht* 3.20). Concerning Samson, Flavius Josephus in *Jewish Antiquities* sees no fault in Samson's causing his own death together with that of the Philistines. He concedes, however, that he showed weakness in being ensnared by a woman. This he considers excusable as owing to the instability of human nature.[18] Aquinas has a reply to the argument that it is lawful to kill oneself since Samson who did so is numbered among the saints (Heb 11:32): "As Augustine says, not even Samson is to be excused that he crushed himself, together with his enemies under the ruins of the house except the Holy Ghost, who had wrought many wonders through him, had secretly commanded him to do this."[19]

The eternal destiny of the Emperor Trajan presented a theological problem. Dante places him in the circle of the just in Paradise in the eye of the eagle, symbol of justice (*Par.* 20, lines 44–46). According to a legend widely believed, Trajan, who died a pagan, was restored to life and converted to Christianity at the prayer of Pope Gregory I. It was on account of his compassion for a poor widow that the pope was moved to pray for him. Aquinas accepts the account that he was restored to life and received the grace of remission of his sins and deliverance from punishment.[20] The *Legenda Aurea* contains a number of variants. One is that Trajan's punishment was simply delayed till the Last Judgment; another, that his sufferings in the next life were mitigated. According to a third version, Gregory himself was punished for praying for a pagan.[21] The fate of Origen was also questionable. In the early Church his works were controversial;

some in fact were condemned. Augustine says, "Origen has rightly been reproved by the Church on more than one account."[22] Such an unqualified verdict no longer prevails. Hans Urs van Balthasar remarks, "The battle against him lasted hundreds of years . . . and in the Middle Ages absurd stories of his apostasy kept circulating."[23]

It was at the request of a friar that Mechtild sought answers to the question of the salvation of these four persons. Her reply, transmitted as from Christ, was "I wish that the dispositions of my mercy toward the soul of Solomon should remain hidden from men so that they may most carefully avoid the sins of the flesh. What my kindness has done for the soul of Samson will also remain unknown so that men may be afraid to take vengeance on their enemies. What I have done for Origen will likewise be concealed so that no one may exalt himself, relying on his knowledge. Finally, what my generosity has provided for Trajan must by my will be unknown to men in order that the Catholic faith may be the more extolled, for that emperor, although endowed with all virtues, had neither Christian faith nor baptism" (*Livre* 5.16.332).

Like Mechtild, Elisabeth of Schönau was also questioned about the salvation of Origen. In answer to her brother's inquiry, she replied, "It is not the Lord's intention that much be revealed to you on this point. You must know that Origen's error did not come from bad will, but from the excessive fervor with which he plunged into the depths of Holy Scripture, which he loved. . . . Therefore the penalty which he endured was not severe."[24] After the reference to Origen, someone has added a marginal note in the St. Gall manuscript of the *Liber:* "What my kindness has done for the soul of Aristotle will remain hidden lest the philosopher limit himself to nature and despise celestial and supernatural things" (*Livre* 5.16.332, n. 1).

Studies of the mystics record many similar experiences. For example, Mechtild was directed to make a dwelling for Christ within her heart: "You could never find a gift more pleasing to me than a home within your heart where I could always live and take my delight. The house should have only one window where I should speak and distribute my gifts." By this image Mechtild understood that she was to speak only to spread the word of God and to teach or console those who came to her (*Livre* 2.33.174). A parallel text is found in Gertrude's *Legatus:* "Nowhere on earth can you find me [Christ] more surely than in the sacrament of the altar and in the heart of my beloved" (*Leg.* 1.3.3). This is a key text: Gertrude's portraits and statues usually show her bearing the image of Christ within her heart. The fourteenth-century recluse, Julian of Norwich, asserts that when God opened her "ghostly eye" she saw her soul in the midst of her heart. "He shall never remove therefrom without end. For in us is his homeliest home and his endless dwelling."[25] A similar passage occurs in the life of Catherine de' Ricci where it is recorded that Christ said to her, "I have come to seek shelter in your heart and in the hearts of all my daughters against the crimes of sinners."[26]

Like many other women mystics, Mechtild and Gertrude were physically frail and beset by illness. Mechtild's violent headaches sometimes lasted for weeks, and she was often sleepless. In her later years she suffered from the stone and, like Gertrude, from some form of hepatitis. Her final illness lasted three years. She also suffered mental pain from a variety of causes: the recollection of her faults; her inability to attend community exercises or perform her usual devotions when she was ill; the conviction that her illness made her useless; and grief over her "wasted life and graces." A long illness was made more trying by the loss of her sense of Christ's presence. She lamented this deprivation so bitterly that her cries could be heard throughout the house (*Livre* 2.26.165).

One of her most intense sufferings was the fright and sadness caused by diabolical temptations. At such times Mechtild wondered whether her spiritual communications were really from God. Overwhelmed and discouraged, she threw herself at the feet of Christ. In the depths of her spirit she heard him call her by name and reassure her: "Fear not . . . do not be surprised to find yourself exposed to these thoughts when you are with me. The devil tempted even me when I was hanging on the cross for you" (*Livre* 2.12.143). On another occasion when Mechtild was again assailed by doubts about the validity of her mystical experiences, she was reassured by the spirit of a Dominican friar whom she had counseled during his lifetime. According to the *Liber*, the friar appeared to her during mass. Calling her by name, he said, "Aha! I now know everything that you hid from me!" "Pray for me," she implored him, "that we may not be deceived by the devil in the gift [of revelation] which is given to us." "Clothe yourself in the armour of faith and believe firmly and steadfastly that the gift comes from God" was the reply (*Livre* 5.7.318–19).

Besides offering her physical and mental sufferings in expiation for her sins and those of others, Mechtild practiced other penances. She had fewer and worse garments than the other nuns; her habit was worn and patched; it was only in obedience that she accepted a veil of good material (*Livre* 5.30.351–52). The Abbess Gertrude sometimes ordered her to sleep after the early morning Office. When she had scarcely recovered from illness, however, Mechtild resumed her attendance at community prayers. In all her penances she remembered the sins committed by members of the Church: clergymen who neglected the study of Scripture or made use of it only for show; "spiritual persons" who disregarded the interior life and gave themselves only to active works; persons who cared neither for the word of God nor the sacraments (*Livre* 4.1.251).

Of the sins for which Mechtild punished herself so sharply, Gertrude knows of only one—in her childhood she had falsely announced that she saw a thief in the courtyard. She regarded this as a serious offence (*Livre* 5.30.351). Among her self-accusations she also included speaking ill of someone and of "inopportune silence." Once, after she had made a general confession, the priest told her to recite for her penance the *Te Deum*, the hymn recited on occasions of solemn thanksgiving for special benefits. After her death and that of her sister the abbess, two confessors testified that they had never encountered more innocent souls (*Livre* 5.30.351). That Gertrude the younger is not included in the commendation is taken as one of the internal evidences of her authorship of the *Liber*.

Mechtild was occasionally scandalized; she could become indignant at a display of ill-temper; she found it hard to be waited on when she was ill; she was afraid of death—the record of these traits shows that with all her mystical experiences she was an intimate member of the community—*nemo communior*, as was said of St. Dominic—no one less singular, more accessible.

4 The *Book of Special Grace*

ECHTILD was at first distressed when she learned that Gertrude and another nun had compiled the *Liber specialis gratiae* from her own account of her mystical experiences. Soon afterward, however, she had a vision of Christ which reassured her. She understood the words, "Do not be disturbed. Let her do what she is doing, for I will be her collaborator and helper" (*Livre* 2.42.186). The use of the feminine singular pronoun points to Gertrude as the chief compiler. This is only one of several indications of her role. Mechtild was made aware that as God had been generous to her, she should also be liberal in sharing the graces she had received. The title of the work, *Liber specialis gratiae*, was to signify not only that Mechtild herself had received special grace, but that reading about her experiences would be an occasion of special grace to others. They would be filled with joy, inspired by divine love, and consoled in their trials (*Livre* 2.43.188). Once Mechtild was convinced that the volume had been written according to the divine will, she was no longer disturbed but willingly read and corrected it. Thereafter she was as little concerned as if it had been written about another person (*Livre* 2.43.187).

It is explicitly stated that two nuns wrote the *Liber*. Mechtild speaks of rays from the Sacred Heart moving toward "the two persons who were writing this book" (*Livre* 5.22.343). Both Paquelin and Doyère in their respective editions of the writings from Helfta agree that Gertrude was one of these persons. Several kinds of evidence support this conclusion. One is the fact that a number of passages in the *Liber* deal with episodes also recorded in Gertrude's *Legatus*. That Gertrude's name is never mentioned in the *Liber* is also circumstantial evidence of her authorship. Such expressions as "the person to whom she told these things" and "another sister had the same experience" indicate Gertrude's identity. Most convincing of all is the style of certain chapters, notably chapter 30 in book 5 of the *Liber*, which gives a summary account of Mechtild's life and virtues. The fluid, clear, and graceful Latin is so similar to that in book 2 of the *Legatus*, admittedly by Gertrude, that both editors have no doubt of their common authorship. That both books were written in Latin is proved by two passages. In the *Legatus*, the word *mansuetudo* is analyzed and interpreted (*Leg.* 1.16.4). In the *Liber*, the two syllables in *ovum* are mentioned (*Livre* 3.42.240–41). A few German words are also used, always in a colloquial context; for instance, *minne* (love), "*quod interpretatur amor*" (*Livre* 2.17.147, n. 1).

The *Liber specialis gratiae* has seven divisions. After a prologue recounting Mechtild's birth, her entry into the monastery, and her various gifts and talents, the first division begins with a consideration of the Annunciation and ends with the feast of the Dedication of a Church. This section contains many suggestions for honoring Christ, his mother, and the saints on their feasts. Twelve chapters on the Virgin Mary are appended to this division. The second division, which includes accounts of many of Mechtild's experiences, deals with the intimate relations of the soul with God. The third and fourth sections are similar in content, but treat more specifically of some circumstances of conventual life. The fifth part deals with the afterlife and refers to a number of persons known to the community at Helfta: the Abbess Gertrude; Mechtild of Magdeburg, the former Beguine; some Dominican friars; and a little girl, E. de Orlamunde. Before her birth this child had been consecrated to God by her mother. Although she died in her second year, she received in heaven the reward of one who had belonged to a religious order, just as an infant who dies after baptism is saved by the faith of its godparents. Mechtild adds that she was so beautiful that had she grown to maturity, her father would have kept her from entering the cloister. Mechtild sees her in a rose-colored tunic and golden mantle embroidered with snow-white lilies (*Livre* 5.12.328–29). Marjorie Rigby comments on the "interesting coincidence that the *Liber*, like the fourteenth-century English poem, *Pearl*, includes a vision in which a child who died before she was two years old appears as a beautiful maiden splendidly arrayed."[1] The sixth and seventh books of the *Liber* tell of the life, death, and heavenly reward of the Abbess Gertrude and of her sister Mechtild.

Wilhelm Oehl lists the following subjects as common to the literature of mysticism: meditation on the birth, sufferings, and death of Christ; mystical love and intoxication; the dance of the soul; the spiritual battle for salvation; eschatology; the symbolism of numbers; criticism of the times; and the theological and symbolic use—derived from antiquity and beloved by the Middle Ages—of zoology, botany, and mineralogy.[2] In its inclusion of these subjects the *Liber* is representative of the literature of medieval mysticism. Such a list of themes gives no idea of the dynamism and color of Mechtild's book. There is nothing static about her descriptions— all is alive, moving and changing. She has the eye of a painter and the fresh mind of a child.

Many passages illustrate Mechtild's figurative use of flowers and animals. The lily ordinarily represents innocence; the violet and crocus, humility; herb bennet, thanksgiving; the sunflower, obedience. The rose, most frequently used in Mechtild's comparisons, is mentioned at least five times as the symbol of patience (*Livre* 4.35.286 and passim). This association is not original with Mechtild. To give only one instance of its occurrence elsewhere, a traditional hymn in honor of St. Dominic hails him as *rosa patientiae*. A familiar proverb is *Geduld bringt Rosen* (Patience wins roses). In other passages Mechtild uses the rose to symbolize charity, love of the divine will, martyrdom, prayer, and the heart of the Virgin Mary. In her morning prayer she offers her own heart as a rose (*Livre* 3.17.212). A five-petaled rose symbolizes the five senses of Christ (*Livre* 3.2.192). The suffering Christ is described as "the rose without thorns yet wounded by thorns" (*Livre* 1.19.68). A green rose represents the Abbess Gertrude's total abandonment to God (*Livre* 6.3.366).

The tree is a perennial symbol in art and theology. Mechtild and Gertrude both use it to illustrate the relationships between divinity and humanity, heaven and earth, virtue and sin. Ordinarily the tree images are associated with the liturgy. On Christmas night, inspired by the Isaian antiphon, "The stock of Jesse has put forth a branch, the branch has put forth a flower," Mechtild visualized the Virgin Mary in the form of a magnificent tree spreading over the entire universe. An exquisite flower grew from its summit, distilling a fragrant balm over the world (*Livre* 1.29.99). This scene is a visual representation of an early identification of the stock of Jesse (*virga*) with the Virgin Mary (*virgo*). Tertullian is one of several

Christian writers who saw in the text of Isaiah (11:1) a prefiguration of the Virgin Mary. He writes, "The rod which proceeds from the root of Jesse is Mary. The flower shall proceed from it. The flower is Christ."[3] A drawing in a twelfth-century manuscript of the *Speculum Virginum* contains an illustration of this concept.[4] Once during Mass, Mechtild seemed to see a great tree rising above the altar, its top reaching heaven, its branches shading the whole universe. The height of the tree signified Christ's divinity, the breadth, the perfection of his human life. Innumerable leaves and fruits symbolized all the good accomplished by his actions. On the leaves, inscribed in golden letters, were phrases designating the events of his life on earth—e.g. *Christ born, Christ circumcised, Christ presented in the temple.* After the Gospel was read, a golden ladder appeared, reaching to heaven. The Virgin Mary descended, carrying the Infant Jesus in her arms, and laid him on the altar (*Livre* 1.9.29–30). On another occasion Mechtild visualized Christ enthroned on a high mountain covered with fruit-bearing trees, each symbolizing a particular virtue. Under each tree were the saints notable for the virtue it symbolized (*Livre* 1.10.30). The *Liber* reports that during the octave of Corpus Christi she saw in the middle of the church a magnificent tree large enough to cover the earth. Three great branches grew in the form of a fleur-de-lis. Under one branch, animals, symbolizing sinners, were eating the fallen fruit. Persons who lived virtuously stood under another branch, eating fruit from the branches. On the upright branch, angels in the form of birds sang joyfully in praise of God. The souls in Purgatory in the likeness of shadowy human forms were refreshed by the fragrance issuing from the tree. Black birds representing demons flew toward it but were driven off by a great cloud of smoke which symbolized the memory of the passion (*Livre* 1.17.49–50). The color, detail, and animation of Mechtild's tree imagery in its relation to Gertrude's will be noted later.

Mechtild's knowledge of medieval animal lore is obvious. Through popular sayings, sermons, and art, the supposed characteristics of animals were employed to inculcate Christian doctrine and morality. The source of this largely fallacious information was the bestiary, a compilation based on the eleventh-century Latin *Physiologus*. For Mechtild, as for her contemporaries, animals often represent sinners. The lion stands for the proud: "the Lion, proud in the strength of his nature."[5] The ostrich symbolizes the hard-hearted, for after laying its eggs in a hole, it covers them with sand and departs, never to return.⁶ Hell is filled with serpents, toads, dogs, and other loathsome creatures who increase the sufferings of sinners. In the hearts of sinners she sees monsters, symbolizing the gnawing conscience. These are long-tailed worms with the heads and paws of dogs (*Livre* 5.22.334). Christ is represented by the lamb, but sheep and lambs also represent souls, Mechtild's among them (*Livre* 3.22.219; 4.60.306). Her soul is likewise said to be like a little hare, "asleep with its eyes open" (*Livre* 3.34.233; cf. Song 5:2). The dog is sometimes shown in a favorable light. Mechtild communicated to another person this advice as received from Christ: "Let her be like a trusty little dog who always returns to its master even after frequent rebuffs. If she is wounded by a word, she should not withdraw impatiently, or if she does so for a moment, let her return, relying on my mercy, which for a single sigh pardons everything" (*Livre* 4.32.283–84). In another comparison, Mechtild refers to the ant. When overwhelmed by the divine revelation, which came "like an impetuous torrent," she said, "Though you come to fulfill me wholly and enlighten me marvelously, I am so tiny a creature that all I know or can make others know about you is no more than an ant can carry away from a vast mountain" (*Livre* 5.22.354). Mechtild of Magdeburg, it will be recalled, used similar language; her examples were a bee and a jar of honey.

In Mechtild's imagery, birds in general represent angels, while black birds are demons and temptations. She frequently mentions doves and eagles, the former symbolizing the Holy Spirit, the souls of the dead, and various individuals. Eagles, in addition to representing the Holy Spirit, are symbols of Christ and of contemplative souls, notably the Abbess Gertrude (*Livre* 1.23.82; 2.27.167; 3.40.239; 5.6.316). The prayers of the community appear under the form of larks (*Livre* 4.22.272). Mechtild uses a comparison to illustrate the individual differences among the many persons she counseled: some are like nightingales, enamored of God; others, who perform their good works with joyous humility, are larks; the doves are simple souls who quietly receive the gifts of God without discussing his doings nor those of others (*Livre* 3.16.210). She sees her own soul under the form of a bird with three feathers, red for desire, green for love, yellow for hope (*Livre* 2.26.166). A Middle English poem, "The Bird with Four Feathers," interprets them as youth, beauty, strength, and wealth.⁷

Richly colored symbolic garments adorned with jewels and golden ornaments often figure in Mechtild's descriptions of her heavenly visitants. The liturgical colors, red, green, white, and purple, are most common. Blue is rare. The following accounts are typical. "The King of glory once appeared in indescribable splendor in the fullness of his joy, wearing a golden robe embroidered with doves and covered by a red mantle. This garment was open on two sides to indicate that the soul has free access to God. The red mantle symbolized the passion." The doves represented the simplicity of the divine Heart, "whose dispositions are unchangeable, although the creature so often fails in faithfulness to him" (*Livre* 3.49.246). "The Queen of virgins was clothed in a golden mantle embroidered with pairs of red doves facing each other, each with a fresh lily in its beak." The golden mantle symbolized her ardent love of God, the red doves her patience in adversity, the lilies her actions and virtues (*Livre* 2.38.181). "On the vigil of a feast day, the Purification, Mary came, carrying her royal child Jesus, clothed in a sky-blue tunic covered with flowers. On his breast, around his neck, and on his arms was written his gracious name, Jesus Christ" (*Livre* 1.12.36). Love, personified as a beautiful maiden, wore a green robe: Suddenly, golden lattices covered her garment, and within each lattice was the image of Christ the King (*Livre* 1.20.70). After Mechtild's death, Gertrude visualized her in a crystalline robe sparkling like the stars. Her golden girdle was set with rubies, emeralds, and other jewels of dazzling colors. The splendor of her attire lit up paradise with a new light, and the sweet harmony of the crystalline garments resounded through the heavens (*Livre* 7.16.396). This is an example of the synesthesia, fusing of sense impressions, that both Mechtild and Gertrude sometimes employ.

Flowers and jewels symbolize the virtues of glorified souls. Mechtild sees a young bride adorned with rings representing wisdom, love, fidelity, and other virtues; her diadem signifies praise and reverence; bracelets, her good actions and labor. She wears on her heart a bouquet made of her loving memory of God's words (*Livre* 4.31.281). After the death of the Abbess Gertrude, she appears to her sister Mechtild in a magnificent green robe adorned with innumerable stars. Pearls and rubies adorn the seams (*Livre* 6.7.372). Another glorified spirit is a friar, "a faithful and intimate friend of the monastery," who wears shoes embroidered exquisitely in honor of his patience during his long tiring journeys as a preacher (*Livre* 5.7.318).

The significance of jewels as set forth in the medieval lapidaries is familiar to both Gertrude and Mechtild. When Mechtild visualizes Christ seated with one foot resting on a sapphire and the other on a garnet, she remembers that as the sapphire has the virtue of driving out malign humors, so the soul is purified through the wounds of Christ, and "as the garnet gladdens the heart, so Christ's wounds bring joy after the forgiveness of sins" (*Livre* 2.1.133). Pearls have the power to cure certain diseases (*Livre* 4.37.287). Mechtild shares the belief that as only blood can break the diamond, so the blood shed in Christ's passion can destroy the fault of Adam (*Livre* 2.17.148). Catherine of Siena employs the same comparison.[8]

During a mass offered for the dead, Mechtild envisioned a graphic representation of Christ's intimate association with material creation and his union with humanity. His crown was set with jewels symbolizing the virtues of men and women. He was wearing a garment covered with a panel which resembled the gremial, an apron-like vestment formerly worn by bishops. This garment was marvelously composed of human hair, tendrils of plants, and the fur of animals, "because the smallest details of creation are reflected in the most holy Trinity through the humanity of Jesus Christ" (*Livre* 4.3.253). A second manifestation of the relationship of creation to the divinity occurred during the chanting of the *Benedicite*. This hymn (Dn 3:52) calls upon all the powers of nature to praise God. As Mechtild wondered how such creatures as the sun, moon, stars, snow, ice, winds, rain—could offer praise, it seemed that she heard the words: "When one chants this canticle or any similar one which invokes creatures to praise me, they come spiritually into my presence like living persons who glorify me for all my benefits" (*Livre* 3.7.200). This spiritual communication evokes an astounding series of images, challenging the imagination.

Pageantry and spectacle illuminate many of Mechtild's mystical communications. Feasts and processions, the throne of God, and the entourage of angels in the New Jerusalem witness to a conception of spiritual magnificence that recalls the paintings of Fra Angelico and the poetry of Dante. One such scene depicts Mechtild's mystical experience of ascending the mountain of virtue in company with Christ. She envisages a house of transparent silver, surrounded by white-robed children "playing delightedly and praising God." These are the souls of children who died before the age of five and are now eternally happy. Next, she sees a mansion of red carved stones surrounded by a singing throng dressed in purple. These are persons who were married or widowed. The third house, of sapphire, is for an innumerable crowd of scarlet-clad saints. These are the ones who battled valiantly for Christ against the devil. The last house, of pure gold, is the dwelling place of charity where Christ and his mother hold court (*Livre* 1.13.44).

Another passage relates Mechtild's interview with "the least saint in heaven." Clothed in a green garment, he was slender, of medium stature, with curly hair, blue eyes, and remarkably fine features. He said to her, "On earth I was a robber and malefactor. I never did any good deed." "Then how is it that you have entered into joy?" she asked. He answered, "My evil deeds were done not out of malice but ignorance. My parents had reared me in wickedness. At the last moment by God's mercy I repented, and after a long time of suffering, by the gracious kindness of God I was led to this eternal peace" (*Livre* 1.33.110–11).

An extended passage recalls in terms of a wedding festival the sufferings of Christ in his passion: "Call to mind my divine love which drew me from my Father's bosom and caused me to serve thirty-three years seeking for you. And when the time of my wedding was at hand I was sold by my own heart's love as the price of the wedding banquet, and I gave myself for bread and meat and drink. I myself was the kithara and organ at the banquet by means of my gentle words; and to entertain the guests I humbled myself at the feet of my disciples. . . . Call to mind what kind of dance I performed after the banquet, when I fell three times, making such powerful bounds that dripping with bloody sweat, I shed great drops of blood. In that dance I clothed all my fellow-soldiers in threefold garments, when I obtained for them the forgiveness of their sins, the sanctification of their souls, and a share in my divine glory. Remember my humble love when the betrayer came near and kissed me. I felt such ardent love that had he repented, I would have taken his soul to be my bride. . . . Call to mind what kind of marriage songs I heard when I stood before the judge and false witness was brought against me. . . . Remember how for your love I adorned myself when I changed my garments so many times, for my vestments were white and purple and scarlet, and instead of a garland of roses I wore a crown of thorns. . . . Remember how I embraced you when I was bound to the column; for your sake I took on myself all the darts of your enemies. Be mindful how I entered the marriage-bed of the cross. And as spouses give their bridal clothes to actors, I gave my garments to the soldiers and my body to those who crucified me. Then fastened by the cruel nails I stretched out my arms for your dear embrace, singing on my bed of love seven songs of marvelous love" (*Livre* 3.1.190–91).

Some passages in the foregoing quotation have parallels in other medieval writings. "I was sold . . . as the price of the marriage banquet, and I gave myself for bread and meat and drink" recalls lines in the twelfth-century ballad of Judas where Christ asks the apostles at the Last Supper:

> Wou sitte ye, postles, ant wi nule ye ete?
> Ic am iboust ant isold today for oure mete.[9]

The reference to the "bounds" and the "dance" of Christ recalls the ancient association of religion with dance. The passage on the "leaping" of the beloved in the *Song of Songs* inspired the commentary of Hippolytus: "What is meant by this 'leaping'? The Logos leapt from heaven into the womb of the Virgin, he leapt from the womb of his mother on to the cross, from the cross into Hades and from Hades once more back on to the earth. . . . And he leapt from the earth into heaven where he sits on the right hand of the Father. And he will again leap on to the earth with glory to bring judgment." This passage inspired later writers, among them Ambrose and Bede. It appears somewhat altered in the *Legenda Aurea* of Jacobus de Varagine and in Caxton's English translation.[10]

In his treatise, *The Chirche*, Wyclif writes, "Crist . . . ledith the daunce of love," and Margery Kempe hears Christ say, "I xal take the be the on hand in Hevyn and my Modyr be the other hand, and so xalt thu dawnsyn in Hevyn wyth other holy maydens and virgynes."[11] While dance imagery occurs in the writings of all three mystics of Helfta, it seems particularly frequent in Mechtild's *Liber*. During the Easter season she envisioned a heavenly wedding banquet at which Christ appeared in green garments adorned with golden roses. The whole celestial assembly was similarly robed. When the feast was ready, Christ asked, "Who will take the part of the jongleur at this banquet?" At once, taking Mechtild in his hands, he led her in the dance (*Livre* 1.19.68). Another description shows Christ in the center of a round dance of virgins with tambourines (*Livre* 5.5.313–14). As noted earlier, on her anniversary the Abbess Gertrude is shown as honored by all the deceased members of the community, who surround her in a choral dance.

The concept of Christ's whole life as a dance of love is developed in the English carol "My Dancing Day," which begins,

> Tomorrow will be my dancing day
> I would my true love did so chance
> To see the legend of my play,
> To call my true love to the dance.[12]

Note that in the preceding example as in those in the writings from Helfta, Christ is not a solitary dancer. He is seeking partners. In Mechtild and her companions he finds them.

Mechtild frequently expressed the conviction that one can share in the merits of Christ. The chapter, "How One Can Play at Dice with Christ," is an ingenious presentation of her teaching. She begins by saying that the Virgin Mary gives her dice to present to a person for whom she [Mechtild] has been praying. "Give them to her from me so that she may play with my Son. When a husband casts dice with his wife, he likes to take from her in game her rings, her jewels, the pretty ornaments she has made for herself; for her part, she claims for herself everything that belongs to her beloved." Then follows a curious exposition of the signification of the marks on the dice. One point stands for the lowliness of the human person who throws this into the game by accepting scorn, contradiction, and willing endurance of dependence on others. By this, one wins what Christ possesses—namely, the exaltation and honor which his Father gave him in compensation for his abasement on earth. Similarly, the two marks on the dice stand for the human body and soul; gambling with these by performing spiritual or bodily works for the love of God, one wins all the merits of Christ's divinity and humanity. Three points signify the powers of the soul: memory, will, and understanding; the image of the Trinity is impressed on the soul that rightly uses these powers. Four points are cast when the soul abandons itself to God in prosperity and adversity for the present and for the future; five points when the five senses are gratified only according to God's good pleasure; six points when one devotes the six ages of his life to the service of God. In return for these plays, one receives the benefits of the creation of the four parts of the earth governed by God's power and wisdom, the five wounds of Christ with all the fruits of his passion, and the virtues and merits of Christ's life on earth (*Livre* 4.27.276–78). In *The Way of Perfection*, Teresa of Avila employs a similar metaphor in her description of the game of chess where the soul gives checkmate to the divine King.[13]

Many other passages in the *Liber* describe the transference of the merits of Christ, his Mother, and the saints. Often this sharing is indicated by similarity of garments (*Livre* e.g., 1.11.33). Once it seemed that Christ placed his hands over Mechtild's to show that he gave her the merits of all his works (*Livre* 1.1.7). At another time she visualized him as a child of five. When she asked the reason, she understood as his answer, "You are now fifty. My first year compensates for your first ten years, my second for your next decade. . . . Thus all your sins are effaced, your years made holy, your entire life perfected by mine" (*Livre* 2.9.141).

The Virgin Mary is also represented as offering her own graces and good works for the benefit of others. Agnes is among the saints whose special graces Mechtild shared. On the saint's feast, she lamented that so young a child should have loved and suffered generously for Christ, whereas she herself after many years had accomplished so little. At this, she sensed that Christ said to Agnes, "Give her everything you have" (*Livre* 1.11.34). Mechtild then understood that God has given the saints the privilege of sharing all the merits they have won and all that Christ has accomplished in them with persons who honor them and thank God for their graces. She also believed that they receive additional glory and happiness in heaven when one pays them special honor. Such insights, besides strengthening Mechtild's realization of the communion of saints, contributed to her confidence in God's mercy and accessibility. "Christ is more easily possessed than a bit of thread or straw," she said, "a single wish, a sigh, is sufficient" (*Livre* 3.35.235).

Not only color and originality but vigorous expression characterizes many parts of the *Liber specialis gratiae*. For example, when Christ's captors advanced to take him, "He went toward them as eagerly as a mother goes to snatch her child from wolves" (*Livre* 1.18.52). Apropos of Mechtild's devotion to the sufferings of Christ, it is said that if anyone spoke of the passion, she was consumed with such fervor that her face and hands became "as red as a boiled crab" (*in modum decocti cancrii appararent; Livre* 5.30.353). The image of a scullion as a symbol of self-will is part of an instruction on obedience as the regulating virtue in monastic life. A sister who had sacrificed her self-will by an act of renunciation asked Mechtild to present her offering to God. As she did so at mass, she saw rising from the ciborium the figure of a small child, who was suddenly transformed into a beautiful young girl, personifying the divine will. At the same time she saw an ugly little scullion in smoky black clothes, the personification of self-will, who tried to attract the attention of the obedient nuns. Some disregarded him, but others began to smile at him, to speak to him, and finally to whisper with him. The description ends with the warning that if those who follow their own inclinations do not repent and become truly obedient, they will suffer eternal poverty with self-will, "that wretched scullion" (*Livre* 4.19.268–69). This scene resembles Gertrude's vision of a "despicable creature" whom she saw attempting to make her pour the poison of vainglory into the cup offered to her by Christ (*Leg.* 2.11.2).

It is not surprising that the *Liber specialis gratiae* had wide dissemination after Mechtild's death. The Dominicans who had known and esteemed her were most active in propagating her work. In Paquelin's preface to the Solesmes edition of the *Liber* he twice mentions Boccaccio's reference to "*la lauda di Donna Matelda*" (*Rev.* 2, preface, ix). The passage occurs in the *Decamerone:* "A carder and vendor of wool, captain of the *laudesi* at Santa Maria Novella, the Dominican church in Florence, used to make gifts of cloth to the friars. In return they taught him the pater noster in the vernacular, and among other prayers and hymns, '*la lauda di Donna Matelda.*'"[14]

The complete text of the original Latin *Liber* as edited by Louis Paquelin of Solesmes Abbey is based on the Guelferbytanus codex of 1370. Within the next century an abridged version was current on the Continent and in England. All have the title, *Liber spiritualis gracie*, the abbreviation *sp* for *specialis* having been incorrectly expanded. Before 1500 both Latin and English copies were in the London area. Theresa A. Halligan, editor of the Middle English translation of this abridged version, considers it possible that the Carthusians brought the work to England soon after the foundation of Sheen in 1414, and that it was translated either by a monk there or by a brother at Syon Abbey. Two copies of this version, *The Booke of Gostlye Grace*, are extant: Oxford, Bodley MS 220 B, in London dialect, and British Library, Egerton MS 2006, in a northern dialect. For her edition, Halligan used the latter with emendations from the Oxford manuscript when it contained superior readings.[15] The translation is generally faithful to the Latin, with few interpolations, none significant. Unlike the original, the work is addressed to men and women in religious orders and the tone is frequently didactic.

Halligan provides evidence of the circulation and popularity of

Mechtild's revelations in England. In addition to the surviving Latin and English manuscripts there are records of other copies. She lists many compilations of devotional material containing excerpts from Mechtild's revelations and prayers. Of several fifteenth-century bequests, the earliest is that of Alianora Roos of York in 1438, who left to Dame Joan Courtenay a work called the "Maulde buke." In 1495, Cicely, duchess of York and mother of Richard III, left to her granddaughter Bridget, a Dominican nun of Dartford, "a boke of sainte Matilde" as well as a life of Catherine of Siena and the *Legenda aurea*. In 1491 Thomas Symson, a secular priest of York, left to another priest, W. Cok, also of York, "*j. librum de Revelatione Beate Matilde, cum aliis tractatibus in eodem.*"[16]

A problem that some Dante scholars call insoluble is the identity of Matelda, the singing lady who appears in canto 28 of the *Purgatorio*. She is seen in a flowery meadow, "all alone, singing and culling flower from flower." When Dante greets her, she turns to him "as a lady turns in the dance with feet close together on the ground." She tells him that the psalm, "*Delectasti,*" "You make me glad, O Lord, by your deeds; at the work of your hands I rejoice" (Ps 92:4), "gives light that may dispel the cloud from your mind." She adds, "I have come ready for all your questions till you are satisfied." When she had finished speaking, she sang "like a lady enamoured '*Beati quorum tecta sunt peccata.*'" Blessed are they whose sins are covered (Ps 31:1). She is answered by a chorus of invisible spirits singing "Hosanna!" After Dante has submitted to the reproaches of Beatrice, Matelda draws him through the waters of Lethe (*Purg.* 27, 29, 31).

One may accept the premise that Dante's singing maiden is not an abstraction representing innocence, unfallen human nature, or the like, although such a conjecture has been made. As John Sinclair says, "it would hardly be possible for so . . . human a figure to be only a symbol" (*Purg.* 374). It was Dante's practice to include among his characters actual historical persons. Among the many suggested as prototypes of Matelda, four have received special attention: the Countess Matilda of Tuscany; an unnamed lady in the *Vita Nuova*; the Beguine Mechtild of Magdeburg; and Mechtild of Hackeborn.[17]

Most of the earliest commentators as well as some modern critics believe that Dante's original was the Countess Matilda of Tuscany (1046–1115). Beautiful and learned, she became an ardent supporter of the beleaguered papacy during the conflict between Church and Empire. As a girl she gave herself to the study of martial arts, learning how to ride with spear and lance, and to fight with pike, sword, and battle-axe. At the head of her own armies she led innumerable expeditions in aid of successive pontiffs. Her contemporary biographer Domnizo (or Donizo), priest and chronicler of Canossa, speaks admiringly of her many battles.[18] Having inherited the wealth of her father Boniface, marquis of Tuscany, she made large contributions to the papacy. Her fortified castle of Canossa, encircled by three walls, was the scene of the famous submission of Henry IV to Gregory VII. There Matilda interceded with the reluctant pope for the temporarily penitent king. On other occasions Canossa served as the site of papal encounters, conferences, and tribunals—"a new Rome" says Domnizo. From this palatial setting Matilda ruled her vast estate with dignity. "No one, of whatsoever rank, might enter her presence without bending the knee."[19]

Matilda's first marriage was to Godfrey of Lorraine, called "the Hunchback." Tradition and legend speak of a son who died in infancy. This marriage ended in separation. Her second marriage, into which she entered reluctantly, was to the eighteen-year-old Guelf V, duke of Bavaria. Matilda was forty-three and had already rejected several other proposals. It was generally recognized that the marriage was simply for the political advantage of the papacy. It also ended in separation. Domnizo says nothing about the two marriages.

In support of his argument that the prototype of Dante's Matelda could be none other than the countess of Tuscany, Ferdinand Koenen emphasizes her piety and asceticism. He gives comparatively little attention to her military exploits. He quotes Domnizo's statement that she fasted rigorously, kept night vigils, and lived the life of a nun.[20] Letters from Gregory VII suggest that she wished to enter the cloister. Domnizo calls her a daughter of St. Peter, and praises her for serving the pope as both Martha and Mary.[21] Especially in her later years she paid many visits to monasteries and was frequently in the company of monks and clerics. Her generous and numerous charities included large donations of land and money to towns and monasteries, contributions to the building of cathedrals, and the founding of the school of jurisprudence at Bologna. In her last hours she liberated all her serfs. Because of her dedication to the papal cause, Koenen considers her the most suitable prototype for Matelda, who guided Dante to the procession of the Church.[22]

There are no authentic contemporary portraits of Matilda. The fresco above her tomb at San Benedetto Polirone near Mantua shows her clad in a long mantle and mounted on a white horse. In her left hand she holds the reins and in her right a pomegranate, symbol of the Church, the many seeds representing the members. A portrait in the cathedral at Mantua depicts a beautiful, helmeted young woman. Koenen suggests that both these paintings may be copies of older portraits.[23] Bernini's heroic statue in St. Peter's shows the countess holding the papal tiara and a large key protectively under her arm. Her right hand grasps a mace. In the first of three inscriptions over her tomb at San Benedetto, Matilda is hailed as a warrior-woman (*virago*) "who disposed her troops like the Amazonian Penthesilea through so many contests in fierce wars."[24]

In the course of her long life Matilda wrote many letters in Latin, signing them, *Matilda Dei gratia si quid est* (Matilda, such as she is, by the grace of God, if she is anything).[25] The signature suggests a depth of self-knowledge and spirituality that challenges some appraisals of her life and character.

Another person proposed as Dante's model for Matelda is one of the gentle maidens in the *Vita Nuova*. Robert Hollander quotes C. S. Grandgent, who notes that "Dante's method of symbolism, proceeding from the actual to the general, makes the most likely conjecture one that would see behind and in Matelda the traces of an actual Florentine girl, a friend of Beatrice, suggesting as a possibility the girl whose untimely death is mourned in the *Vita Nuova* and the sonnet, *Morte villana*.[26] Dorothy Sayers is among those who hold this opinion. She writes, "Matelda's position as an attendant and friend, to whom Beatrice speaks with a kind of intimate and smiling familiarity, lends a certain propriety to this identification."[27] Perhaps, like Beatrice, Matelda is a person from the private life of Dante.

Those who argue that the Beguine, Mechtild of Magdeburg, was Dante's inspiration assume that he knew her writings. They allege her ardent lyricism, her description of mystical dance, and her virginity as their evidence. Ancelet-Hustache is the chief proponent of this identification.[28] It is true that many passages in *Das fliessende Licht* parallel sections in Dante, as Edmund Gardner has demonstrated. He shows however, that Mechtild of Hackeborn's *Liber* contains an approximately equal number of parallels.[29]

In Mechtild of Hackeborn's *Liber specialis gratiae* the most obvious similarities to Dante are the description of the seven-terraced mount with its seven fountains, the melodious voice singing *Venite benedicti Patris mei* (Mt 25:34) and the singing of the *Asperges* (*Livre* 1.13.39–41; 2.19.152; 2.2.135; cf. *Purg.* 10–15, 17, 31). Mechtild's description of Purgatory also contains several images suggestive of Dante's: persons who have been unfaithful to their rule and religious profession walk bowed down as if under crushing burdens; gluttons and drunkards are shriveled up by hunger and thirst (*Livre* 5.20.339; cf. *Purg.* 11, 23). With Dante's description of the three steps made of marble, purple stone, and porphyry before the gate of Purgatory in canto 9, one may compare Mechtild's description of the three steps before the altar of God. Dante's steps have been regarded as symbols of examination of conscience, contrition, and penance. Mechtild's steps are made of gold for charity, blue stone for meditation on heavenly things, and green for energy in performing actions for God's honor (*Purg.* 9; *Livre* 1.31.106).

Most commentators who discuss the relationship of the *Liber* and the *Divine Comedy* confine themselves to the descriptions of Purgatory. Some parallels in the accounts of Paradise may also be cited. When the souls of the blessed manifest themselves to Dante in the various spheres, he is told that they are not actually there; they are really in heaven but show themselves in lower spheres to signify their varying degrees of beatitude (*Par.* 4). So in the *Liber* when Mechtild has a vision symbolizing the praise of the Trinity, she understands as the words of Christ, "What you see is not taking place in heaven itself, but because you see me in whom every creature is contained, you see all creatures as if they were present" (*Livre* 4.15.265). Likewise, with the line in Dante, "Near and far adds not there nor takes away," one may compare St. John's words to Mechtild, who is surprised to see the apostles apparently below married men who possessed worldly goods, "We are not really farther from God, for he dwells in us, just as I wrote, 'The Word was made flesh and dwelt among us'" (Jn 1:14). He added, "And you, are you farther from God because of the place you occupy?" (*Par.* 30; *Livre* 4.8.259).

Another parallel occurs in the sixth book of the *Liber* where the voices of the saints singing joyously enter into a long trumpet from which the sounds emerge as a single voice (*Livre* 6.9.376). This description recalls the image of the eagle, symbol of justice, in the *Paradiso* where the many spirits composing the form of the bird speak with a single voice (*Par.* 19).

Finally, Mechtild's image of the wheel and cord representing the free will of the human person united to the perfect will of God suggests the image with which Dante ends his poem (*Livre* 4.20.269–70):

> To the high imagination force now failed;
> But like to a wheel whose circling nothing jars,
> Already on my desire and will prevailed
> The Love that moves the sun and the other stars.
>
> (*Par.* 33)[30]

Paquelin believes that Mechtild of Hackeborn was Dante's model. He writes, "Compare this chapter [*Livre* 2.2] with canto 28 of the *Purgatorio* and it will become evident that the poet wished to designate St. Mechtild as the Lady Matelda." The chapter in question begins with the chanting of the *Asperges*. In answer to this prayer for purification, Mechtild is permitted to enter the Heart of Christ "as into a vineyard" through which a river of living water flows from east to west. Paquelin considers this episode a parallel to Matelda's drawing Dante through the waters of Lethe (*Livre* 2.2.135).

Sinclair is the strongest contemporary advocate for Mechtild of Hackeborn as Dante's model for his *donna soletta*. Like other critics, he maintains that it is not Dante's habit to create a purely symbolic figure with no human prototype. He considers the most plausible model the nun "whose sweet and gentle visions of the Earthly Paradise are in some respects in agreement with Dante's, and may well have attracted and influenced him" (*Purg.* 374). One might add that the personality of the singing Matelda who graciously instructs the penitent Dante resembles that of "the nightingale of Christ" whom, as Gertrude attests, "everyone loved and wished to be with," whose book is filled with images of fields, gardens, fountains, music, and dance.

Fiorenzo Forti has given an extensive account of the arguments concerning Matelda's prototype. Most of the protagonists are vehemently opposed to those who hold other opinions. Francesco D'Ovidio asserts, "One thing is certain. Matelda is not the countess [of Tuscany] . . . a fiery imperious old woman of seventy, who was twice married."[31] Thomas J. Bergin believes that the early commentators' choice of the countess may appear to modern critics as "unesthetic."[32] Grandgent likewise rejects the "grave ruler" as well as the contemplative nun, Mechtild of Hackeborn.[33] Koenen rejects both Mechtilds as inappropriate representatives of the active life.³⁴ Hans Urs von Balthasar, who calls Mechtild of Magdeburg "the weather-beaten old Sybil who came to Helfta *post multas tribulationes*," obviously would not consider her the prototype of Matelda.³⁵

After mentioning the writings of Gertrude and the two Mechtilds, Karl Vossler comments: "If one considers the similarities and analogues to Dante's *Purgatorio* which these works reveal, especially in reference to his Earthly Paradise and its streams of oblivion and consolation, its successive steps of purification, etc., it is hard to resist the surmise that Dante read the *Revelationes* of these Benedictine nuns or heard of them, or even that the figure of his Matelda was created as a memorial to the two Mechtilds."³⁶ A stronger possibility is that the coincidence of two mystics with the same name, both associated with Helfta, may have led Dante to attribute to a single writer the works of both women.

Having surveyed the array of arguments and counter-arguments, Forti concludes that no one among the contending parties has succeeded in finding an argument capable of silencing his opponents.³⁷ Matelda remains the most mysterious figure in the *Divine Comedy*.

5 From the Land of Unlikeness: Gertrude the Great

In the year 1261 a five-year-old girl was brought to the monastery of Helfta and entrusted to the care of the Abbess Gertrude of Hackeborn. The child was also named Gertrude, but of her family nothing is known. Unlike many of her companions in the convent school, she has no recorded surname and may have been of humble or illegitimate birth. Various passages in her writings suggest that she was an orphan (*Leg.* 1.16.5; 5.17.1). One fact only is noted: she was born on the feast of the Epiphany, 6 January (*Leg.* intr. 13).

At the time of Gertrude's arrival, Helfta was at the height of its achievement and influence. From the days of the first abbess, Cunegund of Halberstadt, the community had won the admiration and confidence of clergy and people. As noted earlier, members of important families of the region had joined the community. The records of donation include gifts from two archbishops of Magdeburg. Among the most constant and generous benefactors were Albert and Louis of Hackeborn, brothers of the Abbess Gertrude.[1] With her sister Mechtild she was to become an important influence in the life of her young namesake.

Despite the charming landscape of Helfta, the stimulating intellectual atmosphere, and the careful observance of monastic regulations, the convent was to become for the young Gertrude a *regio dissimilitudinis*, "a land of unlikeness," where she would wander unhappily until she experienced the mystical intervention of Christ. The change was not sudden. The nun whose biographical account forms the first portion of the *Legatus divinae pietatis* reports that Gertrude loved study. "She distinguished herself by her eager attentiveness and keen intelligence, far surpassing her companions." As she grew to maturity, she became outstanding for eloquence in speech and skill in writing (*Leg.* 1.1.1, 3). Eventually, it seems, her ardor for intellectual activities made the obligations of conventual life wearying. From the eager, attractive child loved by all and devoted to the studies that she mastered so easily, Gertrude gradually changed into a tense and melancholy young woman. "Alas," she writes, "I was a nun in name and appearance only" (*Leg.* 2.1.1).

The change had probably been imperceptible. From all the excellent qualities recorded of Gertrude's abbess, the gift of discernment may have been lacking. Moreover, the younger Gertrude's self-respect and sense of decorum would have kept her from any obvious transgression, while her natural charm and courtesy would have concealed the change from all but an acute observer. "If you [Christ] had not given me a natural aversion to evil and an attraction to good as well as the reproofs of others, I should have lived like a pagan among pagans" (*Leg.* 2.23.1). Her deviation from the monastic ideal she had professed led to anxiety and depression. In the Advent of 1280 her sadness reached a climax.

Gertrude was twenty-six when on 27 January 1281, two months after her most profound depression, she experienced the presence of Christ. "I was in the dormitory, having just bowed to an older nun according to our custom, when standing before me I saw a youth of sixteen years." She relates that he addressed her in the words of the response in the Office for Advent: "Your salvation is at hand. Why are you consumed with sadness? Have you no counselor that you are so changed by sorrow?" When he had said these words, although she knew that she was in the convent dormitory, yet it seemed to her that she was in her usual corner in the chapel where she was accustomed to say her half-hearted prayers. "I shall save you and deliver you. Do not be afraid," she heard him say. "After these words I saw his gentle right hand clasp mine as if in solemn confirmation. 'You have licked the dust with my enemies and have sucked honey among thorns. Now return to me and I shall make you drink of the torrent of my delights.'"[2] As she listened, Gertrude saw between them a tremendous hedge so set with thorns it seemed impossible to surmount. Incapable of approaching Christ and overcome with longing, she suddenly felt herself lifted and set beside him. It was then that in the hand extended to her she saw the wound of the nail (*Leg.* 2.1.1).[3]

With Gertrude's experience of Christ's love, her life changed. "In new peace and joy I began to run in the fragrance of your ointments (Song 1:3) and to understand the sweetness and lightness of your yoke which I had so recently considered insupportable" (*Leg.* 2.1.2). With the insight imparted by her realization of the divine presence, she also acquired a new self-knowledge. "Hitherto I had," as she vigorously phrases it, "given as little thought to my interior life as—if I may say so—to the interior of my feet" (*Leg.* 2.2.1). Now she perceived such disorder and confusion in herself that she felt totally unfit to become God's dwelling-place. As she continued to struggle against her faults, she often refreshed herself by recollecting the signs of Christ's love. She writes, "Although the rose is far lovelier in the spring when it is in full bloom and fragrance, nevertheless in winter when it is withered it can still inspire a little joy by the memory of its former charm. So to praise your love I wish by this comparison to express what I experienced deeply in this vision which overwhelmed me with joy. May any reader who has received similar or greater graces be inspired by remembering them to give thanks" (*Leg.* 2.21.2). In the *Ascent of Mount Carmel*, John of the Cross has written similarly: "For though the effect of the apprehension be not so great afterwards, when it is recalled, as it was on the first occasion when it was communicated, yet, when it is recalled, love is renewed and the mind is lifted up to God. . . . And thus this is a great favor for the soul on which God bestows it, for it is as though it had within itself a mine of blessings."[4]

The early biographer asserts that after the manifestation of Christ in January 1281, Gertrude's attitude toward her studies changed completely. "From a grammarian she became a theologian" (*Leg.* 1.1.2). Doyère qualifies this statement, pointing out that her "conversion" was not a return to God from a life of sin, indifference, or frivolity, but rather a transition from an intellectual to a mystical perspective. Hitherto her youthful enthusiasm for study had been directed to the things of God but as concerns of science. She had faithfully conformed to the rules of monastic observance but simply as fulfilling the obligations of her state of life. On that "blessed day" in January all was changed. The God whom theology strove to explain became a living person, beloved—the only beloved—who wished to reveal himself as a bridegroom to a bride. More convincing than all theological formulas and conclusions, such an experience of love went far beyond intellectual illumination (*Leg.* intr. 32, 33).

Gertrude did not renounce her love of study nor her scholarship. Even in her most exalted spiritual writing she remembered her rhetoric. She remained the student; her frequent prayers called on Christ as "Best of teachers."

In her newfound joy, Gertrude recovered her love of nature. The fertile landscape of Helfta was the setting for a memorable experience. As she writes in the second book of the *Legatus*, "One day between Easter and the feast of the Ascension when I went into the garden before Prime and sat near the fishpond, I was delighting in the beauty of the scene—the clear flowing stream, the foliage of the surrounding trees, the flying birds, especially the doves—but above all, the solitude. As I asked myself what more I could wish to complete my happiness, I realized that without doubt it was a close, congenial, intimate, and loving friend to share my solitude" (*Leg.* 2.3.1). With this realization came the conviction that Christ might indeed make his home within her if like the stream her constant gratitude could return to its source, like the trees she could be fruitful in good works, and like the doves rise above the things of earth. As she knelt for her evening prayers, after reflecting on these thoughts all day, suddenly she recalled the words of the gospel: "If anyone love me, he will keep my word, and my Father will love him and we will come to him and make our dwelling with him" (Jn 14:23). At that moment Gertrude realized that without waiting for her complete purification, Christ had indeed made his home within her. "Within the mire of my heart I felt your presence. Oh that the entire ocean were changed into blood to cover my head and thus drown the depths of the vileness where your unspeakable nobility has chosen to make your dwelling! Or that my heart might be taken out of my body and purified by burning coals that it might be, certainly not worthy, but less unworthy of your dwelling" (*Leg.* 2.3.2).

To Gertrude, the divine patience which watched her fluctuating efforts to amend her life seemed more notable than the patience shown to Judas. It seemed to her that Christ was more grieved than angered by her faults. In his treatment of her he seemed, she says, desirous to spare her embarrassment. Despite her forgetfulness of him, a forgetfulness lasting sometimes for hours, sometimes for days, sometimes even for weeks, on returning to herself she always found Christ present in her heart (*Leg.* 2.3.3). Teresa of Avila has written, "His Majesty is pleased to punish me only by giving me fresh favors, though to one who knows herself even that is no light punishment."⁵ Only once did Gertrude experience Christ's withdrawal, and that was for a period of eleven days after she had indulged in "worldly conversation" (*Leg.* 2.3.3). How could he endure her waywardness, she wondered once after she had yielded to a movement of anger. The answer took the form of one of the "similitudes" by which she received his instructions: he was like a poor invalid who sits quietly through a storm in the hope that sunshine will return (*Leg.* 2.12.2).

Gertrude's new spiritual orientation is evident in the account of her teaching. To enlighten and encourage her sisters, she spent hours in translating, paraphrasing, and explaining the Scriptures and the writings of the Fathers of the Church. Her biographer, who had known her for many years, compares her to a dove carefully gathering grain for its fledglings, a comparison which recalls Gertrude's meditation in the courtyard; she had loved these birds "because of their liberty" (*Leg.* 1.1.2).

Not only by her teaching but also by her example and her writings Gertrude has won her place among medieval German mystics. It was not until 1289 that she wrote of the event that had inaugurated her new life at Helfta. She felt that by the revelation of his love, Christ had prepared an apt remedy for her spiritual sickness. Looking back eight years later, she was overcome by the ingenuity of the love that had brought her to her knees more effectively than any punishment could have done. On the eve of Holy Thursday she was waiting with the community while the eucharist was being taken to a sick nun. Suddenly overcome by an irresistible impulse, she seized the writing tablet she carried at her side and began to describe the mystical communications she had received. It is this account that constitutes book 2 of the *Legatus*, which opens with a lyrical outburst of gratitude and praise of the divine wisdom, power, and kindness (*Leg.* 2, prologue, 226, 227).

Gertrude's biography contains no reference to spectacular miracles. On one occasion, however, her biographer alleges that her prayers brought an end to intense and unseasonable cold. On another, she says, they caused the cessation of rain which threatened to destroy the harvest. It is also recorded that when the community was at work in the court and the gathering clouds made them fear that they could not finish, Gertrude prayed that the storm might be deferred till the work was done. The anonymous narrator says that everyone heard Gertrude ask for this favor (*in audientia omnium*). Her wish was granted to the letter: as soon as the task had been finished, the storm started so promptly that two or three loiterers were drenched (*Leg.* 1.13.1–3). At another time when she asked Christ to stop the high winds that were causing a long drought, she was given to understand that by this hardship he was inducing certain rebellious persons to turn to him in prayer (*Leg.* 1.13.5). Another episode reveals Gertrude's familiarity with Christ. She was at work, seated on a pile of hay when her stylus slipped into it. Everyone heard her say playfully (*velut jocoso*), "Lord, there is no use in my searching for it; help me to find it." Without even looking, she put her hand into the hay and immediately drew out the stylus "as easily as if she had seen it on the pavement" (*Leg.* 1.13.4). According to some translators it was a needle that she had lost, but the Latin reads *stylus vel acus*. Several passages in the *Legatus* refer to the writing tablets that the nuns carried at their sides; they could therefore write without a desk, and evidently some of their writing was done outdoors. From what we know of Gertrude's life, she seems more likely to have been writing than sewing, though like Teresa of Avila and most other nuns, she did some spinning.

Not long after the manifestation of Christ in 1281, Gertrude discovered a prayer which she frequently repeated: "Lord Jesus Christ, Son of the living God, give me the grace to desire you with all my heart.... Lord of infinite mercy, with your precious blood inscribe your wounds on my heart that I may read in them both your suffering and your love.... Let me find my joy in you alone." From that time, contemplation of the wounds of Christ became one of her habitual devotions. She was thinking of the prayer one day while she was in the refectory for collation and suddenly became convinced that her petition had been granted—that the wounds of Christ had been imprinted on her heart (*Leg.* 2.4.1–3). Gertrude's experience is comparable to that of Catherine of Siena and Teresa of Avila in that the wounds, or stigmata, were invisible. The best-known example of visible stigmata is in the life of Francis of Assisi. During the Middle Ages and later, meditation on the passion of Christ was a popular devotion. The appearance of wounds on the hands, feet, and side was taken as a sharing in the sufferings of Christ. As Paul Siwek points out, "There are no convincing reasons for holding that stigmatization, considered in itself, necessarily surpasses all the powers of nature or that it is strictly miraculous."[6] When Gertrude experienced this phenomenon, she was, she says, next to someone who knew the secrets of her soul. This person was almost certainly Mechtild of Hackeborn, sister of the abbess. Immediately after mentioning her friend, Gertrude adds that she has often felt an increase of fervor as a result of imparting her confidence. "I have learned from someone experienced in these matters that it is good to reveal such secrets to a confidant who is not only a kind and faithful friend but whose greater age inspires reverence" (*Leg.* 2.4.2).

Seven years later, toward the end of her life, Gertrude experienced another answer to prayer. She had asked a friend to pray daily for her, using these words: "Most loving Lord, by your own wounded heart, pierce her heart with the dart of your love so that it may hold nothing earthly but be filled only by your divine power." On Gaudete Sunday, the third week in Advent before Christmas, Gertrude had a premonition that her prayer would be granted. As she was about to receive the sacrament, she cried out, "Lord, I confess that by my own merits I am unworthy to receive your smallest gift, but by the merits and desires of all here present I beseech you in your loving kindness to pierce my heart with the arrow of your love." After she had received the sacrament, it seemed to her that from the right side of the crucifix a ray of light in the form of a sharp arrow sprang out, withdrew, and sprang out once more, through this delay gently enkindling her love. Her desire was not fulfilled until the following Wednesday when the Incarnation is commemorated in the gospel, *Missus est Angelus Gabriel.* At this time she received the mystical wound (*Leg.* 2.5.1, 2).

A later portion of the *Legatus* contains a variant account: a friar who was preaching to the nuns told them: "Love is a golden arrow and in some way one is the master of whatever one strikes with it. So it is a folly to attach one's heart to earthly things and neglect the things of heaven." These words made such an impression on Gertrude that she cried out, "O my only love, can I not have this arrow? I should at once shoot it to transfix and win you forever." It seemed to her that Christ, offering her a golden arrow, said, "You would wound me if you had the arrow, but I am the one who has it. I shall wound you so that you will never recover." Thereupon, she felt that he pierced her with a triple-pointed arrow, leaving her more than ever consumed with love of God (*Leg.* 5.25.1, 2).[7] The *Liber specialis gratiae* records the transverberation of Mechtild of Hackeborn which she experienced while prostrating herself on a crucifix (*Livre* 2.25.163). Teresa of Avila likewise records the piercing of her heart by a seraph holding a golden spear tipped with fire.[8] This is the subject of Bernini's sculpture at St. Peter's in Rome.

Among all Gertrude's mystical experiences these two—the impression of Christ's wounds and the piercing of her heart by the arrow of divine love—gave her such joy, she says, that if she were never to receive any other consolation, even were she to live a thousand years, each hour would be filled with inexhaustible joy and thanksgiving (*Leg.* 2.23.7).

Her contemporary biographer attributes two prophecies to Gertrude. Rudolph, emperor of the Romans, had died on 15 July 1291. In May 1292, as stated in the *Legatus*, Gertrude informed the abbess that Adolph of Nassau had been chosen in his place. She added that he would perish at the hands of one who should succeed him—an event which occurred on 2 July 1298, when he fell in battle with Albert of Austria (*Leg.* 1.2.3). The circumstances of this first prophecy prove conclusively that Gertrude was not an abbess. The Abbess Gertrude of Hackeborn had died in 1291. In 1292 Sophia of Mansfeld, a descendant of the founders, was governing the community; she was then "the mother of the monastery" to whom Gertrude told the result of the imperial election. Every year of Gertrude's life is covered by the extant list of abbesses and interregnums; her name does not appear (*Rev.* 2:727, no. 9).

According to the *Legatus*, her second prophecy dates from 1294 when the community was living in dread of an assault by the armed forces which periodically overran the region. In this emergency the nuns decided to recite the psalter with special antiphons in honor of the Holy Spirit. As they prayed, some members of the community recognized their shortcomings and, confiding themselves to the mercy of God, resolved to amend their lives. To Gertrude a mist which spread through the monastery seemed to symbolize the effect of their contrition, putting their enemies to flight. Just as she was assuring the abbess that the danger was averted, a messenger came to confirm her words (*Leg.* 1.2.3; 3.48.1).

Gertrude lived and died as a simple nun. That her contemporary biographer is silent in regard to her family is probably the strongest proof that she was not of the nobility. As a rule, early hagiographers emphasize the worldly advantages of their subjects in order to praise the virtue of foregoing the privileges of high rank. Instead of one of the surnames important in medieval Saxony, Gertrude has the incomparable title "the Great," which distinguishes her from her abbess, Gertrude of Hackeborn. The title was accorded her by Cardinal Prosper Lambertini—later Benedict XIV, "the scholar pope," in his treatise *De servorum Dei beatificatione et beatorum canonizatione,* written in 1738 when he was *promotor fidei.*[9]

It is not because of any prominence in the history of her country or of the Church that Gertrude is "the Great." As a cloistered nun she did not figure in the events of thirteenth-century Saxony. It is true that she suffered with her companions from the political disorders which sometimes involved the convent, but she escaped the ordeal of her companions, Sophia and Elisabeth of Mansfeld, when in 1284 their brother attacked the monastery. Her title, "the Great," is accorded her by virtue of her spiritual history as recorded in the *Legatus,* her influence in furthering the recognition of mystical communication, and her contribution to the understanding of medieval spirituality. Her role in the history of the veneration of the Sacred Heart is the subject of a later chapter.

Once when Gertrude was wishing that she had a relic of the cross of Christ, it seemed to her that he would say, "Read the story of my passion, and consider well the words I spoke with such great love. Write them down and keep them as relics. . . . One who wishes to remind a friend of their long friendship will say, 'Remember how you loved me when you said such and such a thing to me.' He will do this rather then recall the place where they were, the clothes they wore, or the like. Be sure then that the most precious relics you can have are the words that express the deepest love of my heart" (*Leg.* 4.52.3). Paquelin has observed that the words can apply to Gertrude herself (*Leg.* 4.52.3, n. 2). No relics survive and her grave is unknown. She had prayed in her fourth *Spiritual Excercise:* "Absorb my spirit in your spirit so mightily and deeply that I may be completely buried in you [Christ], losing myself in this union and may no one except your love know of my burial place in you" (*Ex.* 4.240–43). While this petition is to be understood in a spiritual context, it is a fact that the site of Gertrude's burial is unknown. Her writings are her best memorial—the intimate record of her interior life and the life of her community. Important in the history of medieval mysticism, they are also valuable as records of the customs, occupations, and circumstances of her day.

Her abbess was chiefly responsible for Gertrude's preparation as a writer. As she had been brought to the monastery at an early age, she must have attained her mastery of Latin there. The Abbess Gertrude, not yet thirty when her young namesake was entrusted to her care, had already established the strong curriculum for which Helfta was known. The literary reputation of Gertrude the Great rests on her two chief works, the *Exercitia* and the *Legatus divinae pietatis*. Although the *Legatus* is commonly called her "revelations," the designation is misleading. The original title, which may be translated *Herald of God's Loving Kindness*, is a far more accurate expression of the theme of the book. As previously noted, Paquelin offers evidence that Gertrude was also the chief author of the *Liber specialis gratiae*, which records the spiritual life of Mechtild of Hackeborn. Although collections of prayers attributed to Gertrude have been circulated, the only genuine ones are those in the *Legatus* and the *Exercitia*. Among Gertrude's lost works are her letters, vernacular treatises, commentaries, paraphrases and explanations of scriptural texts, a treatise on Esther, and a poem in honor of the passion. This last was evidently a cento, since she says it was "composed from the sayings of the saints" (*Leg.* 3.54.2). As her biographer notes, like Mechtild of Hackeborn, she wrote consoling and encouraging letters to persons in distant places. The loss of Gertrude's vernacular treatises is a disadvantage to students of German literature. The survival of these works would have refuted the impression that the vernacular played no part in the intellectual activity of the times.

The second of Gertrude's extant works, the *Exercitia*, deals with the basis of the Christian life, the duties and privileges of persons consecrated to God, and the necessity of preparing for the next life. The first exercise treats of the recovery of baptismal innocence. The second, on spiritual conversion, as Columba Hart observes, reflects St. Bernard's definition of conversion as the act whereby one resolves to enter the monastic life.[10] Gertrude associates this with the reception of the habit. The third and fourth exercises are concerned with the rituals of espousal and consecration, and the renewal of monastic profession. The fifth exercise is on the withdrawal from all that is not God—*vacare Deo*—in order to rekindle the love of God. The most personal of the exercises, the sixth and seventh, are acts of praise and thanksgiving, atonement for sins, and preparation for death. The exultant jubilus in the sixth exercise is climactic in its expression of Gertrude's ecstatic love of God.[11]

Each exercise begins with a directive—e.g., "Desire to be reborn in God by a new holy life and restored to a new infancy, and say. . . ."

These directives continue throughout the exercises. The exercises themselves are all in the first person singular with few exceptions. The final prayer of the second exercise begins, "Almighty and eternal God, listen favorably to our prayers, and grant to your servants who for the honor of your name are gathered in the unity of charity." This prayer is clearly inspired by the liturgy for the consecration of virgins. A litany in the fourth exercise contains the petition "grant all of us who serve you in this place unity of spirit in the bond of charity and peace" and the response, "Lord, be merciful to us" (*Ex.* 1.5–6; 2.102–4; 4.199–200).

Liturgical and scriptural images and phrases abound in the writings from Helfta. In the *Exercises* the responsory *Regnum mundi* from the Office of St. Agnes occurs frequently. As Hart points out, it was sung at funerals and other special occasions.[12] Though it is no longer included in the Office of St. Agnes, it is still sung during the ceremony of profession in some communities. Gertrude quotes it in whole or in part several times in the *Exercises*. At Helfta it followed the versicle, "My heart has uttered a good word" (Ps 44:2). Other passages derived from the Office of St. Agnes are *Induit me*, "The Lord has clothed me with the garment of salvation and girded me with the robe of gladness"; and *Posuit signum*, "He has placed his mark on my countenance that I should admit no other lover." This antiphon is followed by the response, *Amo Christum*, "I love Christ, whose bridal chamber I have entered; his mother is a virgin, his father has no spouse, his voice sings sweetly to me. When I love him I am chaste; when I touch him, I am pure; when I receive him, I am a virgin." The antiphon, *Annulo suo subarrhavit me*: "With his ring he has given me his pledge" also occurs in the *Legatus* (*Leg.* 3.2.1).

Quotations from both the Hebrew and the New Testaments are numerous. The editors of the *Exercises* give as an example of Gertrude's free handling of texts her allusion to the episode of the withering of Jacob's sinew after his wrestling with the angel (Gen 32:25). Addressing love personified as a queenly maiden, she exclaims, "Your ingenuity has touched the sinew of the heart of my Jesus so sharply that wounded by love it has shriveled" (*Ex.* 7.324–26). She also prays that like Naamon she may be washed seven times in the Jordan of Christ's life and passion (*Ex.* 7.590–91). Adapting the petition of the prodigal son, she prays, "I your unworthy and prodigal daughter, who alas, by my inveterate sins have lost the name of daughter . . ." (*Ex.* 4.184–85).

Since both Gertrude and her friend Mechtild of Hackeborn led the choral office, it is not surprising that musical images are prominent in the writings of both nuns.[13] In the *Exercises*, the divinity of Christ is an organ, his humanity a cithara, and his voice resounds like a melodious harp (*Ex.* 5.251; 6.425–26). Gertrude wishes her desires to vibrate like the strings on the lyres of the seraphim (*Ex.* 6.260–64). The sixth exercise in particular is filled with musical images; many show Gertrude herself singing jubilantly. Other passages describe the songs of saints and angels, of all creation, and of Jesus: "the glory of your beautiful voice resounds above all the instruments of heaven" (*Ex.* 6.270). "When," she asks, "shall I hear the new song of the eternal marriage, which you, O king and spouse of virgins, play for them so sweetly on the cithara?" Feeling incapable of offering worthy thanks, Gertrude asks Jesus to sing on her behalf a hymn of thanksgiving (*Ex.* 6.278–85).

Although a tissue of liturgical and scriptural phrases and motifs, the *Exercises* disclose Gertrude's personality in its characteristic liberty and confidence in the divine mercy. Her transcendent outlook sees the immediacy of each liturgical event in the spiritual life. By the renewal of its promises, baptism becomes a daily reality. Similarly, the hour of death is seen as close at hand. While only the last exercise is entitled "Preparation for Death," all the preceding exercises contain explicit references to the last hours.

Some passages in the *Exercises* appear to echo accounts of experiences and attitudes recorded in the *Legatus*. In the third exercise she says, "I am a motherless orphan" (*Ex.* 3.48).[14] At the mass offered for the deceased parents of the community she visualizes the souls of the departed ascending to heaven like sparks and wonders if her parents are among them. The reply that she hears interiorly is an assertion found repeatedly in the writings from Helfta: "I am your closest relative, your father, your brother, your spouse. All my friends are yours—so they [your parents] are among them" (*Leg.* 5.17.1). In the seventh exercise she calls Christ *juvenis amabilis* "a lovable youth" (*Ex.* 7.649). These are the words she uses in book 2 of the *Legatus* to describe the manifestation of Christ in the dormitory. Another reference to this experience is also in the seventh exercise where she calls her heart "a thorny thicket" and prays that it may be transformed into a paradise of virtues (*Ex.* 7.691–94). In the third exercise she prays, "Be my defense in injury" and in the sixth, "that all the treachery and insolence of my enemies may be brought to naught" (*Ex.* 3.246; 6.652–53). In book 2 of the *Legatus* she does not mention enemies or detractors, but the compilers of the remaining books say that she did have some antagonists. She prays for someone who had caused her pain and for one who had received her counsels with contempt.

Her self-accusations probably go far beyond any hostile criticism she experienced. In both the *Exercises* and the *Legatus* she views herself as incorrigibly negligent, distracted, ungrateful, and impatient. She refers to "my indigence, which is so great that I have never corrected my slightest fault as I should have" (*Leg.* 2.20.11–14). Above all, she deeply regrets having wasted the talents entrusted to her: the talent of time, of understanding, and of eloquence. She views her whole life as ruin and destruction. Nevertheless she relies on the divine mercy to supply for all her sins. Like Mechtild of Hackeborn she prays that the actions and sufferings of Christ may combine with hers to redeem them.

The *Exercitia* resembles the *Legatus*, particularly book 2 composed by Gertrude herself. Deeply emotional passages characterize both. In the exercises, emotion is frequently conveyed by repetition: *heu, heu* (alas); *eia, amor, amor* (ah, love); *quam libenter, quam libenter* (how willingly); *quamdiu, quamdiu* (how long). Vocatives are frequent: *O sapientia* (O wisdom); *eia, Jesu, O mors charissima* (O dearest death!). Strong imperatives in the seventh exercise and in book 2 of the *Legatus* reflect the vigor of Gertrude's personality. In the seventh exercise she employs a semidramatic form. Addressing her "ambassadors"—Mercy, Peace, Wisdom, Perseverance, and Love—all designations of God—she charges them to plead for her at the tribunal of Truth (*Ex.* 7.18–328). A stanza in an abecedarian hymn in medieval German breviaries illustrates a similar personification of virtues:

> *Felix, quae sitit Charitas,*
> *Te fontem vitae, Veritas.*
> (*Ex.* 7.10, n. 5)

> Blessed is Charity who
> thirsts for you, O Truth,
> the fountain of life.

Gertrude quotes a stanza from this hymn before each of the divisions of the exercises. The editors point out that in the passages following these stanzas, she is apparently influenced by their rhymes and cadences. The rhymes in *-ore* are one example: *cruore, dolore, sapore, flore*. Another is *perficis, circumvenis*, etc. Alliteration and assonance are also frequent: *amoris alabastrum, sanctissimorum sensuum, misericordiae multitudinem* are examples of the former; *sperem semper tuis sub pennis* and *in mortis hora absque ulla mora* of the latter. The lines *O mors manans dulcedine / tu morti meae provide* echo familiar cadences (*Ex.* 7.183–357 passim).

Comments on the *Exercitia* as distinct from the *Legatus* include Dom Prosper Guéranger's approbation: he sees them as an example of a liberty of spirit which dates from Gregory the Great and ends with Louis of Blois [Blosius].[15] In his autobiographical novel, *En Route*, J. K. Huysmans, speaking in the person of Durtal, finds in the exercises only an echo of the Scriptures with none of the originality he admires in the works of Teresa of Avila or Angela of Foligno. The prior Maximim replies: "That is true. Yet she does resemble St. Angela by her gift of familiar conversation with Christ, and also by the loving vehemence of her assertions. But this is all transformed as it comes from its source; she thinks liturgically to such an extent that her slightest thought presents itself to her clothed in the language of the Gospels and the psalms."[16] John Gray calls the *Exercitia* "an ascetical treatise of the highest value." Echoing the tribute of Johannes Bühler, he says that the work recalls "both the richness of the Areopagite and the exactness of St. Thomas."[17]

In view of the wholesale destruction of books and manuscripts at New Helfta during the Peasants' Revolt of 1525, it is remarkable that any of Gertrude's writings survived. Yet five fifteenth-century manuscripts of the *Legatus* are extant. None of these was the source of the first printed edition published at Cologne in 1536. This was the work of a Carthusian monk, Lanspergius (Johann Gerecht) who entitled it *Insinuationes divinae pietatis libri quinque . . . nunc primum in lucem editi.* A dedicatory letter signed by Dom Theodorus Loher, vicar of the monastery, gives the erroneous impression that he was the editor; the preface makes a complimentary reference to his confrere, "our Lanspergius, a man of superhuman erudition." Two other Latin editions appeared in 1579 and 1599. Several editions followed in the sixteenth and seventeenth centuries, including Spanish, French, Italian, German, and Dutch translations of the *Legatus*. Other volumes contain excerpts (*Leg.* 2, intr. 58–70).

The edition by Lanspergius is not only the first but the most important of the printed editions of the *Legatus*. The lost manuscript used by Lanspergius lacked the prologue and the first book. For these portions he used an early manuscript in Old German. Prior to the edition of the *Legatus* in the series Sources chrétiennes, the definitive text was that of Dom Louis Paquelin; this edition was based on the 1536 Latin version by Lanspergius, supplemented by two of the fifteenth-century manuscripts, one from Vienna, the other from Mayence. For the Sources chrétiennes edition, Doyère had access to two additional manuscripts, from Munich and from Treves. A fifth manuscript, from Darmstadt, came to his attention only a few days after he received the first proofs of his edition, and he could not make a complete collation. Following his death in 1966, two monks of his community completed the collation (*Leg.* 2, intr. 91, n. 1).

The previously cited English translation of the *Legatus*, issued in 1865, was based on the 1662 Latin edition of Nicholas Canteleu. This English edition by M. F. Cusack, a Poor Clare nun, contains some errors which successive reprints perpetuate even to the present date. The most serious of these inaccuracies is the identification of Gertrude of Helfta with her abbess, Gertrude of Hackeborn, an error which Paquelin exposed in 1875 (*Leg.* 2, intr. 65–66, n. 1).

Gertrude's book is known by three different titles. *Liber Legationis divinae pietatis* (or simply *Legatus divinae pietatis*) is the most authentic because it repeats a phrase in book 5, chapter 3. *Revelations*, the title familiar to readers of the English translation, has a misleading connotation. Several editors have used the title *Insinuationes divinae pietatis*. Adding to the confusion, Paquelin's two-volume edition of the works of Gertrude and Mechtild of Hackeborn is titled *Revelationes Gertrudianae ac Mechtildianae*. In the individual volumes, however, each work has its proper title—*Legatus divinae pietatis* and *Liber specialis gratiae*. The four volumes in the series Sources chrétiennes are definitive. Whether considered as the record of unique personalities, as historical documents, or as contributions to the literature of mysticism, the works of both the mystics of Helfta are attracting the attention of twentieth-century readers.

The first book of the *Legatus*, intended as a memorial of Gertrude, was written after her death by one of her friends. Book 2, her spiritual autobiography, is from her own hand. It will be considered in greater detail. The three remaining books, compiled by Gertrude's companions, deal with aspects of the soul's relations with God, with the feasts of the Church, and with the deaths of members and friends of the community. Of the five books of the *Legatus*, therefore, it should be noted that though the entire work is attributed to Gertrude, she actually wrote only the second. The *Legatus*, as Doyère notes, is a composite (*Leg.* 2, intr. 25). Despite the somewhat formal and rhetorical style of book 1, which is largely a panegyric, the work in its entirety does manifest the influence of Gertrude. It seems that portions of the last three books were dictated by her, for they show her characteristic thought and even some of her expressions, though muted and as it were, secondhand. Other parts were probably based on the recollections of her friends. This composite authorship may be accounted for, at least in part, by Gertrude's frequent illnesses, and also by the likelihood that she gave priority to recording the spiritual history of Mechtild of Hackeborn in the *Liber specialis gratiae*. Much of the material in the latter coincides with the four books of the *Legatus* written by Gertrude's companions.

Book 1 focuses on various sayings and actions which demonstrate Gertrude's sanctity. The formal arrangement of topics—e.g., examples of her virtues under the images of sun, moon, and stars—contrasts with the more casual treatment in books 3, 4, and 5. Of these compiled sections, book 3, the longest, contains many chapters on the effects of sacramental communion. Other subjects are the love of God, the utility of prayer, and the importance of a good intention. The trials which beset the community and the more personal afflictions of illness, temptation, and discouragement are also included. Book 3 is notable for a passage that Gerard Manley Hopkins paraphrased. The poem, number 140, is in the section "Unfinished Poems, Fragments, Light Verse" (1876–79). His source was obviously the English translation of 1865: "When I [Christ] behold anyone in his agony who has thought of Me with pleasure, or who has performed any works deserving of reward, I appear to him at the moment of death with a countenance so full of love and mercy that he repents from his inmost heart for ever having offended Me, and he is saved by this repentance."[18] Hopkins's lines are:

> To him who ever thought with love of me
> Or ever did for my sake some good deed
> I will appear, looking such charity
> And kind compassion at his life's last need
> That he will out of hand and heartily
> Repent he sinned and all his sins be freed.[19]

The same English translation is probably the source of Hopkins's reference to Gertrude in "The Wreck of the Deutschland," stanza 20: "Gertrude, lily, and Luther, are two of a town." This repeats the error in the English translation of 1865, namely, that Gertrude was born in Eisleben.[20] That few readers of Hopkins's poem have recognized it as a close paraphrase of Gertrude's lines is one of many evidences that her influence has been, like her cloistered life, hidden.

Book 4 of the *Legatus* contains meditations on the feasts of the Church year. For the most part these meditations are associated with times when Gertrude's illnesses prevented her from attending services in the monastery church. In this section the figures of the saints, often attired in symbolic garments, are like images from the stained-glass windows of thirteenth-century cathedrals. Book 5 differs markedly from book 4 in that it is chiefly devoted to accounts of the deaths of various persons, many of whom have already been mentioned in a previous chapter. Gertrude's own method of preparing for death is also included. The fifth book ends with an approbation of the entire work. The "compilatrix," who had perhaps written from Gertrude's dictation, asserts that Christ held the volume to his heart and called it "my book." When in order to offer the book to God, this sister concealed it in her sleeve as she was about to receive the eucharist, she felt assured that those who read it would be guided as by the finger of Christ to the passages most useful to them. Those who read only to gratify curiosity or who falsify the text are condemned. In reparation for the writer's limited intelligence, lack of zeal, and inexperience, she commends the work to the Sacred Heart. She feels that her defects have impaired her revelation of the secret treasures confided to her. Yet although obliged to omit "an almost infinite number of details," she has experienced the help of the divine mercy. She concludes with the wish that readers of the book be led first to meditation and then to contemplation (*Leg.* 5.33–36).

Because of its central place in the history of Gertrude's mystical life, book 2 stands apart from the remainder of the *Legatus*. The most important section contains the account of her "conversion." Written in the first person and addressed to God, it is a simple but emotional account of her interior life. Her biographer states that Gertrude wrote this spiritual autobiography with great reluctance. When she became convinced that it was God's will, seconded by her superior's, that she should write, she still felt a strong repugnance. Her doubts subsided when she experienced a spiritual compulsion, a divine insistence: "What use do you see in the written record of my [Christ's] words to St. Catherine when I visited her in prison and said to her, 'Courage, my daughter, for I am with you?' Do not these accounts of the saints increase devotion and make known my love for souls?" (*Leg.* 1.15.1). Once she understood that her writing was intended to draw others to God, Gertrude's reluctance diminished somewhat. She still felt an intense surprise that Christ should treat her with such familiarity, and she knew her own community well enough to foresee that some persons would be shocked and mistrustful. Again she became aware of an urgent compulsion, as if Christ were speaking: "I expect an abundant return from the graces I have given you. I wish that those who have neglected similar gifts will remember them when they read what you say and be grateful. Thus my graces will increase in them. If others maliciously scorn them, let their sin be on their heads; you are not responsible" (*Leg.* 1.15.2).

Despite such assurances Gertrude believed that she had not sufficiently valued her gifts from God. Concluding the first section of book 2, she writes: "If you had given me so slight a thing as a thread of flax, I ought to have received it with the deepest reverence. My God, you know my secrets, you know what compels me to write these things against my will. Seeing how little I have profited by your gifts, I cannot believe that they are for me alone since it is impossible for your eternal wisdom to be frustrated. Therefore, O Giver of all good, you who have overwhelmed me with your undeserved gifts, grant that by reading these things the heart of one of your friends may understand the love of souls that made you leave this magnificent jewel in the mire of my polluted heart for so long. May your mercy be praised with heart and voice so that you may receive some compensation for my deficiency" (*Leg.* 2.5.4–5).

Gertrude began the *Legatus* in the spring of 1289. She was again plagued by uncertainty, however, and stopped writing, not resuming until October when she felt herself once more coerced by the divine insistence. She says of her reluctance and its overruling: "It seemed to me so improper to write these things . . . that I delayed till the feast of the Exaltation of the Holy Cross [14 September]. At mass I decided to devote myself to other occupations, but the Savior's words changed my mind: 'Be sure of this: You will never go out from the prison of the body until you pay the last penny you owe.' As I was thinking that I had already repaid his gifts for the benefit of others if not by my writings at least by my words, he reminded me of what I had heard that night at Matins: 'If the Savior had taught his doctrine only to those who heard him, there would have been no Scripture.' He added, 'Do not object. I wish your writings to give clear evidence of my divine love during these last days when I distribute my gifts to a multitude of souls'" (*Leg.* 2.10.1). Overwhelmed by this reproof, Gertrude thought of the difficulty, if not the impossibility, of expressing without scandalizing others, what she had experienced. A torrential rain seemed to fall upon her, weighing her down unbearably. She heard a few portentous words which she could not understand. As she appealed to God, she felt that he said, "Since this great downpour seems useless to you, I shall draw you to my divine heart and inspire you gently according to your capacity." Thereafter she found that every day she could easily write a number of pages, but having completed this portion, could not add one word. On the next day she could quickly continue her work. This experience, which checked her natural impetuosity, recalled the precept, "One should not be so attached to action as to neglect contemplation." Doyère notes that this is not an exact quotation from Scripture, but may derive from the story of Mary and Martha (Lk 10:41). Gertrude writes, "Thus you [Christ] gave me leisure to delight in Rachel's joyful embraces without depriving me of Lia's glorious fruitfulness" (*Leg.* 2.10.3, n. 1). Rachel is traditionally associated with the contemplative and Lia with the active life.

Gertrude often renewed her self-reproaches for having resisted the manifest will of God. She also repeated her intention: "You know my heart and why I have written these pages—it is only to praise your goodness so that after my death many who read them may be touched by the kindness that made you descend to such depths to save us. You have entrusted very great and numerous graces to one who, alas, misprizes all your gifts" (*Leg.* 2.23.22).

Having surmounted her unwillingness to reveal her mystical experiences, Gertrude gave herself wholeheartedly to her task. With profound emotion she recalls how in her twenty-sixth year, "in a blessed hour at the beginning of twilight, you O God of truth, more radiant than any light yet deeper than any secret thing, determined to end the obscurity of my darkness" (*Leg.* 2.1.1). The chiaroscuro of this passage recurs throughout book 2 of the *Legatus*.

6 The Writings of Gertrude

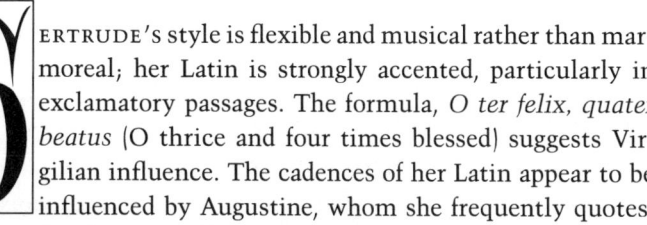ERTRUDE's style is flexible and musical rather than marmoreal; her Latin is strongly accented, particularly in exclamatory passages. The formula, *O ter felix, quater beatus* (O thrice and four times blessed) suggests Virgilian influence. The cadences of her Latin appear to be influenced by Augustine, whom she frequently quotes. An example of a typically Augustinian paronomasia is *sapienti misericordiae et misericordi sapientiae* (wise mercy and merciful wisdom). She also quotes from the Office of the Trinity the grammatical modulations that emphasize various aspects of the Godhead: *vera una Divinitas, una et trina veritas, trina et una Deitas* (*Leg.* 2.8.5; 2.1.2; 2.11.3).

Her vigorous style reflects Gertrude's strong personality. Reproaching herself for disloyalty to God, she writes: "How many times, yielding to malice, levity, or laxity, have I taken back what I had given you [Christ] and snatched it, as it were, from between your teeth to give to your enemy" (*Leg.* 2.13.1). Canteleu's egregious comment on Gertrude's style is that it is "not feminine, that is, not contemptible."[1]

Gertrude's chief literary sources were the Scriptures, liturgical books, the writings of Augustine, and Bernard's sermons on the *Song of Songs*. Evidently she also knew Origen, who is mentioned in the *Liber specialis gratiae*, as are Thomas Aquinas and Albert the Great. Yet she speaks with her own distinctive accent in a style as personal as Bernard's. Many Old Testament themes and persons figure in her writings: Noah's ark, Gideon's fleece, the prodigal son, Joseph, Esther, Abraham, Daniel, Solomon. She adds Abraham, Moses, David, and George to the litany of saints in her *Exercises*.

Numerous scriptural and liturgical quotations appear in her text. She quotes the Isaian text *Tu responde pro me, Domine Deus meus* (38:14) as she remembers the signs of God's love which she had received on Christmas day and reflects with shame that she has not preserved these graces (*Leg.* 2.16.2). Besides the more obvious liturgical expressions, such as *oriens ex alto* and *dator munerum,* Gertrude also quotes several lines from the twelfth-century Christmas sequence, *Laetabundus . . . quo sicut sidus radium protulit virgo filium, verum Deum et hominem* (as the star sends forth its ray so the virgin bore her son, true God and man). A favorite phrase, *creator siderum* or sometimes *vestitor siderum,* is from a hymn for matins.

The *Legatus divinae pietatis* is a hitherto neglected source for details of life in thirteenth-century Germany. Considered from this perspective, Gertrude's choice of illustrative material reveals her as a sympathetic observer, a connoisseur of human experience to whom may be applied the words of Ancelet-Hustache, "They [the mystics] love life under all its forms."[2] As students of mysticism have noted, the language of the mystics must be properly understood; one must not insist on a literal meaning. It is necessary also to take into account the epoch, the milieu, and the intellectual and emotional character of the writer. Doyère warns that to read the language of the great mystics, education is necessary (*Leg.* intr., 47). Gertrude and the two Mechtilds use not only the language of court life and chivalry as was natural for women of their temperament and environment but also many images drawn from domestic life. Evelyn Underhill speaks of "the vividly pictorial visions of Christ and the saints which abound in the writings of the Cistercians of Helfta." She sees as the source of these images the cycle of the liturgical year as well as "the romantic vernacular poetry of the Minnesingers."[3]

Because ordinary language is inadequate to express spiritual realities, it is only by analogies and similitudes that these realities can be conveyed. "St. Thomas," as Walter Ong points out, "discussed the fact that metaphor, which seems to be a device distinctive of poetry and foreign to the physical and mathematical sciences and logic, turns up time and again in Christian theology." He writes: "Thus the symbolic method is common to both (poetry and theology) since neither is of itself accommodated to the human reason."⁴ Angela of Foligno declares that she cannot without some misrepresentation speak of the transcendent experiences she has had: "my words crumble and fall, they blaspheme."⁵

The Roman Catholic church views with reserve the visions and revelations even of highly virtuous persons. Besides the possibility of fraud and delusion, there is also the likelihood that if the manifestation does come from God, the visionary's account of it may be impaired by errors or exaggerations arising from preconceived ideas. "The mud in a torrent is not from its source."⁶ On several occasions Gertrude did not know whether certain ideas came from God or from herself. It is characteristic of true mystics to be distrustful of revelations. The personality and imagination of the visionary enter largely into the vision. Gertrude thought pictorially; her images are colorful and dramatic. Her clear, straightforward descriptions can leave a lasting impression on contemporary readers. It was natural for her to say to Christ: "You have overthrown the tower of my vanity and worldliness . . . you have descended to the valley of my misery" (*Leg.* 2.1.1). The entire *Legatus*, book 2 in particular, is filled with images, many of them liturgical: the hidden manna, the abyss of uncreated wisdom, the rose of patience.

The mystics of Helfta employ a dazzling array of images—rich, colorful garments, silver and gold, jewelry of all kinds. In some passages jewels symbolize the rewards of virtue. As a sign that her negligences in prayer were amended, it seemed to Gertrude that she was given a brilliant piece of enameled jewelry set with precious stones (*Leg.* 4.29.1). She envisioned Christ wearing two jeweled rings representing the joys and sufferings she had offered him (*Leg.* 3.2.1). When she recommenced her recitation of the Divine Office in order to say it with a young nun who was evidently ill, it seemed that she received a jewel for each word that she repeated (*Leg.* 3.61.1).

Spiritual vestments are a recurring motif. In book 3 Gertrude describes the garments with which Christ clothes her in preparation for the eucharist: a white robe for his innocence; a purple tunic for his humility; a green ornament for his hope; a golden mantle for his love of all creatures; a jeweled crown for his joy in their souls; sandals for his confidence in spite of their inconstancy (*Leg.* 3.18.11). In book 4, John the Evangelist is seen wearing a yellow robe strewn with golden eagles from which a red light streams to show that he combined the highest contemplation with the remembrance of Christ's passion. Golden lilies on his shoulders are inscribed "The disciple Jesus loved" and "This is the Guardian of the Virgin." His breastplate bears the first words of his Gospel: *In principio erat verbum* (1:1; *Leg.* 4.4.1, 2).

Benedict is clothed in glory as the father of monasticism; fragrant roses spring from his body, and his scepter is a jeweled cross. Those who faithfully follow his rule are honored (*Leg.* 4.11.1, 2). Magdalen is adorned with golden roses and sparkling gems, corresponding in number to her forgiven sins. The flowers represent the divine mercy, the jewels her penances (*Leg.* 4.46.1). Bernard's robe is tricolored: white for innocence, violet for fidelity to monastic life, crimson for fervent love. He wears golden ornaments set with gems as a sign of his excellent doctrine and preaching. A diadem of many colors crowns his heart to show the profit that others have gained from his writings. As Gertrude thanks God for the graces given to him, small gold shields engraved with the names of virtues appear on his garments (*Leg.* 4.49.1–3). Augustine's vestments glow like pure crystal with colors representing patience, kindness, and the love of God. A radiant globe above his head sends forth rays and stars (*Leg.* 4.50.4, 6). Catherine of Alexandria, seated in royal state, is surrounded by the fifty philosophers she converted, each holding a golden scepter touching the hem of her robe (*Leg.* 4.57.1). John the Baptist wears crimson vestments ornamented with golden lambs (*Leg.* 4.42.2). Dominic and Francis, like Benedict, are shown with roses and glowing scepters (*Leg.* 4.50.8).

On the feast of the Assumption of the Virgin Mary, Gertrude envisions her clothed in a green mantle sparkling with many golden flowers in the form of trefoils. To prepare for this feast, Gertrude had intended to offer Hail Marys corresponding in number to the years of Mary's life. The number is variously given as sixty-three, sixty-six, or seventy. Because of her extreme weakness, Gertrude had been able to say only the three aspirations, *Ave Maria, gratia plena, Dominus tecum*. The trefoils on Mary's robe represented this threefold invocation (*Leg.* 4.48.1, 2). The robes of Christ, as she visualized him on Ascension day, were a green tunic symbolizing the living freshness of the virtues of his humanity, and a scarlet mantle symbolizing the love that led him to his passion (*Leg.* 4.36.3). On the first Sunday of Lent, as she prayed that Christ might make up for the dispensation from the fast which she was obliged to accept, she was consoled as she visualized herself wearing garments representing all the virtues that she desired: a white robe for the innocence which the privations of Christ had won for her, and a red robe for the merits of his abstinence (*Leg.* 4.17.1–2). On 1 November, the feast of All Saints, a golden robe symbolized her share in their merits. When she prayed for others, they seemed to be robed in garments symbolizing the virtues of innocence, humility, and charity—a white tunic, precious stones in the form of violets, and a rose-colored mantle covered with golden flowers (*Leg.* 4.55.5; 4.7.4). As noted earlier, similarly vivid descriptions appear in the writings of Mechtild of Hackeborn.

The popular and religious literature of the Middle Ages offers other descriptions of symbolic garments. One example is "The Garmont of Gude Ladeis" by the fifteenth-century Scots poet, Robert Henryson. Freely translated, representative stanzas read:

> Her shift should be white chastity;
> And laced with lawful love,
> Her kirtle should be steadfastness
> That never will remove.
> Benignity should be the belt
> About her middle set
> Her mantle of humility
> To ward off wind and wet.[7]

References to symbolic garments no doubt derive ultimately from St. Paul's admonition to put on the armor of God (Ephes 6:13–17 and 1 Thes 5:8).

A familiar example of Christian iconography is the Tree of Jesse. Related to it are the Tree of Life and the Tree of the Cross.[8] The twelfth-century treatise, *De fructibus carnis et spiritus* by the pseudo-Hugh of St. Victor was instrumental in popularizing the images of the trees of virtues and of vices. The *Speculum Virginum*, attributed to Conrad of Hirschau contains drawings of the Tree of Jesse and also of the Tree of Virtue and of Vice.[9] To English readers the Tree of Charity in *Piers Plowman* is probably the most familiar example of the genre. In answer to the question, "What is charity?" Anima tells Piers:

> Then to tell you truly, it is a fair tree . . .
> Mercy is the main root of it, and the mid-stock is pity,
> The leaves are loyal words and the law of Holy Church
> The blossoms are obedient speech and a benign bearing

> The tree is plainly called patience and simplicity of living
> And so through God and good men groweth the fruit,
>   charity...
> It grows, said he, in a garden of God's making,
> The shoot is from that stock and shelters in man's body,
> And the heart is the home wherein it rises.[10]

The symbolic trees in the writings of Gertrude and Mechtild represent a neglected development of the traditional iconography of the Tree of Jesse. Mechtild's symbolic trees have been described in chapter 4. The first of Gertrude's images occurs in the second book of the *Legatus* where she visualizes the tree of love. Overcome by weariness at Mass, she was roused by the bell at the elevation of the host. It seemed to her that she saw Jesus holding a tree covered with fruits and leaves which shone like stars and sent forth brilliant rays. He distributed the fruits to the saints and then planted the tree in her heart as in a garden that she might be sustained by its fruits and refreshed by its shade. As she began to pray for a person who had hurt her, a flower appeared on the tree, and she realized that if she persevered in her good will toward this person, the flower would produce the fruit of charity. She relates that on the same day Christ reappeared under the form of a comely young man. He asked her to gather nuts from the tree to offer to him. Gertrude, whose frequent illnesses kept her in a state of extreme fragility, asked, "Why do you wish me to do this? I am weak in virtue as in sex."[11] She was given to understand that obedience to the divine commands must be exact and complete, even to the point of "breaking our own will." She hastened then to gather the nuts and to remove the shells. Gradually she realized the allegorical significance of the experience: the nuts growing among delicious fruits represented persons of hard and bitter disposition to whom as well as to the gentle, charity is due (*Leg.* 3.15.1, 2).

On another occasion she visualized the tree of charity growing from the Sacred Heart. It was tall and fair, filled with fruits among leaves as bright as stars. Both leaves and fruits sent forth an exquisite perfume. From the roots a pure fountain sprang to a great height and then returned to its source. This image, representing the union of the divinity and humanity in Christ, symbolized the spiritual joy and refreshment brought to the human race by the incarnation (*Leg.* 4.35.4). Gertrude saw her own transformation symbolized by a series of images, beginning with a little plant growing near the burning heart of Jesus. Blighted by her faults and negligences, the plant shrank away until it resembled a cinder. As she invoked the mercy of Christ, streams of blood and water from the Sacred Heart revived the lifeless coal, which then assumed the form of a flourishing tree, its branches divided into three parts like a fleur-de-lis. It seemed that as the tree was presented to the Trinity, each of the three persons, Father, Son, and Holy Spirit, attached to one of the branches all the spiritual fruits of wisdom and kindness that Gertrude would have produced had she cooperated fully with the divine inspirations (*Leg.* 3.18.5).

After communion she visualized her soul again under the form of a tree rooted in the wound of Christ's side; a mystical sap arose in it, causing fruits to appear through the strength of his divinity and humanity. The Trinity rejoiced in this tree as did also the company of the saints, who hung crowns on its branches representing their merits. In a representation of the communion of saints, Gertrude saw the fruits of the tree distilling a liquor, of which one part rose to heaven, augmenting the joys of the blessed, another part flowed into purgatory, assuaging the sufferings of the souls there, and a third part spread over the earth, bringing consolation to the good and the healthful bitterness of penance to sinners. This phenomenon seemed to her to be an answer to her prayer that since her negligence had deprived others of benefits, they might have some share in God's gifts to her (*Leg.* 3.18.6).

The life of a woman for whom she was praying also appeared under the form of a tree with leaves brilliant as gold, growing before the throne of God. This person climbed into the tree and cut off branches which had begun to wither. As she removed each one, another grew from the throne of God, and being grafted on the tree, immediately bore crimson fruit which she presented to Christ. The new branches replacing the withered ones represented the life of Christ, whose sufferings and merits compensated for her faults; the fruits represented her good will in correcting them (*Leg.* 3.73.10–11).

Finally, on the feast of Pentecost, as Gertrude prayed for the gifts of the Holy Spirit, she saw these gifts as trees differing in their fruits: fear of the Lord was shown by small spikes from which flowers grew; the trees of knowledge and piety distilled a gentle dew; counsel and fortitude were symbolized by golden cords on the tree; wisdom and understanding were streams of nectar (*Leg.* 4.38.4).

Gertrude's and Mechtild's symbolic trees are basically similar in the graphic representation of the union of divinity and humanity in Christ, the rewards of virtue, and the consequences of evildoing. Ordinarily the images are associated with liturgical seasons or events—Lent, mass, or the choral office. Mechtild often seems a wondering spectator rather than a participant in the scene. Some details in her descriptions resemble the iconography of the Tree of Jesse and its derivatives. The ladder reaching to heaven, inscriptions on the leaves, and animals at the foot of the tree have their analogues in the *Speculum Virginum,* Herrad of Hohenbourg's *Hortus Deliciarum,* and the mosaic "Triumph of the Cross" in San Clemente, Rome. Color, fragrance, and movement characterize her imagery. The focus is not on individual human beings but on the virtuous and sinners. The most notable aspect of Mechtild's scenes is their cosmic scope; the tree reaches from heaven to earth, its branches extend over the whole world.

Gertrude's images are less colorful but more personal. They often center on individuals—herself and others: her own shortcomings, someone who caused her suffering, a nun who tried to atone for her faults. Her visions are instructive, stressing the amendment of life, the conquest of self-will, and the importance of good works. They reflect the difficulties of human relationships and the compensating manifestations of divine love.

Both the *Legatus* and Mechtild's *Liber* contain images associated with spiritual warfare—the lance, the arrow, the shield. When Gertrude was trying to chant the Office devoutly, it seemed to her that her words were darting like lances from her heart to the heart of Jesus, causing him great joy. Rays of light like stars streaming from the points of the lances clothed all the saints in new glory, particularly the saint whose feast was being celebrated (*Leg.* 3.24.1). In book 2 she had told how her desire to pierce the heart of Christ with the arrow of her love had been followed by the piercing of her own heart by the arrow of divine love. Another passage depicts Christ as saying, "The eye of my chosen one pierces my heart by her serene confidence in me" (*Leg.* 3.7.1). As noted earlier, Mechtild of Hackeborn urged a correspondent to clothe herself in the armor of Christ's passion. Mechtild of Magdeburg uses floral imagery in her description of spiritual armor: "your sword, the noble rose, Jesus Christ; your buckler, the white lily, Mary" (*Licht* 2.19).

In descriptions of flowers and jewels, Gertrude makes occasional use of synesthesia. On the feast of the Assumption of Mary, at the singing of the antiphon *Frondete in gratiam* (flower forth in grace), she visualized a field of flowers sending out a joyful melody in homage to the Virgin. Music also issued from the golden wings of the angels stationed to repel the enemies of the monastery. A similar image is found in Mechtild's *Liber.* When Gertrude visualized persons about to receive communion, their garments were adorned with jewels having the shape and fragrance of violets, symbols of humility (*Leg.* 4.48.10; 4.59.2; 4.7.4).

The foregoing examples demonstrate that like Bernard, Gertrude draws on sensory images to express figuratively the delights of the divine union. Her tone is peaceful; *serene* is one of her favorite words.

Another characteristic of Gertrude's writing is her use of comparisons or analogies to elucidate spiritual realities, and in particular, the intimate communication of the human person with divinity. The use of comparisons is of course common in the Scriptures and in the literature of mysticism. Teresa of Avila's images of the watering of the spiritual garden and of the mansions of the soul are familiar examples.[12] By means of comparisons—some chivalric and feudal, some homely and domestic, Gertrude is enabled to write about even the most exalted mystical experiences. She acknowledges the limitations of her analogies by constant use of such phrases as *ad similitudinem* or *verbi gratia.* Her similitudes are to be distinguished on the one hand from imaginative visions, striking and interesting as these are, and on the other, from simple, undeveloped comparisons, whether similes or metaphors. The term similitude is here reserved for a comparison less extended than the exemplum and ordinarily introduced by one of the phrases listed above. As vignettes showing many aspects of thirteenth-century life, Gertrude's similitudes are valuable to students of medieval environments.

In similitudes drawn from nature, the sun is an ancient image of God. Images of fire and water, rain and dew are also familiar in writings of the mystics. Gertrude and both Mechtilds frequently employ them. For example, the soul drawn by God is absorbed as a dewdrop is taken up by the noonday sun; the rain of grace falls with such abundance that Gertrude is weighed down like a young plant (*Leg.* 5.32.8; 2.10.2). Fields, orchards, and gardens, familiar sights to the nuns of Helfta, are often mentioned. Like Mechtild of Hackeborn she represents virtues by flowers: roses, lilies, violets, trefoils—less frequently, crocus and herb bennet.

References to animals are lively and original. When the community chanted *Regnum mundi et omnem ornatum saeculi*, Gertrude visualized the demons fleeing "as quickly as a pack of rabid dogs when someone has thrown hot water on them" (*Leg.* 4.54.6). Mechtild of Magdeburg usually refers to dogs as contemptible, useless, or dangerous. She frequently calls herself a dog: "unblessed, lame dog!" (*Licht* 4.1). Gertrude's similitudes include wolves, foxes, oxen, lambs, doves, the pelican, fish, and bees. A detail of medieval life is evoked by the comment, "If a wife sometimes gives food to her husband's falcons, she will not for that reason be deprived of his embraces" (*Leg.* 2.13.1).

To illustrate the love of God, Gertrude frequently uses images of parents and children. Mechtild of Hackeborn mentions children less frequently. Remembering that Gertrude was only five when she was brought to Helfta, one asks where she learned the intimate details of family life. Intelligent beyond her years, she may have remembered scenes of home. Probably she also listened intently to the reminiscences of her companions. The reunions of parents with children at the convent school must likewise have given her some vicarious experience, as the following similitude may show. Once when she was asked if she had ever seen a mother console a little child, Gertrude was silent because she could not remember. Then she recalled such a scene six months earlier. The child must have been very young, for only the mother could understand what it was saying (*Leg.* 3.30.38). This image impressed her with the realization that God alone fully understands the minds of his creatures.

The similitudes depicting parents and children are to be understood as analogues of the relations between the creator and the creature. These realistic and vivid scenes give an attractive picture of family life. A mother who is working with silk or pearls will put her little child in an elevated place so that he may hold her thread and jewels (*Leg.* 3.6.1). This is to show that God seeks the cooperation of his creatures. A father is glad to see himself surrounded by his many children who arouse the admiration of others. "But seeing among these children the smallest one, who is less attractive than the others, this good father, filled with pity, takes it into his arms and gives it many little presents" (*Leg.* 2.18.1). Gertrude considered herself to be like this little child, less worthy of admiration than her sisters but for that reason favored by God's compassion. She speaks also of a mother who wishes to keep her beloved little son with her. When he desires to run out to play with his companions, she will place masks (*larvas*) or some other terrifying object nearby so that the frightened child may run back to her arms (*Leg.* 3.63.1). A mother would gladly deck her small child with gold and silver, but since he cannot bear their weight, she adorns him with flowers instead (*Leg.* 3.63.2).

Once when Gertrude saw two members of the community disputing, one upholding justice and the other charity, she appealed to Christ and expressed the answer by a similitude: "A father who sees his children arguing in play will not interfere unless there is danger of a real quarrel" (*Leg.* 3.78.2). Other similitudes refer to a father presiding at table and enjoying the skill of the *lusor* who is entertaining the guests; seeing that the cellar is well stocked with wine; teaching a daughter (*Leg.* 3.54.1; 4.59.4; 4.50.10). Mothers are shown guiding a daughter's hand at work; giving medicine to a sick child; selecting ornaments for a girl's holiday attire (*Leg.* 4.5.4; 5.9.1, 6).

Many of Gertrude's comparisons refer to husbands and wives, especially at the time of marriage. Both bride and groom are assumed to be of noble or royal rank. Similitudes of this kind show not only a richly ceremonious setting but also a loving confidence between husband and wife. Several similitudes treat of the preparations for marriage: for example, when a lord is about to celebrate his wedding, he stores up quantities of grain and wine at harvest time, and immediately the rumor flies that he is intending to marry. Likewise, when a girl sees many messengers coming from her bridegroom to negotiate the marriage, she must also make some preparations (*Leg.* 5.26.2; 5.24.1). A king who is going to marry a bride who lives far away will send a great company of nobles to escort her with musical instruments (*tympanis et citharis, diversisque musicis instrumentis*) and many gifts. When she arrives, he will establish her honorably in one of his palaces, and in the presence of all his princes he will give her the ring of betrothal. The phrase *tympana et organa coeteraque suaviter sonantia instrumenta* occurs in the course of this description (*Leg.* 5.27.9, 10). The spiritual teachings underlying these similitudes are obvious. It is in Gertrude's *Legatus* that one finds the serene affirmation of the simple union of the soul with God in terms as homely as those of Julian of Norwich: "A wife knows her husband's mind and all his secrets because they have lived so long together" (*Leg.* 1.17.2).

The affectionate relationship of friends also supplies many

similitudes. The exchange of gifts and confidences, taking meals together, and consoling one another are frequently mentioned. A man will drink gall if thereby he can offer nectar to his friend. Gertrude emphasizes the generosity of true friends: a rich man will open his money-box to supply a friend's needs; he will clothe his friend in fine garments. A friend will rise with alacrity even from a deep sleep for the sake of conversing with his friend (*Leg.* 4.23.5; 4.25.7; 3.34.1; 3.52.3). Gertrude, who suffered from insomnia, adds that such love is the more appreciated if shown by one who ordinarily cannot sleep.

The many families who had contact with Helfta either through blood relationship or benefactions doubtless afforded ample information concerning feudal manners and the customs of court life. The king or emperor and his attendants supplied analogues for members of the heavenly court. Gertrude's similitudes rarely show the sovereign alone, but in actions such as distributing gifts, visiting his queen, clothing and feeding a faithful knight (*Leg.* 3.9.1; 3.18.24; 4.10.3). In a similitude intended to emphasize that a person whom God has honored should have manners conformable to his dignity, she declares that it would be shameful for one who has been asked to serve at the king's table to go out to clean the stable and thereby defile himself. A chamberlain who has been given the honor of supporting an aged or infirm king would behave reprehensibly if, rising hastily to serve, he let his master fall (*Leg.* 3.44.2). All three of the nun-writers at Helfta, Gertrude and the two Mechtilds, employ such feudal comparisons; the latter two emphasize the long and arduous training required for those who would serve at court.

Gertrude's similitudes also show her familiarity with professions, arts, and crafts. As might be expected, many scenes from the schoolroom provide comparisons. She remarks that a kind teacher takes a young child into his arms to point out the letters, correct mistakes, and supply omissions. Students must begin with the alphabet before advancing to logic. A beginner who does not know the chant perfectly fixes his eyes intently on the book. A master addresses various students each in his own tongue; to one he speaks Latin, to another, Greek (*Leg.* 3.30.40; 2.24.1; 2.16.2; 3.48.2). She mentions the use of a transparent stone (beryl) to magnify script (*Leg.* 1.16.6). The activities of the physician, the goldsmith, and the painter also supply illustrations. When a skillful physician gives a potion to a sick man, the onlookers do not see the patient cured nor does he feel himself instantly restored; nevertheless the doctor knows the efficacy of the medicine (*Leg.* 3.72.4; 4.45.1; 5.4.4). A goldsmith must place in his work as many gems as he has prepared settings (*cistellas*) to receive them (*Leg.* 3.85.1). A painter varnishes a rich picture to increase its brilliance. He makes the colors brighter by retouching them and covers a newly painted picture lest it be dulled by dust (*Leg.* 3.72.4; 4.45.1; 5.4.4). A hunter takes greater pleasure in the flesh of a wild beast caught after long pursuit than he does in that of domestic animals (*Leg.* 3.58.2).

Musical instruments and singing are often mentioned in the writings of the mystics. Gertrude is keenly aware of the importance of the chant in the daily Office, the *opus Dei*. As second chantress, after Mechtild of Hackeborn, she was thoroughly familiar with the liturgy. She refers to the discomfort of a singer with a good voice (*multum sonoram et valde flexibilem*), who moreover delights in singing, if someone with a poor voice (*valde gravem et dissonam*) should take her place. The chanting of those who have little devotion or who take a purely natural pleasure in singing is compared to heavy and unmelodious chords from a stringed instrument (*Leg.* 3.25.2; 4.41.5, 2).

Similitudes referring to household tasks are particularly numerous. Such passages convey an idea of the homely atmosphere of the monastery at Helfta and the nuns' familiarity with housework. The descriptions are realistic: a person surrounded by steam from a cooking vessel; the difficulty of handling flour without getting it on oneself; the use of iron hammers to remove rust (*Leg.* 2.15.1; 3.41.4; 5.16.3). Even mishaps are cited: when one is dyeing a cloth with saffron, anything else falling into the dye is likewise colored; a pot used in cooking may catch fire (*Leg.* 3.69.1; 4.4.4). Many references to washing include the observation that muddy hands may more quickly be cleansed in a small amount of water if they are rubbed vigorously than if they are held motionless in a great quantity of water. The appetizing and refreshing odor of good food, the rapidity with which fresh bread soaks up mead, and the uselessness of a wooden knife contribute to the force of some comparisons (*Leg.* 5.15.2; 3.16.4; 4.4.4; 3.16.5). The last similitude illustrates the ineffectiveness of an unjust excommunication.

In such ordinary household experiences the Helfta mystics found a medium for their advice. For instance, someone who cooked for the community complained to Gertrude that her work did not leave her time to pray. When Gertrude prayed for her, she received the response: "Tell her I did not choose her to serve me an hour a day, but to spend the entire day in my presence. She will do this by performing all her work for my glory in the same spirit in which she should pray. She should always desire that those whom her work benefits should not only be physically strengthened but led to love me more and be confirmed in all good. Whenever she does this, she will season every dish with a savory salt that pleases me greatly" (*Leg.* 3.73.14).

Gold and silver figure in some similitudes. More than once Gertrude remarks that gold appears to best advantage when contrasted with black or with colors. A noble maiden who knows how to make artistic ornaments of pearls and other gems to adorn herself and her sister brings honor to her father, her mother, and all the household (*Leg.* 2.23.17; 3.75.1). Gold and silver may be melted together, she says, to form a precious amalgam; this is a figure of the union of divinity and humanity in Christ. Imitation jewelry made of copper and glass can give an appearance of wealth, but persons who wear real gold and gems are accounted richer (*Leg.* 3.10.2; 3.32.3). A passage that has caused some difficulty refers to a precious stone worn in the emperor's crown "by reason of its singularity." Paquelin calls the stone "besant," a word which ordinarily means a Byzantine coin. Doyère has solved the problem by explaining that the German name of the stone in the manuscripts is *wesant*. The gem in the emperor's crown was called "the orphan"—in German, *Waise*—because it was unique. Lansperg wrote *besant*, and his error has been copied by all subsequent editors except Doyère (*Leg.* 4.6.5, n. 1).

Perfumes and spices are frequent metaphors in the writings of the mystics of Helfta. Delicate ladies, Gertrude has learned, prefer perfume to any other gift. Mechtild refers to the refreshing effect of fine perfumes. When a jar of spices is stirred, says Gertrude, it sends out fragrance; whether the stirring is done with a wooden stick or with something more valuable does not matter. So the praise of God is pleasing to him even when offered by an unworthy person (*Leg.* 4.12.2; *Livre* 4.30.280; *Leg.* 4.1.4). Passages associating fragrances with Christ appear to derive from the text: "We shall run after you in the odor of your ointments" (Song 1:3).

Gertrude's frank humility and humor appear when she compares herself to a scarecrow (*tamquam larvam*) in an orchard to protect the fruit from birds. Evidently the fruit trees are her sisters; the birds are evil spirits (*Leg.* 1.11.3). One of the most detailed similitudes describes the manner of preparing for death. One who desires to be gladdened by divine consolation in his last hours should clothe himself in choice garments, ascend the vehicle of his own body, and with a firm rein govern the animal who draws it—namely, his own will (*Leg.* 5.27.12).

Like all mystics, Gertrude realized that spiritual realities can be described only by analogy. In various ways throughout her writings she warns her readers that her language is not to be taken literally: *ut humano more loquar*, she will say. In her account of a mystical experience at Christmas she writes: "As I possessed it [the Divine Infant] within my soul, it seemed to me that all at once I was changed into the color of this Divine Infant, if we may be permitted to call something a color when it cannot be compared to anything visible." A passage from Bernard of Clairvaux supplements Gertrude's explanation and clarifies the nature of such images. "When the spirit is ravished out of itself and granted a vision of God that suddenly flashes into the mind with the swiftness of a lightning flash, immediately, but whence I know not, images of earthly things fill the imagination, either as an aid to understanding or to temper the intensity of the divine light. So well adapted are they to the divinely illuminated senses, that in their shadow the utterly pure and brilliant radiance of the truth is rendered more bearable to the mind and more capable of being communicated to others. My opinion is that they are formed in our imagination by the inspiration of the holy angels" (*Leg.* 2.6.2; 4.26.2).[13]

According to Paquelin, Gertrude's first visions were imaginative. As her union with Christ developed, the mystical communications were not through images but *per puriores illuminationes cognitionum* and at the end of her life were of such a nature that she could hardly express them (*Rev.* 1:4). A passage in book 4 of the *Legatus* indicates that when she wondered why she was so often instructed by means of corporeal visions, she was given to understand that just as in former times the incarnation, passion, and resurrection were prefigured to the prophets by means of mystical figures and similitudes, so now also spiritual and invisible realities which transcend human understanding must be likewise shown by similitudes or analogies. "No one therefore should scorn what is manifested under a corporal likeness but rather endeavor to become worthy of tasting the hidden sweetness" (*Leg.* 4.12.3). The modern historian of mysticism, Juan Arintero, speaks in a similar vein: "Although they [the saints] see that these things are incomprehensible, they are nevertheless . . . able to declare these marvels by means of analogies, especially when God himself suggests certain symbols which are more suitable for representing them."[14]

Some of the dialogues between Christ and the soul, as Felix Vernet notes, are not to be taken as actual, literal conversations. The expression, "Jesus said to me," which one finds in many writers besides Gertrude, "refers to the thoughts which occur during prayer."[15] The limitations of ordinary language have thwarted many saints. Sigrid Undset writes of Catherine of Siena: "She who had the whole of the lovely and rich Tuscan language at her disposal said: 'It is impossible; it is like dipping pearls into mud.'"[16] Arintero expresses the same idea: "The visions and locutions of the spiritual senses, although they offer a certain analogy with the bodily senses, which authorizes the use of the same names, transcend every form and figure."[17]

In "Studies on the Phenomena of Mystical Experience," Augustin Léonard, O.P., points out that mystical experience is linked to objective realities: Scripture, the Church, the sacraments. It "cannot discover new truths; it is detached neither from revelation nor from faith. . . . The mystic can attach no weight to his intuition except in so far as it reveals to him more intensely what he already knows in common with all Christians."[18] The solidity of Gertrude's doctrine, the simplicity of her counsels, and the directness of her expression put her into the mainstream of spirituality. Ardor and serenity are equally characteristic of "this royal soul" as Vernet calls her.[19]

Gertrude came to realize that her mission was to teach not only her own sisters but whoever should read her writings. In the last chapter of book 2 she explains the reason for her pictorial style when she expresses the hope that her readers may be led "through these images to taste for themselves the hidden manna which can be known only by means of figures" (*Leg.* 2.24.1).

The approbation of Gertrude's writings came first from those who had known her. Foremost among these is Theodore of Apoldia, a Dominican whom the Master General had commissioned to write the life of Dominic. Theodore had not only examined Gertrude's writings but had many conversations with her. The superiors of the monastery at Helfta secured also the approval of other theologians, both Dominicans and Franciscans, six of whom are named in the Vienna codex (*Leg.* 1. Approbations. 105–7).

Johannes Bühler has said: "It may well be that the outpourings of love of a St. Hildegard, Gertrude of Helfta, or Mechtild of Hackeborn are not as immediate in their appeal to modern sensibilities as the speculations of a Meister Eckhart are, or the tender expressions of a Suso. Still, their exposition of heart and soul is no less deep and their language—unfortunately Latin—is often just as poetic."[20] Doyère, however, believes that Gertrude has a great appeal to twentieth-century readers because of the affective, subjective, but never sentimental, qualities of her writing. Her spirituality, rooted in Scripture, the sacraments, and monastic liturgy, is impeccably orthodox. Above all, her liberty of spirit exerts a perennial appeal (*Ex.* intr. "*Aspects Modernes,*" 35–36).

Gertrude's final prayer for the readers of her *Legatus* expresses both the largeness of heart and the serene humility attested by her companions: "According to your faithful promise and my lowly desire, grant all who humbly read these writings gratitude for your condescension, pity for my unworthiness and a sincere desire for their own perfection so that from the golden censers of hearts burning with love a fragrant incense may rise to you, atoning fully for all my ingratitude and negligence" (*Leg.* 2.24.2).

7   Gertrude in Her Community

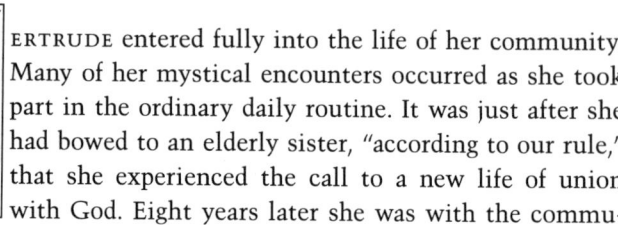ERTRUDE entered fully into the life of her community. Many of her mystical encounters occurred as she took part in the ordinary daily routine. It was just after she had bowed to an elderly sister, "according to our rule," that she experienced the call to a new life of union with God. Eight years later she was with the community awaiting the signal to go to the infirmary where communion was to be given to a sister when she was inspired to write the account of the momentous experience of 27 January 1281. Seized by an irresistible impulse, she snatched the tablet she wore at her side and, overwhelmed by her grateful memory of the presence of Christ, began to write the account now known as the second book of the *Legatus* (*Leg.* 2, prologue, 1).

Her contemporary biographer relates many instances of Gertrude's participation in the common life. When, with the other sisters, she received her portion of food and clothing, she took whatever came first to hand, "with eyes closed." She did, however, value the articles she used in her ministry—her books, her stylus, her writing tablet. When she received presents, she gave them away to the poor or "to persons hostile to her," making such gifts with the alacrity of a miser who receives a hundred coins for one. Whatever was necessary for her physical life—sleep, food, clothing—she used as for God living within her (*Leg.* 1.11 passim). In the same spirit she went from one activity to another, desiring in each to be another humanity for Christ.

Although her role as teacher distinguished her from some of the other members of the community, Gertrude tried to efface herself during her spiritual exercises. When the revelation of God's love moved her to tears, she tried to conceal them. When she was inspired to perform certain ceremonies in honor of the passion, and to pray with arms extended, she remarked, "One who practices such a prayer ought to hide herself in some remote place, for it is not the custom to pray in this way" (*Leg.* 4.26.5).

Gertrude felt special affection for the sisters who had arduous or uncongenial duties. She speaks of one who received a great reward from God because she did not complain when she had to work beyond her strength. When an accident to a sister might have necessitated an amputation, Gertrude prayed fervently that this ordeal might be averted. She experienced the reassurance of Christ and the conviction that the sufferer would be richly recompensed for her patience and that all who helped to relieve her pain would share in her reward (*Leg.* 5.3.7; 3.69.1). To another sister, who wondered why God required her to accept a trial beyond her strength, Gertrude brought this message: "Ask her what trial would be proportioned to her strength. Tell her that since the kingdom of heaven cannot be won without suffering, she shall choose now the sufferings that suit her; then when they come, let her bear them patiently." In consoling her sisters Gertrude drew confidence from her conviction that Christ never permits his own to be tried beyond endurance, "even as a mother who wishes to warm her little child at the fire always holds her hand between the fire and the child" (*Leg.* 3.70.1; 3.83.1).

Gertrude was convinced that God's gifts bore no fruit in her unless she shared them by her words and her writings. The magnificence of the gifts did not lighten the burden of sharing them, and she was often extremely weary. From early morning until evening she was studying, teaching, and writing. She believed that Christ had said to her: "I am always hungry and thirsty for the salvation of souls; anyone who will study some words of Scripture every day will appease my hunger." She worked quickly and with such apparent pleasure that she seemed to be enjoying herself (*Leg.* 4.18.1; 1.11.9). Yet the long hours of study, reading, writing, and teaching sometimes brought her to the point of exhaustion—"my inertia" she calls it. Once when she performed a difficult task, saying, "Lord, I offer this action to you through your only Son, in the strength of your Holy Spirit, and for your eternal glory," she was led to understand that this dedication gave her work an extraordinary value (*Leg.* 2.13.1; 3.30.23). From those whom she served she expected neither thanks nor praise, though even persons who failed to appreciate her holiness could not help admiring her intelligence and eloquence.

She spared no effort in her teaching of the Scriptures, summarizing long passages and commenting on obscure texts so that unlearned sisters could understand them. When encountering passages which tell of sensual actions, she was so impersonal that only a slight flush betrayed her embarrassment. If she needed to treat such matters in order to help someone in spiritual difficulty, she spoke with complete candor and tranquility (*Leg.* 1.7.1; 1.9.1). She invoked God as her teacher in all her studies—*Tu optime magistrorum*, she calls him: "O best of teachers, you who have so many times instructed my ignorance" (*Leg.* 2.18.2).

It was not only by teaching that Gertrude served her sisters. Convinced that the signs of God's love were given to her for the benefit of others, she often asked how her sisters might share her blessings (*Leg.* 3.34.2). She sincerely considered every member of the community to be better than herself. Others, she believed, by the greater purity and holiness of their lives gave more glory to God by a single thought than she could by the holocaust of her life, unworthy and negligent as she was. One is reminded of Teresa of Avila's admonition to her nuns: "If you want to know whether you have made progress or not, sisters, you may be sure that you have, if each of you thinks herself the worst of all."[1]

Gertrude longed to impress on her sisters the importance of fervor and recollection at work and prayer. Characteristically, she taught this by means of a graphic comparison—a portrayal of the Evangelist John writing with different colored inks. Words written in black indicated works performed through custom and routine; those in honor of the passion were recorded in red; those solely for the honor of God to obtain the salvation of all people through the merits of Christ's sufferings, with complete renunciation of all personal merit, were recorded in gold. Gradations of fervor were represented by pearls symbolizing the words of the penitential psalms recited at the chapter of faults. Words spoken through habit and without ardor appeared under the form of dark, lusterless pearls, while those recited devoutly were brilliant (*Leg.* 4.16.2; 4.2.13). A colorful scene is associated with the feast of the Nativity of Mary, when Gertrude visualized each sister's guardian angel standing beside her holding a branch. Various kinds of flowers and fruits, representing the devotion of each nun, grew from the branches (*Leg.* 4.51.3).

Gertrude's admonitions gained force from the realization that her own recitation of the Office was sometimes imperfect. Once when she showed less than her usual attention, she sensed that a demon was beside her, derisively repeating the words, *mirabilia testimonia tua*, in mockery of her careless pronunciation. At the end of the psalm he exclaimed, "Indeed your Creator, your Savior, and your Lover, has done well to give you such facility in speech! You have a great talent for eloquent discourse on any subject whatsoever, but when you speak to God, your words come forth at such a rate that in a single psalm you have left out so many letters, syllables, and words!" (*Leg.* 3.32.4).[2]

As the servant of her sisters, Gertrude taught, advised, consoled, and prayed for them. She had the gift of dispelling doubts and correcting false ideas. Yet though so enlightened in counseling others, she was quick to seek advice, even consulting persons who might have been considered her inferiors and humbly following their recommendations (*Leg.* 1.11.12). Her advice to those who consulted her must have been brief as well as apt, for she spoke to many persons in a single hour. Yet though brief, her words were so effective that sometimes her hearers wept. Her biographer asserts that many found themselves more moved by one of her words than by the long sermons of famous preachers (*Leg.* 1.12.1). Among those whom she directed were "a learned person," "an unlettered person," "one who had entered at an advanced age," "a person tried by temptation," "an invalid," and "one who found great difficulty in the work she had been assigned" (*Leg.* 3.73.13,14,3; 3.76.1; 3.72.4; 3.89.1). Gertrude instructed those who came to her to have confidence in God's merciful love and to recognize the many ways of pleasing him. Once as Mechtild was praying for her friend, she visualized Gertrude's heart as a firm bridge, walled on one side by the divinity, on the other by the humanity of Christ. From this image Mechtild derived a divine promise, "Those who come to me by this bridge will not fall or wander from the right way" (*Leg.* 1.14.6).

To share her gifts by teaching and advising was, Gertrude understood, to make good use of her "talent of intelligence." She accused herself of wasting in useless words the eloquence with which she had been endowed. Moreover, those who came to her for counsel might have applied to her the words of Ecclesiastes (12:11): "Sharp goads these are to sting us, sharp nails driven home, these wise words!" Yet she was cut to the heart if someone, intending to console her, advised her to leave incorrigible persons to suffer the final penalty of their misdeeds. She answered that she would rather die. Such was her burning sincerity that to her contemporary biographer her words seemed to be "dyed in her heart's blood" (*Leg.* 4.17.1; 1.7.1; 1.6.1). She saw her own faults no less clearly than her neighbor's. One is reminded of Bridget of Sweden, who on being asked, "What do the proud ladies say in thy kingdom?" answered, "I am myself one of them and I am ashamed to speak."[3]

Other classes of persons, from the laborers on the convent property to the Dominican fathers and brothers from Halle and Magdeburg, also engaged Gertrude's interest and compassion. Yet her biographer says that she never looked at any man long enough to recognize him on a second meeting (*Leg.* 1.9.1). The affection that she inspired drew her friends to God, and "even rebels" who would not humble themselves before anyone else were overcome by her (*Leg.* 1.12.1). It seemed that she too had heard the divine message, "I have put my words into your mouth" (Jer 1:9). Her gift of dispelling doubts and restoring peace of mind was of particular service to her community. The Abbess Gertrude often consulted her. Sometimes Gertrude herself was unaware of what she had done for her sister companions: a nun who was tormented by temptations which made her hesitate to receive communion felt that she was at once released from her suffering when she secretly possessed herself of a scrap of worn-out cloth from Gertrude's garments. A person in mental distress was advised in a dream to have recourse to her. The contemporary biographer who reports this observes that though the relief of mental pain is less obvious than the cure of bodily disease it may sometimes be as truly miraculous (*Leg.* 1.14.4; 1.2.6; 1.12.2).

Her concern was not limited to the members of her community. She prayed for Jews and pagans, for sinners, for the souls of the dead, for all who suffered, for prelates, and for her superiors. Many persons whom she did not know were recommended to her, and she faithfully interceded for them, sending them sympathetic messages as well. She obtained copies of the Scriptures for places that lacked them (*Leg.* 1.11.11; 1.4.2). Even animals shared her compassion, especially when she saw them undergoing cold, hunger, or thirst. She would offer their sufferings to God, asking him to have pity on the works of his hands. The scope of her charity is expressed in her cry: "O my Savior, I wish to bring to you every soul for your delight. I would go barefoot over the whole world from now till doomsday to carry to you everyone who does not know you and whose love could please you!" (*Leg.* 1.8.1; 4.21.1).

Mechtild once protested to Christ that Gertrude judged the faults of others with a certain severity. She was given to understand that as her friend could not tolerate the least stain on her own soul so she could not endure with indifference the faults of her neighbor (*Leg.* 1.11.9). Gertrude herself sometimes wondered whether she should correct others, though her motive was always the consuming desire that God should have all the honor due him, especially from those who had vowed to serve him. Once when she was reading to the community, she pronounced with great emphasis the words of the commandment, "You shall love the Lord your God with your whole heart, with your whole soul, with your whole mind, and with all your strength" (Mk 12:30). Her biographer cites the incident as evidence of Gertrude's zeal for God's glory. According to one account, she read the text twice (*Leg.* 1.3.6).

The magnanimity shown in her prayers for many classes of people was accompanied by sound practical sense and the realization that there are many states of life. These qualities no doubt attracted her numerous visitors. In the third of her *Exercises* a passage quoted from the Preface for the Consecration of Virgins shows her understanding of human nature and its aspirations: "While no interdiction lessens the honor of marriage, and the original blessing of holy matrimony always remains, there are some loftier spirits who, turning away from the conjugal bond between man and woman, desire the mystery it signifies; and without imitating what is accomplished in marriage, love most of all what it signifies" (*Ex.* 3.222–27). A rubric in the second exercise also shows awareness of those outside the cloister: "Ask the Virgin Mother to be your guide in the monastic state or in whatever your state of life may be" (*Ex.* 2.66–67).

Her biographer states that Gertrude once envisioned Christ supporting a great mansion. He seemed to say, "See with what labor I am holding up this house of religion which is threatened with ruin almost everywhere because there are so few who will work faithfully to defend and sustain it.... All those who by word or act promote the religious state are like columns supporting the weight which crushes me." Deeply moved, Gertrude resolved to work with all her strength to promote the religious state by practicing severe discipline in order to give good example. After she had observed this rigor for some time, her intimate friends persuaded her to relax her austerities and devote herself to peaceful contemplation (*Leg.* 1.7.3). In her zeal for regular monastic life she sometimes ventured to reprove even persons renowned for their virtues. One of the nuns prayed that Christ would moderate this fervor for fear it would give scandal. She was given to understand that he himself had caused scandal: "I acted so when I was on earth. She resembles me in that. Some of the Jews were regarded as the holiest of men and yet they were scandalized by me" (*Leg.* 1.12.1).

On a Sunday when the words *Ubi est frater tuus Abel?* were chanted, Gertrude realized that God will hold each religious responsible for the faults against the rule which she could have prevented by timely correction. The excuse that some give, "It is not my duty to correct him," or "I am worse than he," will be no more acceptable than Cain's words, "Am I my brother's keeper?" Gertrude sought the correction of the faults of her superiors only by recommending them to God. (The masculine pronouns suggest that bishops may be the superiors in question.) As she prayed for the improvement of imperfect superiors, she realized that submission to such persons is more meritorious than submission to the irreproachable. Similarly, superiors profit by the defects as well as by the virtues of their communities (*Leg.* 3.30.18; 3.82.1). As a result of her efforts, Gertrude encountered skepticism and hostility from some of her companions. She mentions detractions but does not give details. One gets the impression that some persons found in her gifts a pretext for resentment. She was sometimes in a dilemma caused by her zeal for God's honor on the one hand and on the other by her unwillingness to offend members of the community who might find her too insistent on minor observances. When she offered to God the pain she foresaw as a result of her actions, she experienced a consoling intuition: "Every time that you incur a reproach for my love, I shall support and fortify you as a city is surrounded by walls and moats so that nothing whatsoever may separate you from me. Moreover, I shall give you the merits that such persons would have acquired by submitting humbly to your remonstrances for my glory" (*Leg.* 4.58.1; 3.62.1).

Gertrude had learned that opposition to injustice does not destroy the virtue of concord. Her biographer cites her zeal for justice and her freedom from human respect: "She would not have defended by a single word her dearest friend even against her own enemy if by doing so she might be guilty of injustice. In fact, if justice demanded it, she would condemn her own mother rather than commit the least injustice even to an enemy" (*Leg.* 4.37.2; 1.6.1). This devotion to justice cost her dear since she loved and esteemed all her sisters. Yet she had no illusions about their shortcomings and once asked Christ why her frequent prayers for her friends appeared to have so little effect. The answer was conveyed by a similitude: "When a young prince returns from the emperor's palace where he has been invested with great possessions, those who meet him see only the weakness of childhood and are unaware of how powerful he will become. Do not be astonished if you see no effect from your prayers. My eternal wisdom disposes of them to greater advantage. The more one prays for another, the more greatly blessed that person will be. Persevering prayer is never without fruit although human beings do not know in what way it will be answered" (*Leg.* 3.30.24).

On another occasion she reported the instruction: "Anyone who loves and defends the truth and thereby loses friends, undergoes suffering, or performs great labor, that person like Mary Magdalen, breaks the alabaster vase and pours on my head a precious perfume, filling the house with its fragrance. Such a one gives good example, and while correcting the faults of others, also corrects her own since she will avoid committing the faults she has condemned in others." Yet it was painful for Gertrude to reprove her companions. "Alas, Lord," she lamented, "that I am the scourge to purify your dear friends" (*Leg.* 4.46.3; 4.5.5).

Gertrude suffered with her sisters from the many troubles which beset the community. Although several threatened assaults on the monastery had been averted, other trials continued. The convent had been robbed more than once, and Gertrude shared her companions' resentment toward their enemies. She felt rebuked for her attitude as she visualized Christ with his arm painfully wounded, saying: "Think how I should suffer if someone were to strike me cruelly on this injured arm. That is how I am treated by those who have no pity for the risk of damnation incurred by your persecutors. Some persons publish the wrongs and damages you suffer, forgetting that these evildoers are also my members. On the other hand, those who are compassionate and who implore my mercy, asking that these sinners may be converted, apply a soothing ointment to my arm. Whoever by wise counsel leads them to the amendment of their lives resembles a skillful physician who restores the arm to its normal state." Gertrude was amazed. "Merciful Lord!" she exclaimed, "how can you call such unworthy persons your arm? They have been cut off from the Church, publicly excommunicated because of the disturbance they have caused in our monastery." "Nevertheless," was the reply, "since they can be reunited to the

Church through absolution, I must take care of them." As Gertrude continued to pray insistently for the protection of the convent, the spiritual instruction also continued: "If you humble yourself under my all-powerful hand and acknowledge that you have deserved these punishments, my fatherly mercy will preserve you from all hostile invasion; but if you rise up proudly against your persecutors, wishing to return evil for evil, then by my just decree I shall allow them to prevail and do you even more harm" (*Leg.* 3.67.1–2). The reference to excommunication suggests that these enemies were under the leadership of Gebhardt, who had already attacked the monastery in 1294. Elsewhere, however, it is said that the convent had many enemies.

It has been mentioned that the monastery was sometimes burdened with debts. The persons in charge of temporal affairs felt great anxiety and Gertrude sympathized with them. A passage in the *Exercises* reflects the urgency of the convent's creditors: "Already the creditor is at the door, demanding from me the loan of life and payment for the time given me. There is no safety in speaking with him, for I have nothing to pay my debt" (*Ex.* 7.149–52). While she prayed earnestly that the convent officials might be enabled to pay the debts in order that they might have more time to pray and fewer distractions, she understood Christ to say: "It does not matter to me whether you perform spiritual exercises or manual labor, provided only that your will is directed to me with a right intention. If I took pleasure only in your spiritual exercises, I should certainly have reformed human nature after Adam's fall so that it would not need food, clothing, or the other things that human beings must make or find with such effort. A mighty emperor is not contented merely to have richly attired ladies-in-waiting in his palace, but he also has men-at-arms, and officials fit for various services always ready to carry out his orders. So I do not find my pleasure merely in the interior exercise of contemplation, but also in various external and useful works, directed to my honor. These too invite me to live among the children of men and to find my delight in them. Furthermore, it is by manual works that they find occasion to practice charity, patience, humility, and other virtues." It seemed to Gertrude then that she saw the chief procurator of the monastery offering to God with great difficulty a piece of gold set with a precious jewel. She heard interiorly Christ's words: "If I lessened his troubles as you ask, I should be deprived of that jewel which pleases me so much and he would lose the reward prepared for him" (*Leg.* 3.68.1).

Gertrude's faults—impetuosity and impatience—are natural to an ardent temperament. Another trait was her apparent absent-mindedness. During the chanting of the office, she was sometimes so lost in contemplation of God that she did not know whether the other sisters were sitting or standing and had to have her attention called to the rubrics. Such abstraction is likely to cause amusement or annoyance. Gertrude prayed that her gift of contemplation might be withdrawn during the time of common prayer. Instead, she found that she was enabled to remain in a state of contemplation while conforming to the actions of the community (*Leg.* 4.15.7). However vehement the accusations of others, they could hardly compare with her self-indictments. Throughout her writings she repeatedly accuses herself of ingratitude, negligence, impatience, and misuse of God's gifts. Although her prayers to Christ are profoundly reverent, she sees herself guilty of "boorish ignorance and discourtesy" (*Leg.* 2.23.17). In the fourth exercise she prays to be delivered from "timidity of spirit and from storminess, from all perversity and sensuality, blindness of heart and aridity of mind, from negligence and waywardness" (*Ex.* 4.174–76). She asked Mechtild to pray for patience and meekness; impatience is evidently her most persistent fault (*Leg.* 1.16.4). Sometimes it was caused by depression or by the neglect of those who took care of her in her illness. Her depression might have been a symptom of the disease, apparently hepatitis, which caused her death. More than once she mentions her disquiet when no one came to take her to the chapel (*Leg.* 3.3.1). She believes that she has been an obstacle to her friends by depending on them instead of God. Failure to thank him for his favors, failure to rejoice with her sisters and to sympathize with them in their sorrows—these are also cited in her self-denunciations. Of those making progress in the spiritual life, it is said that "because of their fervent desire to fulfill faithfully all their obligations and because of their particular psychological state of recollection in God, they may sometimes be inadvertently careless, forgetful of certain details, and perhaps even commit certain faults which they cannot correct, no matter how strenuously they try. These things are an abundant source of complaint and severe reprimands. They cause souls to suffer keenly, for they judge themselves culpable but find that they are helpless to remedy their light imperfections."[4]

It is clear that Gertrude's life was not a triumphal progress; she was not invariably loved and esteemed. She was sometimes hurt by the ingratitude of her friends, sometimes neglected in her illness. It pained her when her words were ineffective. Often, after she had spoken decisively to someone, she doubted the correctness of what she had said, particularly when she had urged a timorous person to receive communion. She was repeatedly given to understand, however, that she had spoken for Christ and that she should be confident of his direction when she gave advice to others (*Leg.* 1.14.2). An especially grievous trial was the temporary loss of her gift of gracious speech and eloquent instruction. When this occurred, she felt that Christ was telling her, "If you still had the gift of eloquence you would perhaps attribute to it your ability to draw souls to me. I have withdrawn it in part to teach you that your power comes from me, and that I have given it to you by a special grace" (*Leg.* 4.30.1).

Gertrude shared fully in all the vicissitudes of the monastery, entering wholeheartedly into the joys and sorrows of community life. Apropos of her love for her sisters, her biographer quotes Gregory the Great who declares that sanctity consists not in working miracles but in loving one's neighbor as oneself (*Leg.* 1.13.5, n. 1). In the *Legatus* the value of mutual support is illustrated by the image of a wall made of precious stones held together by the gold of charity (*Leg.* 4.58.3). Her solicitude for her companions extended to their physical needs. Although apparently she did not have the strength for heavy physical labor, she was not indifferent to the burdens of others in the household but sympathized with them and prayed for them. Even for a person in good health such unremitting labor as Gertrude took on herself would have been taxing. Illness often prevented her from participating in the community exercises; sometimes she could remain for only part of the Office. When it was impossible for her to take an active part in the prayers of the community, Gertrude would go to the choir and sit there during the chanting of the Office so that she might use whatever strength she had in the service of God. It grieved her that at such times she lacked fervor and could scarcely pronounce a few words or chant several notes. She was comforted by the thought that every word and every neume chanted in Christ's honor afforded him more pleasure than she would feel if a friend offered her a delicious and strengthening drink of new mead. Similarly, when she wondered whether she should stand at the Gospel when she felt unable to do so, it seemed to her that Christ said, "When you accomplish something that exceeds your strength, I accept it as indispensable to my honor; but when you omit anything with a right intention,

I accept those omissions as if I myself were infirm. Thus I reward both manners of acting" (*Leg.* 3.59.1–2). Gertrude received a special illumination on this matter when the words *gloriosum sanguinem* were sung on the feast of martyrs. She then reflected that just as blood, which in itself inspires horror, is praised when it is poured forth for the honor of God, so when religious duties are omitted for reasons of charity or obedience, these omissions are pleasing to God and therefore praiseworthy (*Leg.* 3.30.13). Far from cutting her off from the liturgical cycle, Gertrude's illnesses were the occasion for many spiritual illuminations. In her wakeful nights she was encouraged by realizing the value of her sufferings, particularly when the other nuns were too busy to attend to her needs. She thought of Christ as saying to her, "My daughter, you are always with me, and all I have is yours" (*Leg.* 3.30.34).

Her poor health did not deter Gertrude from offering to go with a group of sisters to make a new foundation when the emissaries of a certain nobleman requested this. Yet soon remembering that she had hardly strength enough for her own duties at Helfta, she considered herself foolish to wish for this mission. Nevertheless she believed that Christ was pleased by her desire "as if an ointment had been applied to his wounds." Her biographer says that whatever God permitted seemed right to Gertrude; the fact that the proposed foundation was never made did not disturb her. Her attitude recalls the saying attributed to Bernard, "Whom God pleases, he pleases God" (*Leg.* 3.64.1; 1.16.6).

The names of Gertrude and Mechtild are inseparably linked in the history of mysticism. As noted earlier, Paquelin presents evidence that Gertrude was the chief author of the *Liber specialis gratiae,* the record of Mechtild's spiritual life (*Rev.* 1:13). Sharing the common life at Helfta, they reacted similarly to the trials and sorrows of the community: the interdict imposed by the canons of Halberstadt, the drought which endangered their harvest, the pressure of debt, and the fear of marauding armies, especially in 1294 during the war between the Emperor Adolph and the sons of Albert of Saxony. Both nuns express grief at the death of the Abbess Gertrude. Mechtild had the additional sorrow of being prevented by illness from attendance at her sister's deathbed. On that occasion, Gertrude as second chantress, intoned the antiphon, *Surge, Virgo* (*Leg.* 5.1.24, n. 3). Though the two friends were not sisters as the older biographers mistakenly assert, they were united in a close relationship. Equals in the world of the spirit despite their difference in social rank, they enjoyed a friendship rooted in their monastic commitment and their ardent love of God. Gertrude regarded sentimental friendship as "a deadly poison" and would decline even the most helpful services if she believed that she was being given what was owed to God (*Leg.* 1.6.1). She had no reason to question her relationship with Mechtild. Their love of music was also a bond.

It appears that Gertrude and Mechtild had the same type of constitution. Insomnia and chronic illness are reported of both. Both accepted their physical pain as the chastisements of a loving God, and therefore to be received, as Gertrude says, most willingly and joyfully, "for bodily and spiritual sufferings are the sign of the espousal of the soul to God" (*Leg.* 3.2.1). Mechtild believed that whereas in health one is embraced, as it were, by the right arm of Christ, in sickness it is by his left arm, "which is nearer his heart" (*Livre* 2.32.173).

The two mystics of Helfta have been called the saints of the humanity of Christ, particularly as symbolized by the Sacred Heart.[5] The incarnation, infancy, public life, passion, and death, as brought successively to mind through the liturgical cycle, occupied their thoughts and directed their prayers. Both experienced the presence of Christ presiding at the conventual chapter on Christmas eve. Both experienced his visitation when illness kept them from the community. Both felt deeply convinced of his accessibility. Gertrude believed that even the slightest action was acceptable to him—even such as picking up a straw, speaking a single word, showing a kindness to someone, saying a *Requiem aeternam* for the dead, offering a prayer for sinners or for the just. Christ seemed to say, "How affectionately I shall receive anyone who at the end of a year brings me the fruits of her love in number exceeding her sins!" Gertrude was doubtful that anyone could do this, "since the human heart is so prone to evil." "Why should it be so difficult," was the reply, "since I am pleased by the least sign of zeal and as all-powerful God cooperate with it?" (*Leg.* 4.2.8; *Livre* 1.5.13–14; *Leg.* 4.7.2).

The manifestations of divine love overwhelmed Gertrude and Mechtild. The realization that the supreme being should love and desire the love of his infinitely inferior creatures filled both nuns with passionate incredulity. In book 2 of the *Legatus* Gertrude asks what possible merit on her part could attract such love. As if forgetful of his dignity, bereft of reason and judgment, as if—she dares to say—intoxicated, God driven by love, unites himself to human beings so dissimilar to himself in order to save them (*Leg.* 2.8.3). Mechtild's *Liber* contains a parallel passage: love alone could induce the divine omnipotence so to subject himself, as if demented (*Livre* 2.35.175–76). Catherine of Siena also speaks of Christ as "drunk with love": "O mad lover! You have need of your creature?"[6]

The two mystics performed many of the same ministries, serving others by counseling, teaching, and praying. Gertrude's particular mission was to write and dictate the *Legatus*, the account of her spiritual life; the *Exercitia*; the major portion of the *Liber specialis gratiae*, the memorial of Mechtild of Hackeborn; various treatises, letters, and prayers now lost. Mechtild's particular mission, marked by graces of a unique and intimate character, was to share her experience of the immediacy and accessibility of the divine presence. Each of the mystics had a special responsibility for the other. Mechtild was Gertrude's mentor, enlightening and encouraging her, particularly in the imparting of her mystical experiences. Gertrude's corollary role was the compilation of the *Liber specialis gratiae*, the account of her friend's spiritual life.

A comparison of their imagery suggests some differences of temperament in the two mystics. Though both use domestic, familial, and liturgical images, some of Mechtild's show more color, detail, movement, and scope. For example, she describes the throne of God as made of jasper adorned with gold and rubies, the jasper signifying the eternal youth of the Godhead, the gold his love, the rubies, his passion. In another scene, Mechtild visualizes herself as seizing Christ's hand and tracing an immense cross, large enough to embrace heaven and earth. Later, as she laments that she is unworthy of a spousal relationship with Christ since she has no ring as a sign of fidelity, she sees in spirit Christ, herself, and all creatures in heaven and on earth enclosed in an immense ring set with seven pearls. These symbolize seven ways in which Christ comes at mass (*Livre* 1.10.30; 2.35.178; 3.18.214).

Gertrude the Great has been called "a second Teresa," the Teresa of Germany (*Rev.* 1:xxiv). The writings of the Spanish mystic contain many echoes of Gertrude's, some of which have been noted. The style of both writers—direct, vivid, and graceful—reflects the many resemblances in their spirituality. They both had a special devotion to the infancy of Christ, they experienced a mystical wounding of the heart, they were enjoined to write the accounts of their interior life. Prosper Guéranger in his preface to Gertrude's *Exercises* quotes Francisco Ribera, Teresa's confessor and first biographer, as saying that she had taken Gertrude as her mistress and guide.[7] The statement is not in Ribera's life of Teresa but may have been a verbal communication. The account of Teresa by her confessor, Pedro Ibañez, might apply equally to Gertrude: "Our Lord has given her great compassion for her neighbors, knowledge of her own faults, and self-abasement. She has done much good to many persons of whom I am one."[8] Diego Yepes, also Teresa's confessor, wrote to Leander of Granada, who had translated Gertrude's writings into Castilian: "I hope that His Majesty will grant you the grace that you may be assisted at the hour of your death by His two faithful spouses, who during their lives were always so full of gratitude and courtesy." It was Yepes who commissioned the portrait of Gertrude which has often been copied. He used as a model a painting of Teresa of Avila; to distinguish Gertrude, he had the artist portray the child Jesus in her heart.[9]

Both Gertrude and Teresa had contact with members of the Dominican Order, finding them faithful friends and champions. The Carmelite Order has also been active in propagating the writings of both mystics. In 1633, the Provincial, Denis of the Mother of God, paraphrasing Dante's tribute to Francis and Dominic, said of Gertrude and Teresa, "The conformity of spirit between these two saints is so exact that whoever approves of one approves of the other" (*Rev.* 1:27). Obviously, this resemblance is in the spirit rather than in the vocations of the two mystics. They did not fulfill the same missions in their orders. Yet though Gertrude was without the executive ability of the great Carmelite, it is unquestionable that her influence was also powerful and enduring. Never elected to office as superior, presumably because of her obscure ancestry, Gertrude nevertheless exercised a leadership far more exalted than that of the noble abbesses of the monastery of Helfta: the first superior, Cunegund of Halberstadt, devout and Godfearing; Gertrude of Hackeborn, competent and motherly; and Catherine of Watzdorff, one of the last abbesses, the target of Luther's attack.

8 Aspects of Gertrude's Spirituality

GERTRUDE of Helfta's spirituality is eminently liturgical and therefore eminently Benedictine. Pierre Pourrat observes, "When we read the *Revelationes* we are met on almost every page with lofty thoughts suggested by the phrases chanted in choir, in accordance with the well-known bent of Benedictine piety."[1] The influence of the Dominicans on the spiritual life at Helfta has already been mentioned. In Gertrude the firm doctrinal formation that this contact assured was blended with traditional Benedictine spirituality—the peace which is the motto of the order. With this peace is associated a liberty of spirit to which Frederick Faber has paid tribute. "No one," he writes, "can be at all acquainted with the old-fashioned school of Benedictine writers without perceiving and admiring the beautiful liberty of spirit which pervades and possesses their whole mind. It is just what we should expect from an order of such matured traditions. St. Gertrude is a fair specimen of them. She is thoroughly Benedictine. . . . A spirit of breadth, a spirit of liberty, that is the Catholic spirit; and it was eminently the badge of the old Benedictine ascetics."[2]

Although she has her own highly individual character, the influence of Bernard of Clairvaux pervades many of Gertrude's ideas and expressions. Any discussion of her spirituality must take account of this influence. Like him, she "ruminated" the psalms. Her delight in contemplating the incarnation of Christ also resembles his. His homilies, *Super missus est*, were probably familiar to her. Lepitre has said, "She teaches the theology of the incarnation admirably."[3] Confidence inspired by the birth of Christ characterized both Bernard and Gertrude, particularly at the hour of death. Both had a special devotion to the name of Jesus. Bernard recommended admiration of others' virtues and consideration of one's own lack of virtue.[4] This was Gertrude's habitual attitude. In their writings both mystics combine gentleness with vigor. What Gertrude most admired in the *doctor mellifluus* was his persuasive eloquence; it was a gift she shared. The chief expression of his mysticism is in his sermons on the *Song of Songs*; the Sources chrétiennes edition of the *Legatus* lists more than thirty citations from the sermons.

Both Bernard and Gertrude employ some daring images. Pourrat observes that the true mystics, being dead to the life of the senses and living only for God, express the force of the divine love that consumes them by some comparisons startling to the uninitiated. One who is prepared to read the great mystics has learned "detachment from curiosity about phenomenal manifestations and the ability to discern the universal message distinct from the personal circumstances of the revelations."[5] Teresa of Avila wrote, "it must be realized that the Betrothal has no more to do with the body than if the soul were not in the body, and were nothing but spirit. Between the Spiritual Marriage and the body there is even less connection, for this secret union takes place in the deepest centre of the soul, which must be where God himself dwells."[6]

Bernard's devotion to the Virgin Mary is proverbial. In the *Paradiso* Dante gives him the lines, "The Queen of Heaven, for whom I am all on fire with love, will grant us every grace, since I am her faithful Bernard" (*Par.* 31, lines 99–101). He popularized the idea of Mary as distributor of graces, a concept also found in Gertrude's writings. The chief resemblance between Gertrude and Bernard, her spiritual father, is in their conviction that love unites the spirit of Christ with the human spirit, bringing about a mutual sharing. Bernard's words are, "All things are common to them ... one home, one table, one bed" (*Quibus omnia communia sunt ... una domus, una mensa, unus thorus*).[7] As Ruusbroec explains, "Whenever I write that we are one with God, this is to be understood as a oneness in love and not in being or nature."[8] To Bernard and to Gertrude as to other mystics, the expression "the kiss of the spouse" means the possession of God that is the essence of the mystical union. It is the personified soul that receives on its mouth (*os animae*) the kiss of Christ.[9]

A dissimilarity betwee the two mystics is their attitude toward nature. Gertrude's appreciation of the landscape of Helfta is one of the traits to attract a modern reader. She resembles Francis of Assisi in her love of nature through which she contemplates God, as in the famous "courtyard passage" in book 2 of the *Legatus*. Bernard's indifference to natural beauty is shown in the anecdote of his passing the lake of Lausanne completely unaware of it. His abstraction could be understood not as contempt of nature but as evidence of deep contemplation. He was equally unaware of what he was eating or drinking.

Gertrude found many parallels between her interior life and the lives of certain personages in the Bible. She was particularly attracted to Esther, the Hebrew queen. Her lost treatise on Esther began with the words *Egredimini, filiae Jerusalem* (Song 3:11), a text later associated with the feast of the Sacred Heart. In her preparation for the feast of the Ascension, when she implored Christ to pardon her sins and negligences, it seemed to her that he likened her to the beautiful Esther, saying, "Ask what you will and I shall give it to you" (*Leg.* 4.35.5). In her role as second Esther, Gertrude acted as intercessor for all the members of the Church, seeing in Christ "the true Assuerus" who opened to her the treasury of his Sacred Heart (*Leg.* 4.58.4). She felt that a nun who led the prayers at the chanting of the Office also fulfilled the mission of Esther by praying for her people, her community.

Whereas Esther used diplomacy and her queenly power to outwit the enemies of her people, Gertrude dealt with persecutors by praying for them. She asked the grace of repentance for all those who afflicted the community. On one occasion she was so oppressed by the sense of her unworthiness and weakness that she felt unable either to praise God or aspire to contemplation. All at once it seemed to her that, clothed in the beauty that had adorned Esther before Assuerus, she was presented to Christ, the King of Kings, who greeted her as lady and queen, asking, "What do you wish?" She replied, "I ask and desire with all my heart that your adorable will may be wholly accomplished in me." As Christ recalled to her all the persons who had been recommended to her prayers, she added, "I desire that your loving and peaceable will may be fulfilled in every creature. For this I am willing to endure any suffering" (*Leg.* 3.11.2). Each similarity between herself and the Hebrew queen served to humble Gertrude and make her more uneasy at being revered by her companions.

Both the *Legatus* and the *Exercises* include many other scriptural episodes and phrases. Some of the passages Gertrude quotes or paraphrases are from the liturgy, which might also have suggested to her the linking of texts from the Hebrew and the New Testaments. When she felt unworthy to receive communion and realized that even if she spent a thousand years she could not make herself fit for union with Christ, she adapted the parable of the prodigal son (Lk 15:11–32). She reflected that if she approached Christ humbly, he would perceive her "while she was yet afar off" and clothe her with the garments and jewels of his own innocence, love, humility, hope, and confidence. In the fourth exercise also she sees herself as an unworthy prodigal, "who, alas, by my importunate sins have lost the name of daughter." To express her desire for death and her confidence in God's mercy, she paraphrases the words of Psalm 17:30 and links them with Paul's: "In you, O God my lover, I shall leap over the wall of the body and find myself in that place of security and rejoicing where I shall see you no longer in a dark manner but in truth and face to face" (1 Cor 13:12; *Leg.* 3.18.10, 11; *Ex.* 4.184–85; 5.283–85).

Gertrude's meditations on the details of Christ's life were sustained by the liturgical cycle. Many of her mystical experiences occurred during the mass. She believed that no number of individual prayers and penances can equal the value of the eucharistic offering of the body and blood of Christ. More than once she visualized Christ in priestly or pontifical garments. Several manuscripts of the *Legatus* include the account of a mass celebrated by Christ when Gertrude was unable to attend the community mass. The Beguine, Mechtild of Magdeburg, also reports a visionary experience in which she witnessed a mass celebrated by John the Baptist. Her assertion that she had seen such a mass drew the hostility of many of her contemporaries "because John was not a priest and so could not have said mass" (*Leg.* 5.277–309; *Licht* 2.4; 6.36). This experience predated the account of Gertrude's vision in the *Legatus*.

Second only to the mass in Gertrude's devotions was the Divine Office, the *opus Dei*. At the invitatory on Easter Sunday as she was thinking of the word Alleluia, it seemed to her that Christ said, "You can praise me worthily by uniting your homage with that which the heavenly court offers me through this word. Notice that in the Alleluia you find all the vowels except o, which signifies sorrow" (*Leg.* 4.27.4). As Gertrude continued her recitation of the Office, she understood each verse in reference to the feast of Easter. "Sing to the Lord a new song," a line frequently repeated in the daily Office, underlines the experience of discovering new meanings in words that have been sung daily for many years.

Devotion to the eucharist became intense and widespread during the thirteenth century. In many areas, however, superiors and confessors discouraged frequent communion, particularly for women. Communion once a month was considered frequent. The nuns at Helfta were more fortunate, receiving communion on all Sundays and feast days.[10] The eucharist was brought to the sick. The *Liber* records that after her death the Abbess Gertrude received a special reward for having encouraged frequent communion (*Livre* 5.2.309). The two mystics, Mechtild and Gertrude, also actively encouraged nuns who hesitated to partake of the sacrament. Gertrude herself needed such encouragement when a sermon on God's justice terrified her so that she feared to receive communion. She was reassured when she experienced by a spiritual intuition the words: "Look at the narrowness of the vessel where I enclose myself to come to you, and realize that the strictness of my justice is likewise limited by the mercy that I show in this sacrament." On another occasion she understood the words, "See the smallness of the material form in which I manifest both my divinity and humanity, and compare it with the size of the human body. Judge from this the greatness of my goodness, for as the size of the human body is greater than the [eucharistic] bread which is my body, so my mercy and love in this sacrament cause me in some way to allow the loving human soul to prevail over me" (*Leg.* 3.18.13, 14).

The *Legatus* records an episode emphasizing the importance of humility and community solidarity. Seeing a nun approach communion with an almost fearful reverence, Gertrude disapproved of her. Immediately, however, she believed that Christ was rebuking her with the words, "Do you not see that I deserve respect as well as love? Since human nature is too frail to pay me this double honor and since you are all members of one body, let each by her own disposition supply for what another lacks" (*Leg.* 3.18.19). At a time when she herself had planned to abstain from communion but was driven by ardor to receive the sacrament, she felt that Christ was saying, "Today by your own will you were going to serve me like someone who works with mortar, bricks, and straw, but I have chosen to place you with those who feast at my royal table" (*Leg.* 3.10.2).

The custom of elevating the host immediately after the consecration became general before the end of the thirteenth century. To look at the host was considered a great privilege, and in England especially, "levacion" prayers were composed to greet Christ at the moment of the elevation. A typical prayer begins, "Jesu Lord, welcome thou be / In form of bread as I thee see."[11] Like her contemporaries, Gertrude was eager to see the host. When the number of communicants obstructed her view, she was given to understand that the full delights of sacramental union are gained, not by seeing but by tasting. Although at Helfta the hosts used at mass were large and thick, it once happened that the priest and nuns failed to notice that a host had been dropped. It was not discovered until the sacristan was folding the altar linens. Gertrude knew by a spiritual intuition that the wafer had not been consecrated; nevertheless, she did not say so, preferring that Christ might receive the honor of reparation (*Leg.* 3.18.18; 3.13.1). The ability to distinguish between consecrated and unconsecrated hosts is reported of many mystics, including Catherine of Siena.[12]

At one time the nuns were exposed to the vehemence of someone designated only as "a certain person." The pronoun is masculine, and according to Doyère, refers to a confessor. Carried away by zeal, he used to exclaim against those who, he felt, received communion with too little preparation or devotion. He reproached the nuns and frightened some of them away from the sacrament. Troubled by his behavior, Gertrude appealed to Christ. Her perception of his answer is cast in the form of a similitude: "My delights are to be with the children of men, and in my excelling love I have promised to stay with my faithful ones in this sacrament until the end of time. Whoever keeps from communion someone who is not in mortal sin hinders or interrupts the delight I take in that soul. He is like a harsh tutor who forbids a king's son the delightful companionship of children his own age if they are poor or not of noble birth. He thinks it more fitting that the child should enjoy royal honors than that he should play ball in the street." Gertrude wanted to know if such a person could be pardoned if he resolved not to give such advice again. The answer was reassuring: "I should not only pardon him but I should be as pleased as the king's son would be if his teacher called back his favorite playmates" (*Leg.* 3.77.1, n. 1).

When many of the nuns were abstaining from communion "for various reasons," Gertrude thanked God for having placed her in a situation where neither relatives nor any other consideration could keep her from the sacrament (*Leg.* 3.18.3). This mysterious remark suggests that perhaps family loyalty had led some nuns to forego the sacrament when their relatives were under ecclesiastical censure. When the community could not receive communion because of the interdict, it seemed to Gertrude that she saw Christ spiritually entering into each one. Like other mystics, she also visualized Christ giving himself in the consecrated host, the priest merely making the sign of the cross over each member of the community (*Leg.* 3.16.4; 3.38.3). This experience recalls the words of the hymn *Pange Lingua*, attributed to Thomas Aquinas; it refers to the Last Supper, when Christ distributed the bread to his disciples: *Cibum turbae duodenae / se dat suis manibus* (with his own hands he gives himself as food to the twelve).

Gertrude's desire for the eucharist was so intense that she would have forced her way to it "through drawn swords." Her preparation included watchfulness against sins of speech. "A person who receives communion after sins of speech is like one who greets a guest after having heaped up a great pile of stones at the door" (*Leg.* 3.10.2; 3.18.9). When, in preparation for communion, she wished to offer to God the perfections of Christ on the day of his ascension, she felt assured that he was saying, "In the sight of heaven you are clothed in all the merits you desire. Is it hard for you to believe that I can do this? Does not someone who wishes to honor a friend clothe him in his own garments?" A variation of this image occurred when, at the time of communion, she understood Christ to say, "I will clothe myself with you so that I may extend my hand to sinners. . . . And I will also clothe you with myself in order that all those for whom you pray and those who by nature are like you may be made worthy to receive my royal gifts" (*Leg.* 3.34.1; 3.18.4).

It was immediately after communion that Gertrude experienced an answer to her prayer to be cleansed by Christ. A life-giving tide seemed to flow over her spirit, not only cleansing it but transforming it from a dead ember into a fruitful tree (*Leg.* 3.18.5). All her experiences of eucharistic communion led to the conviction that the demonstrations of human love can give no idea of the rapture of sacramental union with Christ. "The delights of earthly love are passing, but the joy of this union can never diminish; it grows more intense with every renewal" (*Leg.* 5.28.2).

Gertrude once asked, "What advantage have I over those who received you yesterday when I did, but did not do so today?" She sensed the reply: "Among the ancients a person elected a second time to the consulate was more honored than another elected only once. Why should the person more frequently united to me not receive a greater glory?" This question and answer perhaps show Gertrude as spiritual counselor, wishing to encourage frequent communion among those who consulted her. As she felt envious of priests who may communicate daily, she seemed to hear Christ's words, "Certainly, marvelous glory awaits those who receive me worthily. But do not confuse the love of the soul at the time of communion with the glory attached to the celebration of the mass." Gertrude was led to understand that there are various rewards: "one for the heart burning with love and desire; another for the one who makes a long, fervent preparation to receive me. Neither of these gifts is for a priest who celebrates mass routinely and without fervor" (*Leg.* 3.36.1).

Sometimes Gertrude's illness kept her from making her usual preparation for communion. Nevertheless, though she felt unprepared, her intense longing forced her to exclaim, "I know how unworthy I am to receive your body and blood, and I should abstain today from communion if I could find relief and consolation in any creature whatsoever. But from the east to the west, from the north to the south, there is no one but you who can gladden and refresh my body and soul. Behold me now, filled with love and breathless with desire, I run to the fountain of life." A deep conviction that Christ found a unique pleasure in her succeeded this outcry. Her sense of unworthiness was counterbalanced by the conviction that it was his gifts to her that made her pleasing to God (*Leg.* 3.50.1, 2). She came to believe that worthy reception of the eucharist can repair every spiritual loss; as a result, she never became unduly depressed by her faults.

The confidence which is the mark of Gertrude's spirituality was not immediately achieved. Timidity and mistrust frequently caused her to hesitate before receiving the sacrament. Gradually she learned that through Christ's passion she could be cleansed and adorned with the jewels of virtue. She also became aware that one so appareled should walk with dignity. "They behave like fools, who adorned with God's graces and given a share in his merits, still remain fearful" (*Leg.* 3.18.23). Gertrude hoped that the eucharist might be her last nourishment on earth and that she might die in the chapel where she had received the wound of love. Eventually she realized that such desires were inappropriate. Her comment after a dangerous fall shows her changed attitude. When her companions asked how she could express regret that the accident had not caused her death, since if it had, she could not have received the last sacraments, she answered, "With my whole heart I desire the help of those strengthening sacraments, but the will and plan of my Lord seem to me the best preparation. I am certain that whether my death be either sudden or expected, his mercy will never fail me. Without it I could not possibly be saved" (*Leg.* 1.10.4).

Gertrude had also learned that when a sick person receives the eucharist, the effect of the sacrament is not diminished by taking food or drink if the patient's motive is to prolong life for the glory of God. After the reception of communion, every act performed with a good intention is meritorious: to suffer patiently, to eat or drink—all increase the eternal reward because of the continued sacramental union (*Leg.* 3.35.1). When unable to receive communion, Gertrude believed that Christ was, as it were, refreshed by the preparation she had made through her guard over her senses, her moderation in speech, her desires, and her prayers. When she longed to be purified in order to make a spiritual communion, she seemed to see Christ looking at her with a glance like the radiance of the sun. As the sun whitens, softens, and makes fruitful, so the look of Christ purifies, melts, and causes the soul to bring forth the flowers and fruits of virtue (*Leg.* 3.38.2).

Feast days were not invariably joyful occasions for Gertrude and her companions. It was a common experience for her to be without consolation even on great feasts. When another nun complained of the same deprivation, Gertrude shared a spiritual communication with her: "This has not happened by chance but for a reason. On ordinary days and at unexpected moments I [Christ] grant the grace of devotion to arouse the soul from its torpor, but on feast days and at the time of communion I withhold this grace so that the hearts of my chosen ones may be filled with holy desires and humility. This is more helpful to them than the grace of devotion." The contemporary biographer declares that when the presence of Christ was thus withdrawn, Gertrude never fell into depression (*Leg.* 3.18.21; 3.10.1). To serve Christ with faith, reverence, and gratitude when deprived of consolation is, she realized, to serve him at one's own expense, "anxious, like good knights, to serve their King without pay," as Teresa of Avila puts it.[13]

The Church as the "Mystical Body" of Christ is a dominant theme in Gertrude's spirituality. The Fathers of the Church and later theologians frequently employ this image to represent by analogy the union between Christ and the members of the Church. Whereas Gertrude visualized the Mystical Body as a male figure, most others have seen the Church as a female figure, Ecclesia, the bride of Christ, born from his wounded side as Eve was drawn from the side of Adam. Thus Paul regards the union of Christ and the Church as the perfect archetype of Christian marriage (Eph 5:23–33).[14] The female image of the Church is sometimes represented as wounded by sin. Hildegard of Bingen sees the Church as the bride of Christ abused by unworthy clergy. She describes Ecclesia as a beautiful woman richly clothed, "yet her face was spattered with dust and her robe torn on the right side, her mantle had lost its elegance, and her shoes were blackened with mud." She cries out, "Those [the priests] who should have made me beautiful in every part have despoiled me in all."[15] Mechtild of Magdeburg sees Christendom as a poor maid. "I looked at her and saw our Lord also look at her. And I was bitterly ashamed of her. The Lord said: 'Is it seemly that I should take this poor maid to me as my bride? . . . For she is half-blind in understanding and crippled in her hands which do no good works. She is lame in the feet of her desire, for she thinks seldom and idly of me. Her skin is unhealthy, unclean, and impure.'" In answer to Mechtild's question, "What counsel can I give her?" the answer was, "I will wash her in my own blood" (*Licht* 5.34). Catherine of Siena also speaks of the Church as a sickly woman whose condition is caused by corrupt pastors. She writes to Gregory XI: "you will bring back to her faded face the color of blazing charity, for so much blood has been sucked from her by wicked gluttons that she is all pale."[16] Of the seventeenth-century Dominican Catherine de Ricci, the convent annals report, "Holy Church often appeared to her, covered symbolically with horrible, disfiguring wounds."[17]

Unlike these visionaries, Gertrude conceived of the Mystical Body as a male figure whose condition represented the state of the Church. His right side was covered with magnificent regal garments, but his left side was bare and deeply wounded. The right side symbolized those who belong to the Church and have been preserved by the grace of God and their personal merits. The left side represented imperfect members still weighed down by their defects and vices. The adornments on the right side signified the homage and services which some persons offer to those whom they see excelling in virtue and gifts from God. Some persons, Gertrude understood, willingly perform services for the good but show such bitter zeal toward the imperfect and wicked that they aggravate instead of correcting their faults. Such persons seem to strike the Mystical Body with their fists, while disfiguring their own faces with the blood from these wounds. Nevertheless, moved by love for them, Christ behaves as if he had not observed their actions. He pays heed rather to the benefits received by his friends, and with his royal vestments he wipes away the stains from the faces of the others. It seemed to Gertrude that an instruction accompanied this vision of Christ: "Let them learn how to heal the ulcers of my body; that is, how to correct their neighbors' faults. They should touch them gently by charitable admonitions. Then if these methods do not succeed, they must resort to more stringent ones.

"But some of them have no care for my wounds; they know their neighbor's defects and scorn him, yet they will not speak a single word for fear of bringing trouble upon themselves. With Cain they ask, 'Am I my brother's keeper?' These persons seem to spread an ointment on my wounds, but it inflames and infects instead of healing. Under cover of silence they let their neighbor's faults grow worse, when by their words they might have corrected them. Others point out his faults to their neighbor, but not seeing immediate improvement, they are outraged and resolve never to advise anyone in the future since their words are not heeded. Yet they will not hesitate to condemn others secretly and even to injure them by detraction without saying a single word of counsel or reproof. These also seem to anoint my wounds, whereas they are tearing them with burning irons" (*Leg.* 3.74). Catherine of Siena in her letters to religious superiors frequently uses the same image of ointments applied to spiritual wounds that actually require cautery.[18]

"Some refrain from correcting others not so much from malice as from indifference; these persons tread on my feet. Some care for nothing but their own will; it does not matter to them that they may scandalize my chosen ones, provided that everything goes according to their liking; these pierce my hands with flaming awls. Some love and venerate good clergymen, and rightly praise their words and actions; by so doing they adorn my right side with jeweled ornaments and pearls. Yet these same people are rigorous in their judgment of those who do not keep their rule or who have many faults; by this behavior they shower blows upon my lacerated left side, which I desire them to support by kindness. Others actually applaud the ill deeds of prelates and superiors in order to win their favor and permission to do what they please; these turn my head violently and cause me extreme anguish—worse, they insult me in my sufferings and seem to mock the wounds that cover my face" (*Leg.* 3.74). This image of the Mystical Body is a far more extended comparison than the one previously described in which the injured arm of Christ symbolized the persecutors of the community.

Gertrude's numerous references show the Virgin Mary under three aspects: first, as active, interceding for human beings but also ardently praising, thanking, and adoring God; second, as receiving homage from the saints and from Christ; third, as sharing freely with all, particularly sinners, the gifts she has received. Gertrude's first allusion to Mary is in the account of her "conversion": "on the Monday before the feast of the Purification of your [Christ's] most chaste mother." At another time, when she feared that illness would keep her from receiving communion, she experienced the Virgin Mary's consoling presence. Gertrude regarded as one of her greatest privileges the assurance that Mary was her special guardian, given to her by Christ with the urgent affection of a bridegroom commending his bride to his mother. The eighth lesson in the office for the feast of Gertrude the Great refers to this event: *Deiparam Virginem peculiari beneficio in matrem et procuratricem sibi a Cristo datam* (*Leg.* 2.1.1; 2.23.11).

In her third exercise Gertrude asks Christ to present her to his mother as to her abbess (*Ex.* 3.338–40). It is possible that she made this petition during the interregnum of 1298–1303 when there was no "mother of the monastery." Gertrude most often refers to Mary as intercessor for sinners—for example, on the feast of the Assumption when she visualized sinners in the form of various animals running to conceal themselves under Mary's mantle. She sheltered them kindly and stroked them affectionately "as one strokes a little dog" (*Leg.* 4.48.5). Alphonsus Liguori cites this episode.[19] A symbol of the range of the Virgin's charity was shown to Gertrude in the form of a beautiful garden in which she was standing. The flowers close to her were less brilliant and fragrant than those farther off. This signified that actions prompted by far-reaching charity are more worthy than those of more limited scope (*Leg.* 4.48.14).

Both Gertrude of Helfta and Mechtild of Hackeborn were particularly attracted to the feast of Christ's nativity. Like Bernard of Clairvaux, Gertrude meditated on the text "A bundle of myrrh is my beloved to me" (Song 1:12), and like him, she associated it with the weakness and discomforts of the Christ child. Bernard wrote "I have been careful to gather for myself and place on my breast a bundle formed of all the anguish and bitterness which my Lord has undergone, first of all, his privations as a child."[20] On the vigil of Christmas, as Gertrude prayed that her heart might be prepared for the birth of Christ, she visualized the power, wisdom, and mercy of God as forming the walls and roof of the stable. Bells hanging from the walls symbolized all the good works performed in honor of the feast (*Leg.* 4.2.7). One of her visions anticipates Dali's painting "The Madonna of Port Lligat." Gertrude saw spiritually the Child Jesus in his mother's womb, which was as transparent as crystal, and it seemed to her that as his humanity was nourished by Mary's milk, so his divinity was served by her love and purity (*Leg.* 4.3.4). Dali's surrealist painting shows the Christ child within his mother. An icon-like opening in him reveals a radiant crust of bread symbolizing the eucharist. Close by, a vessel represents the blood of Christ. Dali says, "The open spaces cut through the human body become "Mystical and Virginal Tabernacles."[21]

The spirituality of the Middle Ages was marked by contemplation of Christ's passion and the desire to make atonement for the sins of the world. Gertrude's writings reflect this compulsion. One of her lost works, a poem on the passion, may have been a song (*carmen*). Her contemporary biographer says that Christ, responding to her desire for atonement, sought to find repose in her (*Leg.* 1.3.6). A similar experience is recorded of other mystics, including Mechtild of Hackeborn and Catherine de Ricci (*Livre* 2.33.174). The latter understood as the words of Christ, "I wish to take refuge in your heart and in the hearts of my other daughters from the crimes of sinners."[22]

Gertrude was ingenious in devising ways to offer reparation to Christ for the pains and insults he had endured; many of these practices she taught to others. She was accustomed to venerate the wounds of Christ individually, each with a special intention—for example, the wound in the right hand to expiate her lack of virtue. Doubtless at such times she remembered the first manifestation of Christ when, as she was lifted over the thorny hedge, she recognized the wounded hand extended to her. When performing acts of charity beyond her strength, she recalled what Christ suffered when his hands and feet were stretched on the cross (*Leg.* 2.4.4; 4.26.8). She also practiced devotions in honor of his anticipation of his passion, his crown of thorns, his words on the cross, and his death. In all these exercises she remembered the needs of others, sinners in particular.

Scriptural and liturgical texts inspired Gertrude's contemplation of the face of Christ. Many of her prayers echo the verses, "Of you my heart has said, 'Seek his face.' It is your face, O Jahweh, that I seek. Do not hide your face from me" (Ps 26:8). The *Exercises* contain similar entreaties: "Reveal to me the beauty of your gracious face that I may pour out my soul in your sight." "Come quickly, that in the presence of your loveable countenance I may utterly forget all the sorrows of my heart" (*Ex.* 6.20–21; 6.72–73). The eucharistic hymn, *Adoro te devote*, attributed to Thomas Aquinas, expresses the same urgency:

*Jesu, quem velatum nunc adspicio
Oro fiat illud quod tam sitio
Ut te revelata cernens facie
Visu sim beata tuae gloriae.*

Jesu, whom I look at shrouded here below,
I beseech thee send me what I thirst for so,
Some day to gaze on thee face to face in light
And be blest for ever with thy glory's sight.[23]

A mystical experience that Gertrude records in book 2 of the *Legatus* is an intellectual vision of the face of Christ. It was a Sunday in Lent, she writes, during the chanting of the response, "I saw the Lord face to face," that "my spirit being illuminated, it seemed to me that as if touching my face there was that face of which Bernard has said, 'not having been formed, but forming all things; not appearing to bodily eyes, but rejoicing the heart's countenance by the gracious gift of love, not by any visible color' " (*Leg.* 2.21.1). Gertrude's sixth exercise refers to this experience: "My king and my God . . . fount of eternal light, your gracious face has imprinted its radiance on me, unworthy as I am" (*Ex.* 6.201–5). The first antiphon for second vespers of the feast of St. Gertrude reads, "Christ spoke to his beloved Gertrude as a man speaks in secret to his friend."

Not only the transcendent image of the divine countenance but also the human face of Christ, bruised and disfigured as it appeared during his passion, was the object of Gertrude's contemplation. When she asked, "How can we soothe the anguish of your gracious face?" she received by spiritual intuition the reply, "If anyone meditates devoutly on my passion with loving repentance and charitable prayer for sinners, his heart is to me like a soothing ointment which relieves all my sufferings" (*Leg.* 4.15.5).

The sight of a crucifix always moved Gertrude profoundly. It seemed to her that every loving glance directed toward it was reciprocated by the merciful gaze of Christ as if he were saying, "See how for your love I have been fastened to the cross, naked and scorned, my whole body covered with wounds, and all my limbs dislocated. Yet my heart is so filled with love that if it were necessary for your salvation, I should be willing to undergo for you alone all the pain that I suffered for the whole world." One of Gertrude's sayings is that no one ever looks at a crucifix except by the special providence of God, nor does anyone ever look at one devoutly without receiving some great benefit (*Leg.* 3.41.2, 3).

The contemporary biographer says that someone who asked Christ what most pleased him in Gertrude received the reply, "Her liberty of spirit" (*Leg.* 1.11.7). As Doyère notes, the accounts of her actions and deportment in a variety of situations make it difficult at first to understand her thoughts and behavior. He also finds the narrative style to be involved (*touffue*).[24] It seems that her companions were surprised by the variety and adaptability of her attitudes—for example, her willingness to die without the sacraments if an accident were to cause her death. When Mechtild of Hackeborn visualized Gertrude always facing the throne of God as she moved from one activity to another, she heard spiritually the words, "What you see is an image of her life. She always walks before me, constantly attentive to my will. Whenever it is evident, she instantly obeys it. . . . Thus her whole life is devoted to my praise and glory" (*Leg.* 1.11.9). Gertrude's total abandonment to the divine will resolves the apparent opposition between her talent for teaching and counseling on the one hand, and on the other, her mystical graces and the need to reveal to others the riches of divine love. Her confidence in Christ's power to compensate for her deficiencies enables her to speak with authority in the name of God.[25] It is in this liberty of spirit that one may find the fundamental virtue underlying all Gertrude's words and actions.

The spiritual freedom that prevailed in the medieval cloister contrasts sharply with the atmosphere in some convents during later centuries, the seventeenth in particular. Without fear of novelty, many men and women of the Middle Ages expressed their devotion in imaginative, even naive ways. Gertrude once replaced the nails in her crucifix with sweet-smelling cloves (*Leg.* 3.45.1); Henry

Suso crowned the statue of the Virgin Mary with the first flowers of spring; Francis of Assisi would take a piece of wood from the ground and draw another stick across it as if playing a viol, "then suiting his action to the rhythm, he would sing of our Lord Jesus in the language of France."[26] These innovations were an expression of youth and vitality, the energetic fervor of individuals at a time when, as John Gray puts it, "all living people were young."[27] The same imaginative fervor is found in Céline Martin's account of her sister, Thérèse of Lisieux: "One day I saw her touching the crown of thorns and the nails of her crucifix very attentively and I asked her what she was doing. In the tone of one taken by surprise she answered, "I'm taking out his nails and removing his crown of thorns."[28]

Gertrude's forthright expression of her liberty of spirit is paralleled in the lives of other women mystics. Catherine of Siena said to Christ, "I want the Ancient Enemy to lose them, every one of these brothers of mine, and I want you to win them."[29] Mezzi Sibriwin, a Dominican nun at Töss, anticipated the epitaph of Martin Elmerod when she exclaimed, "Lord, if you were Mezzi Sibriwin and I were God, I should let you be God, and I would be Mezzi." Thérèse of Lisieux's last written words echo this declaration but with reference to the Virgin Mary.[30]

These are more or less superficial manifestations of the liberty of spirit which, Vernet asserts, is found only in the highest forms of the mystical state.[31] When the moment of intense union has passed—*rara hora, parva mora,* writes Bernard, and Gertrude echoes him—the person reenters the common life, walking by the light of faith, often uncertain, doubtful, even tormented by human weaknesses, and needing the counsel of others. Such a condition may have inspired Gertrude's prayer: "by your love restore to me that liberty of spirit in which you set me free . . . at the price of your blood" (*Ex.* 7.495–97).[32]

Associated with freedom of spirit is vigor or energy—a classic trait which may coexist with physical infirmity. It is seen in the valiant woman of the Book of Proverbs, in the mother of the Macchabees, in Judith. In the New Dispensation it is found in the child-martyr Agnes, in Agatha, Catherine of Siena, Joan of Arc, Teresa of Avila. In her fifth exercise Gertrude prays, "Gird my thigh with the sword of your spirit, O most mighty, and give me a valiant heart so that I may act bravely and vigorously in all virtue, firmly rooted and inseparable from you, persevering with an indomitable mind" (*Ex.*

5.390–93). Fearless in matters concerning God's honor or the spiritual welfare of others, she acted and spoke uncompromisingly. Yet this vigor was never directed to her own defense. The mysterious sentence of her contemporary biographer testifies that Gertrude had enemies whom she did not resist: "She sought only the glory of God, not her own; indeed, she not only sought it, she pursued it with such ardor that she would sacrifice to it her honor, her life, and in a certain sense, her soul." With this testimony one may associate Gertrude's own declaration: "Although I should undergo the torments of hell as I deserve, nevertheless I should rejoice if through my labors the Lord God might receive honor from others" (*Leg.* 1.4.1; 1.11.1).

Léonard writes: "The consciousness of the abyss which separates the uncreated Being from the creature, the still more unmeasurable distance which divides the sinner from absolute Holiness, characterize Christian mysticism. Recognition of the necessity of grace, of a benevolent inclination on God's part before the abyss can be bridged, springs inevitably from this."[33] One such bridging of the abyss through communication of the merits of Christ is symbolized by Gertrude's experience on an Easter Monday, perhaps the anniversary of her reception of the habit. She had asked Christ to supply by the merits of the eucharist for all her negligences in obeying the rule. It then seemed to her that he presented her to his Father. She was wearing her habit, which appeared to be made of as many pieces as she had spent years in the order. In each year she could distinguish all her thoughts, words, and actions, good and bad; moreover, the motive of each was apparent. Among her imperfections was an occasional use of diplomacy to get her own way. When, however, Christ had offered for her to his Father all the merits of his life, the habit appeared to be covered with plates of gold (*Leg.* 4.28.1).

The confidence inspired by such intimations of divine mercy was the basis of Gertrude's intimacy with Christ. Her inquiries as to why some evils were unremedied, her respectful demands as to why some prayers are unanswered, her insistence that her dying sisters be consoled in their last moments, all show the confidence of a daughter at ease with a loving father. With both Gertrude and Teresa the confidence sometimes approached playfulness. Gertrude made her request for finding her lost stylus *quasi jocosa.* Teresa composed a mock litany imploring God to protect the nuns' new habits from vermin.[34] Although Gertrude's humor was less robust than Teresa's, she enjoyed community recreations, being assured that God delights in the joy of his servants just as a father takes pleasure in a minstrel who is entertaining the family. It is said that Christ answered her *subridens* (smilingly) (*Leg.* 3.44.1; 4.14.8). Yet Gertrude is invariably reverent. As to Teresa of Avila so to her, God is king or emperor, the divine majesty. Gertrude's confidence was reinforced when she became convinced that her poems in Christ's honor gave him as much pleasure "as a person whose friend leads him through a garden filled with music, fruit, and fragrant flowers." Moreover, she was given to understand that not the least movement of her finger, not even a single loving thought should be unrewarded (*Leg.* 3.54.2). This recalls Jean Cocteau's saying, "If he [God] counts us, if he counts our hairs, he counts also the syllables of our poems."[35]

The alternate acknowledgments of God's transcendence and her own incapacity to love and honor him worthily are the systole and diastole of Gertrude's spiritual life. She echoes the cry of Bernard in the *De diligendo Deo:* "My God, my help, I will love you because of your mercy as much as I am able, not as much as I should, but at least as much as I am able."[36] Her gratitude for God's gifts breaks forth in almost every line of book 2. She carefully observes not only the days but often the very hours when she received these favors. Her complete abandonment to the divine will inspires her response to the words of Christ as she records them in the *Legatus:* "If you wish me to find complete delight in your heart, permit me to do with it whatever I wish, without caring whether I give you consolation or bitterness." Again and again she was spiritually instructed: "Your will is the key to your heart. Give it to me" (*Leg.* 4.26.6; 4.23.9).

"Gertrude was truly the spouse of Christ," says Pourrat. "Transformed in him, she had no other desire than to accomplish his holy will in all things."[37] Vernet ranks her with Angela of Foligno and Catherine of Siena as "a star of the first magnitude."[38] Among the canonized saints who have admired and cited her teachings are Alphonsus Liguori, Francis de Sales, and John Eudes.[39] In later times, Columba Marmion, Jacques Maritain, and Dorothy Day show familiarity with her writings.[40]

9   Veneration of the Sacred Heart

VENERATION of the Sacred Heart, based on belief in the incarnation, is rooted in Scripture, Christian tradition, and liturgy. The theology of the first Christian millennium makes repeated mention of the fountain of living water from the wound in the side of Christ crucified. In the torrent of sacramental grace the Latin Fathers saw a fulfillment of the prophecy of Isaiah (12:3): "You shall draw waters with joy from the fountain of the Savior." The birth of the Church *ex aqua et sanguine* from the wounded side of the new Adam asleep in death was, they affirmed, a parallel to the birth of Eve from the side of the sleeping Adam. "Both dogmatically and historically, this vision of the Church proceeding from the Heart of our Lord was a fundamental notion of the early Christians."[1] The image of the wound in the side of Christ as an inexhaustible fountain of redemptive life through the Church and the sacraments sums up the history of patristic thought on the subject. It is an objective attitude which looks back to the time of the crucifixion. Although in the Middle Ages it was supplemented by another concept, it was not supplanted, and this objective attitude remains basic to the theology and liturgy of the Sacred Heart.

Concomitant with the image of the wound in Christ's side as a fountain of life was a particular devotion to the apostle John who, Augustine writes, "received from the Lord on whose breast he lay at the Last Supper (in order thereby to signify that he drew loftier mysteries from his inmost Heart) a special and peculiar gift, namely, the ability to communicate the spirit of Jesus."[2] So too, Paulinus writes, "John, who rested blissfully on the breast of our Lord, was inebriated with the Holy Spirit; from the Heart of all-creating Wisdom he quaffed an understanding that transcends any creature's."[3] In the transition from patristic times to the Middle Ages, John is a key figure, uniting the earlier objective concept with an emerging deeply emotional and subjective veneration.

Meditation on the *Song of Songs* played a major part among the influences contributing to this synthesis. As early as the sixth century, Gregory the Great had applied the words, "Come, my dove in the clefts of the rocks, in the hollow places of the wall," to the wounded side of Christ as the refuge of the soul.[4] By the eleventh century the number of such reflections was considerable. Anselm of Canterbury, meditating on the passion of Christ, exclaimed: "What sweetness in his pierced side! That wound has given us a glimpse of the treasure house of his goodness, that is to say, of the love of his Heart for us."[5] Bernard of Clairvaux likewise spoke of the mystery of the Sacred Heart: "The secret of his Heart lies visible through the clefts of his body; visible too the great mystery of his love."[6]

The influence of Bernard's commentary on the *Song of Songs* gave new impetus to the concept of the heart of Christ as an immediate presence. Gilbert of Hoyland, who continued Bernard's unfinished treatise, found his greatest inspiration in the verse, "You have wounded my heart, my sister, my spouse." In a passage which recalls the fulfillment of Gertrude's prayer, he writes: "Shall we not call that soul blessed which pierces with its fervent love the very Heart of our Lord Jesus Christ? . . . Do not cease wounding your Spouse. Use your ardent acts of love as darts to pierce him."[7]

Among Gertrude's predecessors in the veneration of the Sacred Heart is Lutgard of Aywières, a Cistercian stigmatic of the early thirteenth century. The Dominican, Thomas of Cantimpré, her confessor, has recorded her history. At the age of fifteen she had a mystical encounter with Christ, who showed her his wounded side. Thereafter she became deeply contemplative. Thomas, who knew her for at least fifteen years, tells of a later experience. She had prayed for an understanding of Scripture, but after acquiring this ability, she felt that she was making no progress. Her *Vita* records the following dialogue with Christ:

"What am I doing, unlettered as I am,
a rustic nun and layperson,
acquainting myself with secrets of Scripture?"

The Lord replied: "What do you wish?"

She answered: "I want your Heart."

The Lord said, "Nay, rather it is I
Who want your heart." . . .
And so from that moment
there was an exchange of hearts between them,
or rather a union of created and uncreated spirits
resulting from an overwhelming gift of grace.

Thomas adds: "This is what the apostle meant in saying that whoever adheres to God becomes one spirit with him."[8]

The names of Gertrude the Great and Mechtild of Hackeborn are linked in the history of veneration of the Sacred Heart. Through their influence as well as that of the former Beguine, Mechtild of Magdeburg, Helfta became a center of this devotion. It may even be maintained that Helfta provides the first instance of communal acceptance of the cult; Gertrude, its chief advocate, did not meet the opposition that was to assail Margaret Mary Alacoque four centuries later.

Gertrude regarded the apostle John as her chosen friend and patron. His paramount role in the history of the objective devotion to the Sacred Heart has already been noted. On a day in Advent she visualized him wearing a mantle adorned with golden eagles, and a breastplate inscribed: *In principio erat Verbum*. Again, on his own feast, pointing reverently to the bosom of Christ, he seemed to say: "Behold, this is the Holy of Holies, drawing to itself all that is good in heaven and on earth." As Gertrude asked why he had not spoken of what he experienced when leaning against the heart of Christ at the Last Supper, she heard interiorly the words, "It was my task to present to the first age of the Church the doctrine of the Word made flesh, which no human intellect can ever fully comprehend. The eloquence of that loving pulsation of his Heart is reserved for the modern age so that the world grown old and torpid may be rekindled by the love of God" (*Leg.* 4.4.1–4). The first sentence of John's reply recalls the patristic theology described earlier in this chapter. His next conveys the subjective devotion which became dominant in the Middle Ages. This juxtaposition of the two aspects of the veneration of the heart of Christ makes Gertrude's vision unique. As Jean Bainvel writes, "It forms an epoch in the history of the devotion to the Sacred Heart."[9]

Between the apostle John and Gertrude the Great as saints of the Sacred Heart are the others, such as Anselm, Bernard, and Francis of Assisi, whose meditations and mystical intuitions prepared the spiritual climate for the flowering of the devotion in Gertrude and Mechtild. It is evident that the women of Helfta are not isolated from the devotional atmosphere of their era. Nevertheless, the eminence of their convent, their personalities, and their outstanding gifts make them instrumental in communicating the warmly personal, immediate, and contemporary quality of their association with the Sacred Heart.

As shown by earlier quotations in this chapter, it was contemplation of the wound in Christ's side that led directly to the image of the Sacred Heart. It seems pointless, therefore, to speak of an "originator" of the devotion. Without doubt, the mystics of Helfta are outstanding in their concentration on the divine heart, and as Neumann asserts, Mechtild of Magdeburg certainly influenced the cult.[10] Like many mystics before her, she honored the wounds of Christ, and often spoke ardently of his "heart's blood" as a sign of his love. The pierced heart of Christ was for her the incarnation of his inner life. In the first part of her work, *Das fliessende Licht*, the chapter "Of the Presence at Court of the Soul to Whom God Shows Himself" contains the lines: "He with great desire shows her his Divine Heart. It glows like red gold in a great fire. And God lays the soul in his glowing Heart so that he, the great God, and she, the humble maid, embrace and are one as water with wine." In the same section Mechtild represents Christ as saying, "How fiery my Heart!" and again, "Your heart's desire you shall lay nowhere but in my own Divine Heart" (*Licht* 1.4, 29, 43). A more characteristic sentence occurs in one of her prayers: "Together with all your creatures, I long here and now for your glory in all things and through all things, as they flowed spotless from your loving Heart" (*Licht* 5.35). This is one of many examples of the dominant image in her book as expressed in the title *The Flowing Light of the Godhead*.

A comparison of her writing with that of her companions, Gertrude and Mechtild of Hackeborn, shows that as Doyère observes, her "spiritual orientation" is somewhat different (*Leg.* 1, intr., 15). As Evelyn Underhill asserts, Mechtild of Magdeburg is "a true Minnesinger of the Holy Ghost," an "exquisite poet and visionary."[11] If there is insufficient evidence for Ancelet-Hustache's assertion that she originated the veneration of the Sacred Heart at Helfta, she is nevertheless a participant in this devotion and certainly one of the luminaries of medieval German mysticism.

Like Gertrude's *Legatus*, Mechtild of Hackeborn's *Liber* is permeated by expressions of devotion to the Sacred Heart. Gertrude testified after her friend's death: "This angelic maiden is most fittingly compared to the seraphim, for she was so directly united to God who is love itself, so ardently attached to his flaming heart that she was made one fiery spirit with him" (*Livre* 5.30.356).

Even more often than Gertrude, Mechtild visualized the Sacred Heart as a magnificent dwelling, a house of gold, the abode of four beautiful maidens—Humility, Patience, Mildness, and Charity. As in spirit she entered the house, she perceived a great cross engraved on the pavement. Prostrating herself upon it, she felt herself pierced to the soul by a golden dart from the center of the cross. Paquelin relates this to the transverberations of Gertrude and Teresa of Avila, as indicating a relationship in their mystical states (*Livre* 2.25.163; *Rev.* 2.25.163, n. 1). In her painful illnesses, Mechtild prayed that she might take refuge in the heart of Christ as in a house of repose. She also visualized the Sacred Heart as the gate of heaven, at which one might knock three times by praising the power of the Father, the wisdom of the Son, and the goodness of the Holy Spirit (*Livre* 2.27.167–68; 3.4.194).

One image of the Sacred Heart is unique in its informality. After receiving a special blessing—which she does not describe—Mechtild, overcome by a sense of her unworthiness, exclaimed: "O generous King! So magnificent a gift is not suitable for me. I am not worthy to serve in your kitchen and wash the vessels there." It seemed to her that Christ asked her kindly, "And what is my kitchen and what are the vessels you want to cleanse?" As she did not know what to say, she felt that he himself was answering his question: "The kitchen is my divine heart. As the kitchen is a place open to all, to slaves as well as to free men, so my heart is always open to all, and ready to fulfill everyone's desires. The ruler in the kitchen is the Holy Spirit whose inexpressible kindness fills my heart with overflowing generosity. My vessels are the hearts of my saints and my chosen ones who continually share in the ravishing abundance of my divine heart" (*Livre* 2.23.161–62).

Once after receiving the eucharist, Mechtild experienced an interior communication: "Thou in me and I in thee. Be submerged in my omnipotence like the fish in the ocean." "O Lord," she answered, "fish are often caught in the net. What if that should happen to me?" She understood as an answer, "You cannot be drawn forth from me. You will make your nest in my divine heart. . . .

The nest is sincere humility, maintained among all the gifts and favors I have given you" (*Livre* 2.24.162). As will be shown later, the image of the soul as a fish submerged in God occurs frequently in the writings from Helfta.

Mechtild's prayers give constant evidence of her veneration of the Sacred Heart. Every morning she greeted Christ with the salutation, "Praise, benediction, glory, and salvation to the most gentle and benevolent heart of Jesus, my true lover. I thank you for your faithful watch surrounding me this night in which you have offered to God the Father the thanksgiving and homage that I owe him. And now I offer you my heart like a fresh rose that its fragrance may delight your divine heart" (*Livre* 3.17.21–22). When any suffering came to her, she would say, "O love, the bearer to me of these pains from the heart of God, I offer this to you" (*Livre* 2.36.178–79). She also advised others to make this offering.

Mechtild believed that the Virgin Mary inspired her to venerate the wounds of Christ, saying, "Come and greet the wound in the dear heart of my Son, for it is his heart that felt the suffering of all the wounds of his body" (*Livre* 4.5.255). In a letter to a friend she wrote: "God gives his divine heart to the soul in order that it may give him its heart in return. One ought carefully to keep the heart of God and consider well what most pleases him" (*Livre* 4.59.305).

Both Mechtild of Hackeborn and Gertrude frequently describe the Sacred Heart as sending forth streams of light or rivers of crystal clarity. Mechtild represents the heart as producing three fragrant streams of allegorical significance: the first has the perfume of rosewater to represent the love distilled from "that most noble rose," the Sacred Heart; the second has the fragrance of rich wine from the royal blood shed on the winepress of the cross; the third has the odor of sweet balm from the divine heart, "which even death cannot make bitter." In the odor of these three ointments the soul runs in love and desire, according to the text: "We will run to thee in the odor of thy ointments" (*Song* 1:4; *Livre* 3.25.222–23).

Mechtild uses many other images for the Sacred Heart: a lyre or other instrument on which she plays in honor of God, a lamp, a vineyard, a furnace, a fountain (*Livre* 7.14.394; 3.25.1; 2.2.135; 4.15.265; 1.22.78). Stringed instruments, in particular, the harp or lyre, are prominent images in the writings of both Gertrude and Mechtild. In the latter, the harp becomes a symbol of the transcendent interplay of the human and divine intimacies.

Like Gertrude, Mechtild experienced by a spiritual intuition the pulsations of the heart of Christ. On the feast of the Nativity it seemed to her that she embraced the Christ child, marveling as she did so at the strange beating of his infant heart—a strong triple pulsation followed by a lighter one. Interiorly, she sensed the words: "My heart did not beat like those of other men; from my infancy to my death the pulsations were as you hear. That is why I died so quickly on the cross." It seemed that the impetuosity of his love accounted for the three vehement pulsations; the fourth represented his mildness and gentleness toward human beings, giving them an example that they could imitate. At another time, Mechtild seemed to hear in the vigorous beating of the divine heart a repeated invitation: "Come and repent, come and be reconciled, come and be consoled, come and be blessed. Come, my sister, to possess the eternal inheritance that I obtained for you by my blood. Come, my spouse, to rejoice in my divinity." Again, after communion, the three pulsations of the heart of Christ were interpreted as three words addressed to her: "Come; that is to say, separate yourself from all creatures; Enter, with confidence, as a spouse; Into the bridal chamber, that is, the divine heart" (*Livre* 1.5.18; 2.1.134; 2.20.154). Another interpretation of the pulsations of the Heart of Christ occurs in the encyclical, "*Haurietis Aquas,*" of Pius XII. He writes: "we must lovingly meditate on the pulsations of his most Sacred Heart by which, so to say, he himself kept on measuring the time of his sojourn on earth up to the last minute."[12]

The gift of the Sacred Heart as a pledge of love is recorded in both Gertrude's *Legatus* and Mechtild's *Liber.* It is apparently one of Mechtild's first mystical experiences. During Easter week as she intoned the antiphon *Venite, benedicti* (Come, you blessed), she felt a sudden extraordinary joy and exclaimed, "Oh, if only I could be one of the blessed ones to hear that gracious word!" It seemed to her that she received an answer: "Be assured of that. I shall give you my heart as pledge. You will always have it with you, and on the day when your desire is to be granted, you will restore it to me. I give you my heart also to be your refuge so that at the hour of death, no other road will open to you but my heart where you will rest forever" (*Livre* 2.19.152).

This image of the Sacred Heart as a door or portal through which the dying may enter occurs in several other passages. The elaborate description relating the stages of Christ's passion to the parts of a dance ends, "After this, I opened my heart for you to enter" (*Livre* 3.1.191). Mechtild's *Liber* reports that when her sister, the Abbess

Gertrude, was dying, Mechtild saw her enter into the Sacred Heart as into an open sanctuary. Later, when the bereaved community sang the line "You who repose in the shadow of the Beloved" (from the responsory, *Surge, Virgo*), the voice of the dead abbess seemed to answer, "It would not be enough for me to be in his shadow; it is in the heart of the Well-Beloved that I rest in sweetness, serenity, and peace" (*Livre* 6.6.370–71). It was Mechtild also who visualized a great concourse of the members of the congregation gathering in a festal dance around the abbess on the anniversary of her death. Their song, *O Mater nostra*, entered into the heart of Christ from which it emerged as a single melody of marvelous beauty (*Livre* 6.9.376).

During Mechtild's last days it seemed to her friend Gertrude that after her anointing she lived in an aura of spiritual light sent forth from the heart of Christ. Moreover, her acts of love appeared to elicit a torrent of blessings on the whole Church. At the moment of her death on the feast of Elizabeth of Hungary, 19 November, Gertrude believed that Christ reminded Mechtild of the gift of his heart and gently asked, "Where is my pledge?" At these words it seemed to Gertrude that Mechtild offered her own heart to Christ and breathed her last as he received it (*Livre* 7.11.391–92).

One of Gertrude's first references to the heart of Christ occurs seven years after the account of her "conversion." As noted in chapter 5, it was after Mechtild of Hackeborn had invoked the Sacred Heart on her behalf that Gertrude experienced the mystical wounding of her own heart by the "arrow of love." Two variant accounts of this event witness to her fervent gratitude.

Her seventh exercise contains a series of invocations: "O Heart abounding in loving kindness! . . . O Heart filled with compassion! . . . O Heart supremely dear, I implore you, absorb my heart totally" (*Ex.* 7.380–84). On a night preceding the vigil of Christmas, she envisioned a light issuing from the Sacred Heart and forming a path leading to him. On another occasion when she had been left alone in her illness because the other sisters were engaged in their occupations, she visualized Christ showing her the wound in his side. From it issued a pure stream, solid as crystal, which formed on his breast a precious ornament alternating in color between gold and rose. She heard interiorly the words, "This illness has so sanctified you that whenever you seem to go away from me to serve your neighbor by thought, word, or deed, you will be no more separated from me than this stream is separated from my heart. As the gold and rose shine together with the crystal, so my divinity symbolized by the gold, and the patience of my humanity symbolized by the rose, will make all your actions pleasing to me" (*Leg.* 4.1.1; 2.9.1).

When she prayed that she might banish the thoughts distracting her as she prepared for communion, she felt that Christ was saying to her, "If anyone who is tempted takes refuge with me, I can say of that person: 'One is my dove, chosen among thousands; with one glance she has pierced my divine heart. . . . The glance of my beloved which pierces my heart is her serene confidence, that I can and will help her faithfully in everything.' " As she prayed for someone recommended to her, she saw a crystal-clear stream from the Sacred Heart flowing into the person. At another time she sensed that a golden channel poured the virtue and beauty of the divine perfections into her own soul. During a rapture she seemed to be mysteriously drawn into the heart of Christ which she had chosen for her temple. She remembered the example of St. Dominic as she heard the words, "Have you not read of some of my saints, such as my servant Dominic, who did not leave my temple but even ate and slept there?" (*Leg.* 3.7.1; 3.9.4; 3.26.2; 3.28.1).[13]

Gertrude believed that she received from the Sacred Heart everything that she needed, including physical strength. When she had passed a sleepless night, she prayed: "By the tranquility in which you reposed for endless ages in the bosom of the Father; by the nine months in the womb of the Virgin Mary; by the joys that you experience in dwelling with a loving soul; I beseech you, O merciful God, grant me a little rest, not for my own satisfaction, but for your eternal praise so that my exhausted strength may be restored." She felt that her prayer was answered by an inspiration to rest in the divine heart and by an interior admonition: "Anyone who is worn out by long wakefulness should say this prayer that you have just offered in order to regain the strength to sing my praises. If I do not grant his prayer and he endures weariness with patience and humility, my divine kindness will receive him with great joy" (*Leg.* 3.52.1–3).

When Gertrude was grieving over the behavior of a friend who had repaid her kindness with contempt, she felt consoled by sensing that Christ was offering her his heart and saying: "Consider, my well-beloved, the secrets of my heart. See now, whether you can ever reproach me for the slightest infidelity" (*Leg.* 3.63.1–2). After she had prayed for someone who had sought her intercession, Gertrude gave her this instruction as from Christ: "Let her make her nest in the crevice of the rock, that is to say, in the Sacred Heart, that she may rest in the depths of that cavern and taste the honey of the rock—namely, the aspirations of the divine heart." These images are clearly a development of those in the meditations of Gregory and Anselm quoted earlier in this chapter (*Leg.* 3.73.7).

On one occasion Gertrude visualized the consolations of the Holy Spirit under the figure of a stream of honey flowing from the Sacred Heart; at another time she was surprised that the stream had become bitter. As she wondered about the meaning of this change, she seemed to hear the words: "When someone gives money to a friend, the one who receives it is free to buy whatever he wishes. If he can buy either sweet or sour apples for the same price, he may prefer to buy the sour ones because they will keep better. Likewise, when I hear the prayers of my chosen ones, I send the grace which will be of most benefit. For example, it is better for some persons to have trials rather than consolations in this life; therefore when I pour out my blessings on them, they will have more bitter sorrows and tribulations, whereby they will receive ever more graces according to my pleasure. The consolation stored up for them is hidden from them at present so that they may labor the more faithfully, bearing their adversities patiently for the love of my name" (*Leg.* 4.58.5).

As she offered her heart to Christ, it seemed to Gertrude that it was united to his under the form of a chalice. "Grant, O loving God," she prayed, "that my heart may be always before you like those flasks that are carried to the master's table, that you may have it filled or emptied whenever and for whomever you wish." She believed that Christ, pleased with this prayer, said to his Father: "O holy Father, for your eternal praise may this heart pour forth over the world all that my human heart contained." That the offering of her heart to God appeared to add to the joy of the saints in heaven and to the advancement of the just on earth convinced Gertrude that it was God's will for her to help many persons by her writings (*Leg.* 3.30.2).

Some paintings depict Gertrude the Great with seven rings on her right hand. A seventeenth-century work in the style of Lazaro Pardo de Lagos of Cuzco shows this detail. The painting, now at Potosí in the Casa de la Moneda, commemorates an episode told in the *Legatus*. One day as Gertrude was thinking of all that Christ had done for her, "I was so audacious," she says, "as to reproach him with not having sealed his promise by putting his hand in mine as is customary with those who make a contract." Thereupon, she says, opening his heart, he enclosed her right hand within it, solemnly promising to confirm in her all the graces he had given. When she withdrew her hand, it seemed to her that the fingers were encircled by seven gold rings symbolizing her privileges. An antiphon in honor of Gertrude recalls this favor by the words *annulis septem*. Later, however, it seemed to her that she had acted perversely by demanding "signs and wonders" (*Leg.* 2.20.14–15). This event recalls Mechtild's similar request which was answered by the mystical bestowal of a ring set with seven gems—a ring of cosmic dimensions, enclosing both Christ and Mechtild (*Livre* 3.18.214).

Remembering the many special favors she had received and wondering which of them would be most useful to others, Gertrude experienced a spiritual locution in which Christ instructed her: "The greatest advantage for human beings is to remember always that I, son of a virgin, stand before God the Father to plead the cause of the human race. If they defile their hearts through human frailty, I offer my Sacred Heart in reparation. If they sin with their mouths, I offer my innocent mouth for them. If they offend him by their actions, I offer my pierced hands for them. . . . I wish, therefore, that after they have so easily obtained my forgiveness, they would thank me for it" (*Leg.* 3.40.1).

Even in her preparation for the feast of the Nativity, Gertrude venerated the wounds of Christ, concluding her prayer with an act of homage to the wound in his side. She greeted the Sacred Heart with profound love, honoring it as containing all the mysteries of the divinity. A few days after this feast, when she was reflecting on the graces John the Evangelist had received at the Last Supper, she envisioned his beatitude in heaven: within the bosom of Christ there was an immense ocean, and in it the beloved apostle in the form of a bee floated "like a fish" in perfect joy and freedom. As noted earlier, this image is frequent in the literature of mysticism. Mechtild uses it at least four times—e.g., "to her intimate confidant" (probably Gertrude): she said, "My spirit swims in the divinity like a fish in the ocean" (*Leg.* 4.2.4, 5; 4.4.5). Likewise, Catherine of Siena longed for communion "for then the soul is in God and God in the soul just as the fish is in the sea and the sea in the fish."[14]

Gertrude's prayers for others were frequently associated with the liturgical seasons. During the days of Carnival before Lent, she was inspired to say the *Laudate Dominum* while offering to Christ all the weariness and labors of his Sacred Heart for the salvation of the human race. When she prayed for others, it seemed to her that for each person she had enkindled a flame of love in the heart of Christ. As she wished to know how she could enkindle this flame for everyone in the Church, she felt that Christ was responding: "In four ways: first, by praising me for creating all in my image; second, by thanking me for all the benefits I have already given them and those I shall yet give; third, by sorrowing over the obstacles they put in the way of my grace; fourth, by praying for all who, according to my providence strive for perfection for the sake of my honor and glory" (*Leg.* 4.15.4; 4.25.4).

Gertrude visualized the unceasing efficacy of the Sacred Heart for the salvation of the world under the figure of two pulsations: one brought about the salvation of sinners, the other the sanctification of the just. She considered that as no human activity, such as seeing, hearing, or working can interrupt the movement of the human heart, so the interceding pulsation of the Sacred Heart will continue until the end of time (*Leg.* 3.51.1–2). As she meditated on the coming of the Holy Spirit to the disciples, she thought of Christ as saying to her, "If you wish to receive him, you must touch my side and my hands as the disciples did." She understood these words to mean that "to touch the side of Christ is to acknowledge thankfully the love of the Sacred Heart notwithstanding human ingratitude" (*Leg.* 4.32.1).

The feast of the Dedication of the Church was the occasion for many spiritual insights regarding the Sacred Heart. It was then that Gertrude visualized it as a mansion of delight which she was permitted to enter. "My Lord," she exclaimed, "it would have been enough for me to stand where your feet had stood, but how can I thank you for this overwhelming privilege?" It seemed to her that Christ responded, "Since you so often give me your noblest possession, your heart, it is only just that you should find your delight in mine. I am your God, all in all to you—strength, life, knowledge, nourishment, clothing—all that you can desire" (*Leg.* 4.58.2).

Like Mechtild, Gertrude felt that she had been remiss in honoring the Virgin Mary. Having appealed to Christ to offer his mother the homage she deserved, it seemed to her that as she chanted the antiphon *Tota pulchra es* on the feast of the Assumption, she saw a shower of stars passing from the Sacred Heart to adorn her. They were so numerous that many fell to the ground and the saints joyfully gathered them. This signified that all the blessed share in the merits of the Virgin Mary (*Leg.* 4.48.8).

As recorded in the *Legatus,* Gertrude's mystical experiences are closely associated with the veneration of the Sacred Heart. In recapitulating all that she has received, she says, "You have granted me the priceless grace of your familiar friendship by giving me to my great joy the noble ark of your divinity, namely, your divine heart. You have even—most precious sign of our intimacy—exchanged it for mine. How often through this divine heart have you revealed your secret judgments and your joys, overwhelming me with your tenderness. If I did not know your inexhaustible goodness I could scarcely comprehend the unique dignity you have accorded to your blessed mother who reigns with you in heaven" (*Leg.* 2.23.8).

All three of the mystics of Helfta had assimilated the patristic, objective attitude toward the Sacred Heart as described at the beginning of this chapter. Their personal relations with Christ did not supersede, but rather reinforced the traditional veneration. In their astonishing familiarity with the Sacred Heart each of the three mystics has a distinct personality. Mechtild of Magdeburg has been called "the poet of a transfigured, glorified sorrow, most acceptable offering to the divine Heart of Jesus."[15] Mechtild of Hackeborn, on the other hand, is captivated by the glorified heart of the triumphant Christ. For Gertrude, the association of the passion and the eucharist with the Sacred Heart inspires a multitude of images, striking in their range and richness. She perceives it, as does Mechtild of Hackeborn, under the aspect of an instrument played on by the Holy Spirit; as an organ, source of delight for the Trinity; as a chalice from which the elect drink; as a censer through which the prayers of the faithful mount to God in fragrance; as a burning lamp; a treasure house of the divinity; a golden altar; a portal of salvation; a stream flowing with honey; a marvelous palace (*Leg.* 2, 3, 4 passim).

Most notable, however, is the atmosphere of mystical love, unwavering confidence, and simple intimacy pervading the *Legatus divinae pietatis* which makes it a central document in the theological and devotional literature of the Sacred Heart.

10 The Death of Gertrude

ONE of the proofs of the genuineness of mystical union is that the mystic desires "to be dissolved and to be with Christ" (Phil 1:23). "True union can always be identified by the soul's ardent longings for death, if it should be the will of God, and meanwhile, the desire to suffer, to work, and to endure reproaches for his sake without any regard for human considerations."[1] Both these desires are found in Gertrude. When she wished to recover her health in order to follow the rule more exactly, she felt rebuked by Christ for opposing his will. "But my only wish is to praise you," she protested. She sensed the response: "Your prayer is like a little girl's. If you were to persist, I should not accept it." At one time Gertrude had wanted to die so as to release God from the burden of giving her the many graces that his ardent love provided for her salvation. At other times she was made to understand that such longing should be united to perfect submission to God's will. One who desires death yet is content to live as long as Providence ordains will receive in recompense all the merits of Christ's life (*Leg.* 3.50.3).

Having learned this lesson of tranquil resignation to the will of Christ, Gertrude expressed it in a similitude: "When a bridegroom leads his bride into a garden of roses to gather them for a garland, she takes so much pleasure in his conversation that she never pauses to ask which of the roses he wishes her to gather, but she takes whichever flower her bridegroom gives her and places it in her garland. So also the faithful soul" (*Leg.* 3.56.1).

Gertrude's frequent illnesses and the deaths of her companions kept her constantly reminded of the importance of a good preparation for eternity. Accordingly, she was accustomed to perform a number of special devotions with this intention. Every Friday at noon she withdrew to say for herself the prayers for those in their last agony. After she had done this for some time, she experienced an anticipation of her own death. She seemed to see herself in the arms of Christ, her head supported by the Virgin Mary. The celestial choir held censers from which issued the prayers of the entire Church. Her guardian angel under the aspect of a noble prince rejoiced at the happiness soon to be hers. The demons under the forms of hideous toads and serpents were so powerless that they vanished at the sight of a column of fire mounting from the dying nun to the throne of God. Each saint invoked in the litany for the dying came forth to assist her. The description of these celestial allies, each with an appropriate symbol, creates a pageant-like effect: the patriarchs have fresh green palm branches representing their good works; the prophets have golden mirrors depicting their revelations; the martyrs, golden bracelets; the confessors, golden flowers; the virgins, roses with gold thorns; the widows, golden caskets. Gertrude's special patron, John the Evangelist, offered her two golden rings. The other apostles also gave her rings to symbolize their fidelity to Christ. All these gifts signified that the saints were sharing their merits with her. At the climax of this mystical panorama, Gertrude envisioned Christ drawing her into eternal life "as a dewdrop is absorbed by the sun" (*Leg.* 5.32.8). The entire fifth book of the *Legatus* is a mystical exposition; the writer, Gertrude's unknown friend, has in only a few passages given any information about the actual circumstances of her death.

In addition to her weekly preparation, Gertrude made a five-day retreat every year with the intention of obtaining the grace of a good death. Mechtild also made it a practice to follow these exercises. As her illness became more serious, Gertrude redoubled the fervor of her preparations, endeavoring to unite all her actions to those performed by Christ (*Leg.* 5.27.1). Her *Spiritual Exercises*, as previously noted, contain many passages in preparation for death.

One of the most vivid mystical manifestations of the Sacred Heart is associated with the last days of Gertrude's life. At the elevation of the consecrated host at Mass, Christ appeared to open his heart with both hands. Flames coming forth from it fused her heart with his. From the two hearts a tree with double trunks, one of gold and one of silver, sprang up, shining like the sun. She understood the words, "This tree has grown from the union of your heart with mine." The branches were hung with magnificent fruits which bowed down over all those for whom she had prayed. In answer to her question, "Is this illness taking me to you?" she sensed the reply, "It brings you nearer to me" (*Leg.* 5.27.7, 9). The *Legatus* records a continuing dialogue with Christ during Gertrude's last days. According to this account, on the feast of Martin of Tours, 11 November, Gertrude felt an intense desire to die when she read the response, "Blessed Martin knew the hour of his death long beforehand." "When will you grant me the same news, O Lord?" she asked. "Soon," was the reply. During the next Easter week the same question and answer were repeated with the added admonition, "In the time that remains to you, do not live for yourself but for my glory" (*Leg.* 5.23.1).

At a later time she received the message, "Choose whichever you wish—either to die at once or to have the merit of a long illness though you fear that thereby you may commit more faults." Gertrude felt that Christ was pleased when she left the choice entirely to him. "If for my love you consent to live here longer, I shall dwell in you and you in me like a dove in the rocks until I lead you into the land of eternal spring." Thereafter, whenever Gertrude grew impatient for death, she seemed to hear the words, "What true bride would desire to reach the place where her spouse can no longer add to her adornment nor she prepare gifts for him?" (*Leg.* 5.23.2–3).

Another dialogue, allegorical in its detail, illustrates Gertrude's intimacy with Christ. She believed that he had promised to provide her with a spiritual conveyance at the time of her death. As recorded in the *Legatus*, two angels were to sound the trumpet to announce the tidings: "Behold the bridegroom is coming. Go forth to meet him" (Mt 25:6). The dialogue follows: "What will be the chariot?" "My divine desire." "Where shall I be seated?" "Your confidence in my goodness will be the seat." "And the reins?" "Fervent love." "Lord, you know that I don't understand what other things are necessary. I don't know what else to ask." "No matter what you were to ask, I promise that your joys will go beyond all that you could see or imagine. The human mind cannot conceive what I have prepared for my chosen ones, and this inability is my delight" (Cf. I Cor 2:9; *Leg.* 5.24.1–2).

When Gertrude expressed a desire to die in the church where she had received the mystical wound of love, it seemed to her that Christ said: "When your soul goes forth from this world, I shall place you under the shadow of my fatherly protection and with motherly care carry and cover you as a woman protects her beloved infant when she is crossing a stormy sea. When the journey is over, I shall fill you with unspeakable joys in heaven, just as the mother does not mean merely to save her child from the sea, but to bring it to shore." Thereupon Gertrude left it to the divine will to determine the place as well as the time of her death (*Leg.* 5.25.3).

It seemed to her that at an earlier date she had been better prepared to die but since then had become negligent because of Christ's delay in calling her. As she reflected on this, she heard interiorly the words, "All things have their time according to my wisdom. I have faithfully kept for you whatever you have already done, and nothing that you have added to it will be lost." From this admonition she learned that one may prepare for death long in advance, just as a prince may store wine and grain in his cellar to make ready for his marriage (*Leg.* 5.26.1, 2).

Gertrude was habitually conscious of her membership in the universal Church and never more so than in her last days. She praised God for the graces, gifts, and glory given to the Virgin Mary, and for the merits and joys of all the saints. She felt confident that Christ had promised to draw to himself a multitude of sinners on the day of her death. She was also sure that those who assisted her in her last illness would be richly rewarded; that many souls would be released from Purgatory and enter heaven with her; that those who prayed for her or thanked God for his goodness to her should receive most abundant graces and favors (*Leg.* 5.29 passim).

Years before, Gertrude had understood that adversity is the spiritual ring that espouses the soul to Christ. Now in her last sufferings it was in union with his passion that she prepared herself for eternal life. The Sacred Heart became for her the source of strength, peace, and consolation, changing her sufferings into joy. Meditating on her obligations as a religious and her imperfect performance of her duties, she said prayers of reparation, particularly for her negligence in the recitation of the Office. She also acknowledged her faults against her neighbors—specifically, want of consideration, neglecting to give thanks, rejoice, or grieve with them. She reread her rule, endeavoring to atone for her failure to observe it, and for failing to offer praise, thanksgiving, supplication, and reparation for the whole Church. The consolation that she experienced was so great that the nuns desired to be near her in order to receive her instructions, and they said many prayers that her life might be prolonged (*Leg.* 5.30.5–10).

Among the prayers that she often repeated were stanzas from the Jubilus on the Holy Name of Jesus, the hymn best known by its first line, *Jesu dulcis memoria*. Formerly ascribed to Bernard, it is now believed to be the work of a twelfth-century anonymous English Cistercian. Among the stanzas that Gertrude recited from memory, one in particular echoes a thought frequently expressed in her writings:

> *Desiderate millies*
> *mi Jesu, quando venies,*
> *me laetum quando facies*
> *de te me quando saties?*

> Jesu, a thousand times desired,
> My own, when will you come to me?
> When will you make me glad again?
> When fulfill me utterly?

As she had so often done, she once more grieved for her insufficient devotion to the Virgin Mary, and once more experienced the consolation of Christ, who confided her last hour to the care of his mother (*Leg.* 5.31.1).

Gertrude died in 1301 or 1302. Although her sisters had said, "She should be put on the altar with the relics of the saints," she was probably buried in the convent cemetery. The site of her grave is not recorded. In her fourth exercise she had prayed that her grave might be unknown, but this refers to a mystical burial of her spirit within the Spirit of God (*Ex.* 4.240–43).

Despite her reputation for holiness and the approval of her writings by several theologians, Gertrude, unlike Mechtild of Hackeborn, did not attract general interest immediately after her death. As noted earlier, her *Legatus* survives in few manuscripts, and it was not till the edition of Lanspergius in 1536 that she began to become illustrious. From 1560, vernacular editions were published in Italy, Germany, France, and Spain. The Spanish edition of 1601 was "crowned with the approbation of the most renowned theologians: Diego Yepes S.J. and Domingo Bañez O.P. [both confessors of Teresa of Avila]; Francisco Suarez S.J.; and other religious, Carmelites, Franciscans, and Benedictines."[2] The first official evidence of a cult dates from 7 October 1606, when the Apostolic See gave permission to the nuns of St. John the Evangelist in Licenza to recite an Office in honor of Gertrude. The association of Gertrude with St. John in the veneration of the Sacred Heart gives significance to this event. In 1689, a community in Mexico, the nuns of the Conception of the Blessed Virgin, also received this permission. In the same year Gertrude was declared patroness of the West Indies. In 1654, the Benedictine monks and nuns of the Congregation of Monte Cassino, and soon thereafter all Benedictine congregations were allowed to say the Office of St. Gertrude.[3]

Although never formally canonized, Gertrude was included in the Roman martyrology in 1677 with the entry: "*17 Novembris in Germania, S. Gertrudis Virginis Ordinis S. Benedicti, quae dono revelationum clara exstitit.*" In the next century the kingdom of Poland and the duchy of Saxony were permitted to establish a mass and Office in honor of St. Gertrude. As noted earlier, her title, *la magna*, was given to her by Prosper, Cardinal Lambertini, later Benedict XIV, in 1738. On 20 July 1738 her feast was extended to the entire Church (*Leg.* 1, intro., 31). The Office of St. Gertrude commemorates her humility, her devotion to the eucharist and the passion, and her stigmata. The line *Adjuvabat eam Deus vultu suo* (God has helped her by his countenance) alludes to her vision of the face of Christ. This is an adaptation of Psalm 45:6, *Adjuvabit eam mane diluculo* (God will help her at break of dawn). One of the responsories in the Office perpetuates the words often inscribed in a banderole on her portraits, *In corde Gertrudis invenietis me* (You will find me in the heart of Gertrude).

The feast of St. Gertrude has been celebrated at various times on 15, 16, and 17 November. When she was to be assigned a day in the Roman calendar, 17 November was at first proposed. That day, however, was already assigned to St. Gregory the Wonderworker. The Pontiff, Clement XII, was of the opinion that a saint who had moved mountains should not himself be moved; moreover, it was improper that a bishop and doctor should yield his place to a virgin.[4] Since neither the exact date nor year of Gertrude's death is given in the *Legatus*—it is said only that she died shortly after the feast of St. Lebuin on 12 November—it was decided that her feast should be on 15 November. At present, the Roman calendar lists it on 16 November; some Benedictine communities, however, keep it on the following day, Gregory Thaumaturgus notwithstanding.

The title of Gertrude's book, *Legatus divinae pietatis* (The Messenger of the Divine Loving Kindness), expresses the theme of her life and teaching. That much of the work was dictated to her companions at Helfta assured at least local dissemination of her message. Engelbert Krebs asserts that through her veneration of the Sacred Heart, Gertrude has had a strong influence on the "baroque mysticism" of the seventeenth and eighteenth centuries.[5] As to Margaret Mary Alacoque and Claude de la Colombière, the two seventeenth-century proponents of devotion to the Sacred Heart, it seems that their revelations only amplified and confirmed those of Gertrude.

Commenting on Gertrude's role, Ledos has emphasized that at first she did not understand it—hence her difficulty in submitting to what she finally accepted as a divine command.[6] Her superiors and companions also reinforced this injunction. Her gradual realization that she must share what she had received had the twofold effect of making her docile to spiritual inspiration and humble in recognizing that she was called to assist others. She grieved over her failure to appreciate the divine gift: "By my useless words I have wasted the talent you so liberally gave me. But now I may gain at least some merit by sharing your bounty" (*Leg.* 2.20.5). It was largely through the admonitions of her friend Mechtild of Hackeborn that she began to understand her obligation as a messenger, *legatus*, of the merciful love of God.

When Gertrude complained that she had a thousand desires that she could not fulfill because of her health and circumstances, she received in spirit the explanation for her apparently incompatible aspirations: "I have done this so that in your book each person will find instruction and consolation" (*Leg.* 3.64.3). This episode recalls a passage in the autobiography of Thérèse of Lisieux: "I feel called to the priesthood and to the apostolate—I would be a martyr, a doctor of the Church. . . . One mission alone would not satisfy my longings."[7]

Gertrude of Helfta's particular gifts and opportunities—her studies, her familiarity with the Scriptures and the works of the Fathers of the Church, her conversations with her friends, and especially the guidance and companionship of Mechtild of Hackeborn—all combined to form the unique personality reflected in her writings. Helfta, where she experienced and shared the common life as well as the secrets of her mystical intuitions, assumes in her narrative and the testimony of her companions a lively reality. The community headed by the Abbess Gertrude; her sister, Mechtild of Hackeborn; the storm-beaten Mechtild of Magdeburg; a host of others, among them Gertrude's friend, the unnamed *compilatrix*—"another learned virgin," as Lanspergius calls her—are all present in the pages of both the *Legatus divinae pietatis* and the *Liber specialis gratiae*. Yet companioned and befriended as she was, the final image is of a solitary figure, transfixed in adoration and love as she listens in spirit to the words, "I am your closest relative, *ego propinquissimus sum*—your father, your brother, your spouse."

Notes

Preface

1 Giles Constable, *Medieval Monasticism: A Select Bibliography* (Toronto and Buffalo: University of Toronto Press, 1976), xvii.
2 Bernard of Clairvaux, Sermon for the Vigil of Christmas, in *Sancti Bernardi Opera: Sermones super Cantica Canticorum*, ed. Jean Leclercq, C. H. Talbot, and H. M. Rochais (Rome: Editiones Cistercienses, 1975–77), vol. 4, sermon 5, section 6; Jean Leclercq, *Bernard of Clairvaux and the Cistercian Spirit*, trans. Claire Lavoie (Kalamazoo: Cistercian Publications, 1976), 90.
3 *Leg.* 4.23.8.

1 Helfta

1 Heinrich Grössler, *Die Blütezeit des Klosters Helfta bei Eisleben*, Jahres-Bericht über das Königliche Gymnasium zu Eisleben von Ostern 1886 bis Ostern 1887 (Eisleben, 1887), 9; Caroline Walker Bynum, *Jesus as Mother: Studies in the Spirituality of the High Middle Ages* (Berkeley and Los Angeles: University of California Press, 1982), 252–53.
2 Max Krühne, ed., *Urkundenbuch der Kloster der Graftschaft Mansfeld*, Geschichtsquellen der Provinz Sachsen und angrenzender Gebiete 20 (Halle, 1888), 179–81.
3 Josef Stierli, "Devotion to the Sacred Heart from the End of Patristic Times to St. Margaret Mary," in Stierli, *Heart of the Saviour: A Symposium on Devotion to the Sacred Heart* (New York: Herder and Herder, 1958), 72.
4 For the five books of the *Legatus divinae pietatis* by Gertrude the Great, I have used the bilingual Latin and French editions in the series *Sources chrétiennes*, nos. 127, 139, 143, 255, 331 (Paris, 1967, 1968, 1978, 1986). Because the page numbers differ in the Latin and French texts, I have used the section numbers, which are identical. Books 1, 2, and 3 were edited by Pierre Doyère; books 4 and 5 by Jean-Marie Clément, the nuns of Wisques, and Bernard de Vregille.
5 Krühne, *Unkundenbuch*, 179–81.
6 Grössler, *Blütezeit*, 7 n. 1.
7 Ibid., 35.

8 Gerhard Fittkau, Essen-Werden, letter to author, 16 October 1960.
9 Pierre Doyère, introduction to *Leg.* 1, 10.
10 P. Heinrich Denifle, "Uber die Anfänge der Predigtweise der deutschen Mystiker," *Archiv für Literatur und Kirchengeschichte des Mittelalters* (Berlin) 2 (1886): 641–52.
11 Jeanne Ancelet-Hustache, *Mechtilde de Magdeburg (1207–1282): Etude de psychologie religieuse* (Paris, 1926), 22, 23.
12 Gertrude's preference for short prayers has ample precedent as shown by Thomas Bestul, "Chaucer's Parson's Tale and the Late-Medieval Tradition of Religious Meditation," *Speculum* 64 (July 1989): 604 n. 14.
13 Rudolf of Fulda, "The Life of St. Lioba," in *The Anglo-Saxon Missionaries in Germany*, by C. H. Talbot (New York: Sheed and Ward, 1954), 215.
14 George Sarton, *Introduction to the History of Science* (Baltimore: Williams and Wilkins, 1931), 2:389.
15 Franz Anton Specht, *Geschichte des Unterrichtswesen in Deutschland von den ältesten Zeiten bis zur Mitte des XIII Jahrhunderts* (Stuttgart, 1885), 256–57.
16 George Haven Putnam, *Books and Their Makers During the Middle Ages*, 2 vols. (1896–97; reprint, New York: Hilary House, 1962), 1:52.
17 Ibid., 1:79–80.
18 Jean Leclercq, *The Love of Learning and the Desire for God*, trans. Catherine Misrahi (New York: Fordham University Press, 1960), 154.
19 Charles, comte de Montalembert, *The Monks of the West*, trans. Aurelien de Courson (London: Longmans, Green, 1896), 5:151.

2 *The Women of Helfta*

1 Grössler, *Blütezeit*, 9; *Rev.* 1:vi.
2 Putnam, *Books*, 1:34.
3 Bernard of Clairvaux, *On the Song of Songs: Sermons 1–86*, in *The Works of Bernard of Clairvaux*, trans. Kilian Walsh, Cistercian Fathers Series, no. 7 (Kalamazoo: Cistercian Publications, 1983), 2:189 (sermon 38, section 3).
4 Krühne, *Urkundenbuch*, 131–51 passim.
5 Ibid., 133.
6 Gerard Manley Hopkins, "The Wreck of the Deutschland," in *Poems*, ed. W. H. Gardner and N. H. Mackenzie (London: Oxford University Press, 1967), 58, line 20.
7 Hans Neumann, "Mechthild von Magdeburg" in *Verfasserlexikon*, ed. Wolfgang Stammler (Berlin, 1987) 6: cols. 260–62.
8 Neumann, "Mechthild," col. 260.
9 Cited by Ancelet-Hustache, *Mechtilde*, 54–55.
10 Lucy Menzies, *The Revelations of Mechtild of Magdeburg* (London: Longmans, Green, 1953), xix.
11 Ancelet-Hustache, *Mechtilde*, 54–55.
12 Neumann, "Mechthild," cols. 260–61.
13 Carola Sharp, "The Faith of Mechthild von Magdeburg and Her Life Under Cistercian Rule" (Paper presented at the International Conference on Medieval Studies, Western Michigan University, Kalamazoo, Michigan, 11 May 1987).

14 Lincoln Kirstein, *Dance: A Short History of Classical Theatrical Dancing* (New York: G. P. Putnam, 1935), 108.
15 Translation by John Howard from "The German Mystic: Mechtild of Magdeburg," in *Medieval Women Writers*, ed. Katharina M. Wilson (Athens: University of Georgia Press, 1984), 178.
16 Neumann, "Mechthild," 261.
17 James C. Franklin, *Mystical Transformations: The Imagery of Liquids in the Work of Mechthild von Magdeburg* (Cranbury, N.J.: Fairleigh Dickinson University Press, 1978), 114, 116, and passim.
18 Susan L. Clark, "Ze Glicher Wis": Mechthild von Magdeburg and the Concept of Likeness," in *The Worlds of Medieval Women: Creativity, Influence, and Imagination*, ed. Constance H. Berman, Charles W. Connell, and Judith Rice Rothschild (Morgantown: West Virginia University Press, 1985), 42, 46.
19 Philipp Strauch, "Kleine Beiträge zur Geschichte der deutschen Mystik" *Zeitschrift für deutsches Altertum und deutsche Literatur* (Berlin) 27 (1883): 368–81.
20 Grössler, *Blütezeit*, 10.
21 Gertrude the Great of Helfta, *The Life and Revelations of Saint Gertrude, Virgin and Abbess of the Order of St. Benedict*, trans. M. F. Cusack (1865; reprint, Westminster, Md.: Newman, 1952), 310 n. 1. Hereafter cited as *Life*.

3 "The Nightingale of Christ"

1 Philipp Strauch, "Mechthild von Hackeborn," *Allgemeine deutsche Biographie* (Berlin) 21 (1970):156.
2 David Knowles, *The Religious Orders in England* (Cambridge: Cambridge University Press, 1948), 285.
3 William of St. Thierry et al, *Vitae Sancti Bernardi Abbatis. Vita prima*, PL 185:225.
4 Robert Brentano, *Rome before Avignon* (New York: Basic Books, 1974), 175.
5 Julian of Norwich, *Showings*, trans. Edmund Colledge and James Walsh (New York: Paulist Press, 1978), 194–95.
6 Eileen Power, *Medieval People* (New York: Barnes and Noble, 1963), 94.
7 Mechtild of Hackeborn, *The Booke of Gostlye Grace of Mechtild of Hackeborn*, ed. Theresa A. Halligan (Toronto: Pontifical Institute of Medieval Studies, 1979, microfiche), p. 303. Hereafter cited as *Gostlye Grace*. This is a fifteenth-century translation of an abridged version of the *Liber specialis gratiae*.
8 Jean Leclercq, "Le genre épistolaire au moyen âge," *Revue du moyen âge latin* 2 (April 1946):63–70.
9 Benedict, *Rule of St. Benedict*, ed. Timothy Fry (Collegeville, Minn.: Liturgical Press, 1981), 183, no. 21.
10 *Gostlye Grace*, 39.
11 Leclercq, *Love of Learning*, 301.
12 Frederick Raby, *History of Secular Latin Poetry in the Middle Ages* (Oxford: Clarendon Press, 1934), 2:269.
13 Augusta Theodosia Drane, *The History of St. Catherine of Siena and Her*

Companions, 2 vols. (London: Longmans Green, 1915), 1:218–19.
14　Teresa of Jesus, *The Way of Perfection*, in *Complete Works*, trans. and ed. E. Allison Peers, 3 vols. (New York: Sheed and Ward, 1946), 2:185.
15　Ida Fredericke Görres, *The Hidden Face: A Study of St. Thérèse of Lisieux*, trans. Richard Winston and Clara Winston (New York: Pantheon, 1959), 279–80.
16　Gregory the Great, *Morals on the Book of Job*, trans. Members of the English Church, Library of Fathers of the Holy Catholic Church (Oxford and London, 1838–61), vol. 18, bk. 2, p. 69.
17　Augustine, *De Civitate Dei contra Paganos*, ed. J. E. C. Welldon, Society for Promoting Christian Knowledge (London: Macmillan, 1924), vol. 2, bk. 17, ch. 20, p. 296.
18　Josephus, *Jewish Antiquities* trans. H. St. John Thackeray and Ralph Marcus (Cambridge: Harvard University Press, 1966), 5:143.
19　Thomas Aquinas, *Summa Theologica*, trans. Fathers of the English Dominican Province (New York: Benziger, 1947), 2: question 64, article 6, 1470. See also Augustine, *De Civitate Dei*, 1:21.
20　Aquinas, *Summa* 3, supplement 71.5.
21　Jacobus de Varagine, *Legenda Aurea*, ed. Th. Graesse (Vratislava: Koerner, 1890), *de beato Gregorio*, ch. 46, sec. 10.
22　Augustine, *De Civitate Dei*, vol. 2, bk. 21, ch. 17, p. 551.
23　Rowan A. Green, trans., *Origen*, preface by Hans Urs von Balthasar (New York: Paulist Press, 1979), xii.
24　Elisabeth of Schönau, *Die Visionem der hl. Elisabeth und die Schriften der Aebte Ekbert und Emecho von Schönau*, ed. F. W. E. Roth (Brunn, 1884), 62–63.
25　Julian of Norwich, *Showings*, 60.
26　Florence Mary Capes, *St. Catherine de' Ricci: Her Life, Her Letters, Her Community* (London: Burns and Oates, 1905), 85.

4　The Book of Special Grace

1　Marjorie Rigby, review of *The Booke of Gostlye Grace of Mechtild of Hackeborn*, ed. Theresa A. Halligan, *Review of English Studies*, n.s., 33 (1982): 194–95.
2　Wilhelm Oehl, *Mechthild von Magdeburg, Deutsche Mystiker*, (Munich: Kosel, n.d.), 2:28–29.
3　Arthur Watson, *The Early Iconography of the Tree of Jesse* (London: Oxford University Press, Humphrey Milford, 1934), chapter 1; Eleanor Simmons Greenhill, "The Child in the Tree: A Study of the Cosmological Tree in Christian Tradition," *Traditio* 10 (1954): 345.
4　Watson, *Early Iconography*, plate 30.
5　Terence Hanbury White, *Bestiary* (New York: Putnam, 1954), 7.
6　Ibid., 121.
7　Carleton Fairchild Brown, ed., *Religious Lyrics of the Fourteenth Century* (Oxford: Clarendon Press, 1924), 208–15.
8　Catherine of Siena, *The Dialogue*, trans. Suzanne Noffke (New York: Paulist Press, 1980), 31 n. 5.

9   Carleton Fairchild Brown, ed., *English Lyrics of the Thirteenth Century* (Oxford: Clarendon Press, 1932), 38–39.
10 Hugo Rahner, *Man at Play*, trans. Brian Battershaw and Edward Quinn (New York: Herder and Herder, 1967), 76–77.
11 John Wyclif, *Select English Works of Wyclif*, ed. T. Arnold, 3 vols. (Oxford, 1869–71), 3:360. Margery Kempe, *The Book of Margery Kempe*, ed. Sanford Brown Meech, EETS, o.s., 212 (London: Oxford University Press, 1940), 52.
12 Percy Dearmer, R. Vaughan Williams, and Martin Shaw, eds., *Oxford Book of Carols* (London: Oxford University Press, Humphrey Milford, 1928), 94–96.
13 Teresa of Jesus, *The Way of Perfection*, in *Complete Works*, 2:63.
14 Giovanni Boccaccio, *Decameron* (day 7, novella 1, 5), in *Tutte le Opere di Giovanni Boccaccio*, ed. Vittore Branca (Milan: Mondadori, 1976), 4:587–88. Branca, citing Ancelet-Hustache, believes that the reference is to Mechtild of Magdeburg, 1360–61, n. 3.
15 *Gostlye Grace*, 7–10, 52–53.
16 Ibid., 47–52.
17 Fiorenzo Forti, "Matelda," *Enciclopedia Dantesca* (Rome: Istituto della Enciclopedia Italiana, 1971), 3:854–60.
18 Nora Duff, *Matilda of Tuscany (1046–1115)* (London: Methuen, 1909), 1, 5.
19 Ibid., 79.
20 Ferdinand Koenen, "Matelda," *Deutsches Dante-Jahrbuch* 10 (1928): 160–61.
21 Ibid., 157, 159.
22 Ibid., 161–62.
23 Ibid., 166; J. C. Cooper, *An Illustrated Encyclopedia of Traditional Symbols* (London: Thames and Hudson, 1978), 134.
24 Duff, *Matilda*, 275.
25 Ibid., 269.
26 Robert Hollander, *Allegory in Dante's Commedia* (Princeton: Princeton University Press, 1969), 152–53.
27 Dorothy Sayers, *The Divine Comedy: Purgatory* (Baltimore: Penguin, 1955), 347–48, note E: "The Identity of Matilda."
28 Ancelet-Hustache, *Mechtilde*, 307.
29 Edmund Gardner, *Dante and the Mystics* (London: Dent, 1913; reprint, New York: Octagon Books, 1968), 342–48.
30 Cf. canto 33 in Dante Alighieri, *The Divine Comedy*, trans. Lawrence Binyon (New York: Viking, 1947), 544.
31 Forti, "Matelda," 854.
32 Thomas J. Bergin, *Dante* (New York: Orion, 1965), 233–34.
33 Hollander, *Allegory*, 152 n. 18.
34 Koenen, "Matelda," 155.
35 Hans Urs von Balthasar, "Mechthilds kirklicher Auftrag" in *Licht*, 20.
36 Karl Vossler, *Mediaeval Culture*, trans. William Cranston Lawton (New York: Harcourt, Brace, 1929), 2:117.
37 Forti, "Matelda," 855.

5 *From the Land of Unlikeness: Gertrude the Great*

1   Krühne, *Urkundenbuch*, 132, 145, 148.
2   The expression "to suck honey among thorns" was proverbial in England as early as the twelfth century. It occurs in a homily, circa 1175: "Nis nan blisse . . . that ne beo / To bitter aboht / thet et huni ther-in / beoth licked of thornes." It is one of the proverbs of Hendyng, circa 1300: "Dere is boht the hony that is licked of the thorne." The most explicit statement occurs in the lyric, "Worldes Blis Ne Last No Throwe": "thu likest huni of thorn iwis / that seest thi love on worldes blis / for ful of bitternis hit is" (Brown, *English Lyrics*, 88, 201 n. 20).
3   Cf. Teresa of Jesus: "He revealed himself to me . . . and he gave me his right hand, saying to me: 'Behold this nail'" (*Spiritual Relations*, in *Complete Works*, 1:352).
4   John of the Cross, *Ascent of Mount Carmel*, in *Complete Works*, ed. and trans. E. Allison Peers (Westminster, Md.: Newman, 1945), 1:237–38.
5   Teresa of Jesus, *The Letters of Saint Teresa of Jesus*, trans. and ed. E. Allison Peers (London: Burns, Oates, and Washbourne, 1951), 2:889.
6   P. Siwek, "Stigmatization," *NCE* 13:713.
7   Cf. *An Epistle of Discretion*: "He may not be gotten by thought, nor concluded by understanding; but he may be loved and chosen with the true lovely will of thine heart. . . . Such a blind shot with the sharp dart of longing may never fail." Evelyn Underhill, *Mysticism: A Study in the Nature and Development of Man's Spiritual Consciousness* (New York: New American Library, 1955), 85 n. 5.
8   Teresa of Jesus, *Life*, in *Complete Works*, 1:192–93.
9   Ludwig von Pastor, *The History of the Popes*, trans. E. F. Peeler (St. Louis: Herder, 1949), 35:25.
10 Gertrude the Great of Helfta, *The Exercises of Saint Gertrude*, introduction, commentary, and translation by a Benedictine nun of Regina Laudis [Columba Hart] (Westminster, Md.: Newman, 1956), 17. Hereafter cited as Hart, *Exercises*.
11 Gertrud Jaron Lewis, trans., "The Mystical *Jubilus* by Gertrud of Helfta," *Vox Benedictina* 1, no. 4 (October 1984): 237–47.
12 Hart, *Exercises*, 175.
13 Therese Schroeder-Sheker, "The Alchemical Harp of Mechthild of Hackeborn," *Vox Benedictina* 6 (January 1989): 49–55.
14 The editors question this mysterious precision—a "motherless orphan." Cf. Lam. 5:3, "We have become orphans, fatherless."
15 Prosper Guéranger, preface to *The Exercises of Saint Gertrude*, trans. Thomas Alder Pope (London: Burns and Oates, 1863), xx.
16 J. K. Huysmans, *En Route* (Paris: P. V. Stock, 1907), 430.
17 Felix Vernet, "Gertrude la Grande," *DTC* 6:1333.
18 *Life*, 201.
19 Hopkins, *Poems*, 178; Sister Mary Jeremy [Finnegan], Letters, *Times Literary Supplement*, 14 November 1952.
20 *Life*, 2.

6 The Writings of Gertrude

1. Nicolas Canteleu, *Insinuationes divinae pietatis seu revelationes S. Gertrudis virginis et abbatissae ordinis S. Benedicti* (Paris: Leonard, 1662), bk. 1, p. 4.
2. Ancelet-Hustache, *Mechtilde*, 383.
3. Evelyn Underhill, "Medieval Mysticism," in *Cambridge Medieval History* (Cambridge: Cambridge University Press, 1932), 7:796.
4. Walter J. Ong, "Wit and Mystery: A Revaluation in Medieval Latin Hymnody" *Speculum* 22 (July 1947): 324.
5. Angela of Foligno, *Il Libro della Beata Angela da Foligno*, ed. Ludger Thier and Abbe Calufetti, (Rome: Collegii S. Bonaventurae ad Claras Aquas, Grottaferrata, 1985), 386. Unpublished translation by Paul Lachance.
6. Gabriel Ledos, *Sainte Gertrude* (Paris: Lecoffre, 1907), 160.
7. Robert Henryson, *Poems*, selected and ed. Charles Elliott (Oxford: Clarendon Press, 1974), 125–26.
8. Watson, *Early Iconography*.
9. Arthur Watson, "The *Speculum Virginum* with Special Reference to the Tree of Jesse" *Speculum* 3 (1928): 445–69.
10. William Langland, *The Vision of Piers Plowman*, trans. Henry W. Wells (London: Sheed and Ward, 1938), passus 16, line 215.
11. Is the French translation, *pourquoi me demander cela a moi dont la faiblesse des vertus est celle de mon sexe* warranted by the Latin: *quare hoc poscis a me quae sum tenera tam virtutibus quam sexu?* Is not Gertrude simply saying that her virtue is as frail as her physical condition?
12. Teresa of Jesus, *Life*, in *Complete Works*, 1:127–28; *The Interior Castle*, in *Complete Works*, 2:187–351.
13. Bernard, *Song of Songs*, 2:206–7 (sermon 41, section 3).
14. Juan Gonzalez Arintero, *The Mystical Evolution in the Development and Vitality of the Church*, trans. Jordan Aumann (St. Louis: Herder, 1949), 2:355.
15. Felix Vernet, *La Spiritualité Médiévale* (Paris: Librairie Bloud et Gay, 1928), 195.
16. Sigrid Undset, *Catherine of Siena*, trans. Kate Austin-Lund (New York: Sheed and Ward, 1954), 92.
17. Arintero, *Mystical Evolution*, 2:340.
18. Augustin Léonard, "Studies in the Phenomena of Mystical Experience," in *Mystery and Mysticism: A Symposium* (London: Blackfriars, 1956), 92–93.
19. Vernet, *Spiritualité*, 147.
20. Johannes Bühler, *Klosterleben in deutschen Mittelalter nach zeitgenössischen Aufzeichnungen* (Leipzig: Insel-Verlag, 1923), 248.

7 Gertrude in Her Community

1. Teresa of Jesus, *Way of Perfection*, in *Complete Works*, 2:74–75.
2. The demon must be Tutivillus, who collected the syllables omitted by priests and monks during the mass and office. Tutivillus appears in the Towneley play of the Judgment. He introduces himself to the devils, saying, "*fragmenta verborum colligit horum*" (he collects the fragments of words).

In Martial Rose's edition of the Wakefield-Towneley plays, the first demon says to Tutivillus, "Now thou art my own chorister, ye live with the nuns" (James Orchard Halliwell-Phillips, *A Dictionary of Archaic and Provincial Words*, 7th ed. [New York: Dutton, 1924], 896. George England, ed., *The Towneley Plays*, notes and introduction by Alfred W. Pollard, EETS extra series, 71 [1897; reprint, London: Humphrey Milford, 1952], "The Judgment," lines 206–13. Martial Rose, ed., *The Wakefield Mystery Plays*, [Garden City: Doubleday, 1962], 528, 530.
3   Johannes Jorgensen, *Saint Bridget of Sweden*, trans. Ingeborg Lund (London: Longmans Green, 1954), 1:150.
4   Arintero, *Mystical Evolution*, 2:106.
5   Vernet, "Gertrude la Grande" *DTC* 6:1333.
6   Caterina da Siena, *Dialogo*, ch. 151, 435; ch. 153, 442.
7   Prosper Guéranger, preface to *The Exercises of Saint Gertrude*, trans. Thomas Alder Pope (London: Burns and Oates, 1863), xvi.
8   P. Pedro Ibañez, "Statement of P. Pedro Ibañez on the Spirit of Saint Teresa," in *Santa Teresa de Jesús y la Orden de Predicatores*, by Felipe Martin (Avila, 1909), 664, no. 29.
9   Gertrude, *Life*, xxxiv, xxxiii.

8   Aspects of Gertrude's Spirituality

1   Pierre Pourrat, *Christian Spirituality in the Middle Ages*, trans. S. P. Jacques (Westminster, Md.: Newman, 1953), 2:86.
2   Frederick William Faber, *All for Jesus* (Baltimore: John Murphy, 1854), 354.
3   Albert Lepitre, quoted by Vernet, "Gertrude la Grande" *DTC* 6:1333.
4   Bernard, *Sancti Bernardi Opera*, sermon 37, section 7.
5   Pourrat, *Christian Spirituality*, 2:66 n. 1; Doyère, *Leg.*, Intr., 47.
6   Teresa of Jesus, *Interior Castle*, in *Complete Works*, 2:234.
7   Bernard, *Sancti Bernardi Opera*, sermon 7, section 2.
8   John Ruusbroec, *The Spiritual Espousals and Other Works*, intr. and trans. James A. Wiseman, Classics of Western Spirituality (New York: Paulist Press, 1985), 247.
9   Pourrat, *Christian Spirituality*, 2:88 n. 1.
10 Joseph Duhr, "Communion fréquente," *DS* 3:1262.
11 Reginald Thorne Davies, ed., *Medieval English Lyrics* (Evanston: Northwestern University Press, 1964), 115.
12 Drane, *History of St. Catherine*, 1:331–33 n. 1.
13 Teresa of Jesus, *Life*, in *Complete Works*, 1:93.
14 E. Dublanchy, "Eglise, corps de Jésu-Christ," *DTC* 4:2150, sec. 4.
15 Barbara Newman, *Sister of Wisdom: St. Hildegarde's Theology of the Feminine* (Berkeley and Los Angeles: University of California Press, 1987), 241–42 n. 114.
16 Catherine of Siena, *The Letters of St. Catherine of Siena*, trans., intr., notes, Suzanne Noffke, Medieval and Renaissance Texts and Studies, 52 (Binghamton: State University of New York, 1988), 1:202, letter 63.
17 Capes, *St. Catherine de' Ricci*, 176.
18 Catherine of Siena, *Letters*, 1:167.
19 Alphonsus Liguori, *Glories of Mary* (New York: P. J. Kenedy, 1952), 86.

20 Bernard, *Sancti Bernardi Opera*, sermon 43, section 3.
21 Paul Bird, "Dali Orthodoxy," *Art News* 83 (February 1984): 122.
22 Capes, *St. Catherine de' Ricci*, 85.
23 *Rhythmus ad SS. Sacramentum*, translated by Hopkins in *Poems* 211–12.
24 Doyère, "Gertrude d'Helfta: Libertas cordis," *DS* 6:336.
25 Ibid.
26 Henry Suso, *The Exemplar*, ed. Nicholas Heller, trans. M. Ann Edward (Dubuque: Priory Press, 1962), 1:107; Pourrat, *Christian Spirituality*, 2:165 n. 3.
27 John Gray, trans., *The True Prayers of St. Gertrude and St. Mechtilde* (New York: Sheed and Ward, 1936), Intr. 5.
28 Christopher O'Mahony, ed. and trans., *St. Thérèse of Lisieux by Those Who Knew Her* (1975; reprint, Dublin: Veritas Publications, 1989), 150.
29 Raymond of Capua, *Life of Catherine of Siena*, trans. Conleth Kearns (Wilmington: Michael Glazier, 1980), 14.
30 Elsbet Stagel, *Das Leben der Schwestern zu Töss*, ed. Ferdinand Vetter. Deutsche Texte des Mittelalters 6. (Berlin: Weidmannsche Buchhandlung, 1906), 29.
31 Vernet, *Spiritualité*, 185.
32 Bernard, *Sancti Bernardi Opera*, sermon 23, section 15.
33 Léonard, "Studies in the Phenomena of Mystical Experience," 111, 112.
34 Teresa of Jesus, *Poems*, in *Complete Works*, 3:311–12.
35 Jean Cocteau, *Art and Faith: Letters between Jacques Maritain and Jean Cocteau*, trans. John Coleman (New York: Philosophical Library, 1948), 49.
36 Bernard, *Liber de diligendo Deo*, in *Sancti Bernardi Opera*, vol. 3, sermon 6, section 16.
37 Pourrat, *Christian Spirituality*, 2:91.
38 Vernet, *Spiritualité*, 70.
39 Liguori, *Glories of Mary*, e.g., 41, 146–47; Francis de Sales, *Vrais Entretiens Spirituels*, ed. J. Gabolda (Paris: Lecoffre, 1927), Entretien 15:333–35; John Eudes, *The Sacred Heart of Jesus*, trans. Richard Flower (New York: P. J. Kenedy, 1946), 55, 63, 75.
40 Columba Marmion, *Sponsa Verbi* (Paris: Lethielleux, 1923), 32–34; Jacques Maritain and Raïssa Maritain, *Prayer and Intelligence*, trans. Algar Thorold (New York: Sheed and Ward, 1943), 4, 28; William D. Miller, *Dorothy Day: A Biography* (San Francisco: Harper and Row, 1982), 286.

9 Veneration of the Sacred Heart

1 Hugo Rahner, "The Beginnings of the Devotion in Patristic Times," in *Heart of the Savior: A Symposium*, ed. Josef Stierli, trans. Paul Andrews (New York: Herder and Herder, 1958), 51.
2 Augustine, *Tractatus in Joannis Evangelium*, PL 35:1536.
3 Paulinus of Nola, *Letters of St. Paulinus of Nola*, trans. and annotated, P. G. Walsh, Ancient Christian Writers 35 (Westminster, Md.: Newman, 1966), 1:193 letter 21, section 4.
4 Gregory, *Super Cantica Canticorum Expositio*, PL 79:499.
5 Anselm, *De passione Christi*, PL 158:762.
6 Bernard, *Sancti Bernardi Opera*, vol. 2, sermon 16, section 4.

7 Gilbert of Hoyland, *Sermo 30 on Canticle 4:9* (Paris: Migne, 1854), *PL* 184:155, section 2.
8 Martinus Cawley, trans. and ed. *Lives of Ida of Nivelles, Lutgard, and Alice the Leper*, Guadalupe Translations (Lafayette, Ore.: Guadalupe Abbey, 1987), 5–6, 13.
9 Jean Bainvel, "Devotion to the Heart of Jesus," in *Catholic Encyclopedia* (New York: Appleton, 1910), 7:165.
10 Neumann, "Mechthild von Magdeburg," 6: col. 267.
11 Evelyn Underhill, "Medieval Mysticism," in *Cambridge Medieval History* (Cambridge: Cambridge University Press, 1932), 7:796.
12 Pius XII, "*Haurietis Aquas*," in *The Papal Encyclicals*, ed. Claudia Carlen, Consortium Books (Wilmington, N.C.: McGrath, 1981), 4:299.
13 According to Varagine, Dominic slept either before the altar or with his head on a stone. There is no reference to his eating in church (*Legenda Aurea*, 477). See also M. H. Vicaire, *St. Dominic and His Times*, trans. Kathleen Pond (New York: McGraw-Hill, 1964), 351.
14 Catherine of Siena, *Dialogue*, prologue, 27.
15 Eric Colledge, "Mechtild of Magdeburg," *The Month* 211 (June 1961), 335.

10 The Death of Gertrude

1 Arintero, *Mystical Evolution*, 2:162.
2 Ledos, *Sainte Gertrude*, 203.
3 Doyère, "Gertrude d'Helfta," *DS* 16:338.
4 Alban Butler, *Lives of the Saints*, ed. Herbert Thurston and Donald Attwater, (New York: P. J. Kenedy, 1956), 4:363 n.
5 Engelbert Krebs, "Gertrude v. Helfta," in *Die Deutsche Literatur des Mittelalters Verfasserlexikon*, ed. Wolfgang Stammler (Berlin, 1936), vol. 2, cols. 43–44.
6 Ledos, *Sainte Gertrude*, 164.
7 Thérèse of Lisieux, *Story of a Soul*, trans. John Clarke, 2d ed. (Washington, D.C.: ICS [Institute of Carmelite Studies] Publications, 1976), 192–93.

Bibliography

Acta sanctorum. 85 vols., in 67. Paris: V. Palmé, 1863–1940.
Ancelet-Hustache, Jeanne. *Mechtilde de Magdebourg (1207–1282): Etude de psychologie religieuse.* Paris, 1926.
Angela of Foligno. *Il Libro della Beata Angela da Foligno.* Edited by Ludger Thier and Abele Calufetti. Rome: Collegii S. Bonaventurae ad Claras Aquas, Grottaferrata, 1985.
Anselm. *De passione Christi. Liber Meditationum et Orationum.* PL 709–1016.
Aquinas, Thomas. *Summa Theologica.* Translated by Fathers of the English Dominican Province. 3 vols. New York: Benziger, 1947.
Arintero, Juan Gonzalez. *The Mystical Evolution in the Development and Vitality of the Church.* Translated by Jordan Aumann. 2 vols. St. Louis: Herder, 1949.
Augustine. *De Civitate Dei contra Paganos.* Edited by J. E. C. Welldon. 2 vols. Society for Promoting Christian Knowledge. London: Macmillan, 1924.
———. *Tractatus in Joannis Evangelium.* PL 35:1535–43.
Bainvel, Jean. "*Dévotion au Coeur Sacré de Jésus.*" DTC 3:271–351.
———. "Devotion to the Heart of Jesus." In *Catholic Encyclopedia,* 7:165. New York: Appleton, 1910.
Balthasar, Hans Urs von. "Mechthilds kirchlicher Auftrag." In *Das fliessende Licht der Gottheit,* by Mechthild von Magdeburg. Edited by Margot Schmidt. Einsiedeln: Benziger, 1956.
Benedict. *The Rule of St. Benedict.* Edited by Timothy Fry. Collegeville, Minn.: Liturgical Press, 1981.
Bergin, Thomas G. *Dante.* New York: Orion, 1965.
Bernard of Clairvaux. *On the Song of Songs: Sermons 1–86.* In *The Works of Bernard of Clairvaux,* translated by Kilian Walsh, 4 vols. Cistercian Fathers Series, no. 7. Kalamazoo: Cistercian Publications, 1983.
———. *Sancti Bernardi Opera: Sermones super Cantica Canticorum.* Edited by Jean Leclercq, C. H. Talbot, and H. M. Rochais. 8 vols., in 9. Rome: Editiones Cistercienses, 1957–77.
Bestul, Thomas. "Chaucer's Parson's Tale and the Late-Medieval Tradition of Religious Meditation." *Speculum* 64 (July 1989): 600–619.
Biblia Sacra. Rome: Desclée, 1947.

Bird, Paul. "Dali Orthodoxy." *Art Digest* 25 (15 December 1950): 17.
Boccaccio, Giovanni. *Decameron*. In *Tutte le Opere di Giovanni Boccaccio*, edited by Vittore Branca, vol. 4. Milan: Mondadori, 1976.
Brentano, Robert. *Rome before Avignon*. New York: Basic Books, 1974.
Browe, Peter. *Die Eucharistischen Wunder des Mittelalters*. Breslau: Muller and Seiffert, 1938.
Brown, Carleton Fairchild, ed. *English Lyrics of the Thirteenth Century*. Oxford: Clarendon Press, 1932.
———. *Religious Lyrics of the Fourteenth Century*. Oxford: Clarendon Press, 1924.
Bühler, Johannes. *Klosterleben im deutschen Mittelalter nach zeitgenössischen Aufzeichnungen*. Leipzig: Insel-Verlag, 1923.
Butler, Alban. *Lives of the Saints*. Edited, revised, and supplemented by Herbert Thurston and Donald Attwater. 4 vols. New York: P. J. Kenedy, 1956.
Bynum, Caroline Walker. *Jesus as Mother: Studies in the Spirituality of the High Middle Ages*. Berkeley and Los Angeles: University of California Press, 1982.
———. "Women Mystics and Eucharistic Devotion in the 13th Century." *Women's Studies* 2 (1984): 179–214.
Canteleu. Nicolas. *Insinuationes divinae pietatis seu revelationes S. Gertrudis virginis et abbatissae ordinis S. Benedicti*. Paris: Leonard, 1662.
Capes, Florence Mary. *St. Catherine de' Ricci: Her Life, Her Letters, Her Community*. London: Burns and Oates, 1905.
Caterina da Siena. *Il Dialogo*. Edited by G. Cavallini. Roma: Edizioni Cateriniae, 1968.
Catherine of Siena. *The Dialogue*. Translated by Suzanne Noffke. New York: Paulist Press, 1980.
———. *The Letters of St. Catherine of Siena*. Translated with introduction and notes by Suzanne Noffke. Medieval and Renaissance Texts and Studies, 52. Binghamton: State University of New York, 1988.
Cawley, Martinus, trans. and ed. *Lives of Ida of Nivelles, Lutgard, and Alice the Leper*. Guadalupe Translations. Lafayette, Ore.: Guadalupe Abbey, 1987.
Clark, Susan L. "Ze Glicher Wis": Mechthild von Magdeburg and the Concept of Likeness." In *The Worlds of Medieval Women: Creativity, Influence, and Imagination*, edited by Constance H. Berman, Charles W. Connell, and Judith Rice Rothschild, 41–50. Morgantown: West Virginia University Press, 1985.
Cocteau, Jean. *Art and Faith: Letters between Jacques Maritain and Jean Cocteau*. Translated by John Coleman. New York: Philosophical Library, 1948.
Colledge, Eric. "Mechtild of Magdeburg." *The Month* 211 (June 1961): 325–36.
Constable, Giles. *Medieval Monasticism: A Select Bibliography*. Toronto and Buffalo: University of Toronto Press, 1976.
Cooper, J. C. *An Illustrated Encyclopaedia of Traditional Symbols*. London: Thames and Hudson, 1978.
Dante Alighieri. *Dante's Paradiso*. Italian text with English translation and comment by John D. Sinclair. New York: Oxford University Press, 1961.
———. *Dante's Purgatorio*. Italian text with English translation and comment by John D. Sinclair. New York: Oxford University Press. 1961.

———. *The Divine Comedy*. Translated by Lawrence Binyon. New York: Viking, 1947.
Davies, Reginald Thorne, ed. *Medieval English Lyrics*. Evanston: Northwestern University Press, 1964.
Dearmer, Percy, R. Vaughn Williams, and Martin Shaw, eds. *Oxford Book of Carols*. London: Oxford University Press, Humphrey Milford, 1928.
Denifle, P. Heinrich. "Uber die Anfänge der Predigtweise der deutschen Mystiker." *Archiv für Literatur und Kirchengeschichte des Mittelalters* (Berlin) 2 (1886):641–52.
Dictionnaire de spiritualité, ascétique et mystique, doctrine et histoire. 14 vols. and fascicle. Paris: Beauchesne, 1937.
Dictionnaire de théologie catholique. 15 vols. Paris: Letouzey, 1909–50.
Dolan, Gilbert. *St. Gertrude the Great*. St. Louis: Herder, 1916.
Doyère, Pierre. "Gertrude d'Helfta: Libertas cordis." *DS* 6:336.
———. "St. Gertrude, Mystic and Nun." *Worship* 34 (October 1960): 536–43.
Drane, Augusta Theodosia. *The History of St. Catherine of Siena and Her Companions*. 2 vols. London: Longmans Green, 1915.
Dublanchy, E. "Eglise, corps de Jésu-Christ." *DTC* 4:2150.
Duff, Nora. *Matilda of Tuscany (1046–1115)*. London: Methuen, 1909.
Duhr, Joseph. "Communion fréquente." *DS* 3:1262.
Elisabeth of Schönau. *Die Visionem der hl. Elisabeth und die Schriften der Aebte Ekbert und Emecho von Schönau*. Edited by W. E. Roth. Brunn, 1884.
England, George, ed. *The Towneley Plays*. Notes and introduction by Alfred W. Pollard. EETS extra series, 71. 1897. Reprint. London: Humphrey Milford, 1952.
Eudes, John. *The Sacred Heart of Jesus*. Translated by Richard Flower. New York: P. J. Kenedy, 1946.
Faber, Frederick William. *All for Jesus*. Baltimore: John Murphy, 1854.
[Finnegan,] Mary Jeremy. "Idiom of Women Mystics." *Mystics Quarterly* 13 (June 1987): 65–72.
———. Letters. *Times Literary Supplement*, 14 November 1952.
———. "Mechtild of Hackeborn: *Nemo Communior*." In *Peace Weavers: Medieval Religious Women*, edited by Lillian Thomas Shank and John A. Nichols, 2:213–21. Cistercian Studies Series, no. 72. Kalamazoo: Cistercian Publications, 1987.
———. "'Similitudes' in the Writing of St. Gertrude of Helfta." *Mediaeval Studies* 19 (1957): 48–54.
Forti, Fiorenzo. "Matelda." *Enciclopedia Dantesca*. Rome: Istituto della Enciclopedia Italiana, 1971.
Francis de Sales. *Vrais Entretiens Spirituels*. Edited by J. Gabolda. Paris: Lecoffre, 1927.
Franklin, James C. *Mystical Transformations: The Imagery of Liquids in the Work of Mechthild von Magdeburg*. Cranbury, N.J.: Farleigh Dickinson University Press, 1978.
Gardner, Edmund. *Dante and the Mystics*. London: Dent, 1913. Reprint. New York: Octagon Books, 1968.
Gertrude the Great of Helfta. *Les Exercices*. Vol. 1 of *Oeuvres Spirituelles*. Edited by Jacques Hourlier and Albert Schmitt. Sources chrétiennes 127. Paris: Editions du Cerf, 1967.

———. *The Exercises of St. Gertrude*. Translated by Thomas Alder Pope. London: Burns and Oates, 1863.

———. *The Exercises of Saint Gertrude*. Introduction, commentary, and translation by a Benedictine nun of Regina Laudis [Columba Hart]. Westminster, Md.: Newman, 1956.

———. *Exercitia*. In *Revelationes Gertrudianae ac Mechtildianae*, vol. 1. Edited by monks of Solesmes [Louis Paquelin]. Poitiers-Paris, 1875.

———. *Gertrud the Great of Helfta: Spiritual Exercises*. Translation, notes, and indexes by Gertrud Jaron Lewis and Jack Lewis. Cistercian Fathers Series 49. Kalamazoo: Cistercian Publications, 1989.

———. *Le Héraut* [Legatus divinae pietatis]. Vol. 2 of *Oeuvres Spirituelles*. Edited by Pierre Doyère. Sources chrétiennes 139. Paris: Editions du Cerf, 1968.

———. *Legatus divinae pietatis*. In *Revelationes Gertrudianae ac Mechtildianae*, vol. 1. Edited by monks of Solesmes [Louis Paquelin]. Poitiers-Paris, 1875.

———. *The Life and Revelations of Saint Gertrude, Virgin and Abbess of the Order of St. Benedict*. Translated by M. F. Cusack. 1865. Reprint. Westminster, Md.: Newman, 1952.

———. *Oeuvres Spirituelles*. Latin/French. 5 vols. Sources chrétiennes 127, 139, 143, 255, 331. Paris: Editions du Cerf, 1967–86.

———. *The True Prayers of St. Gertrude and St. Mechtilde*. Translated by Canon John Gray. New York: Sheed and Ward, 1936.

Gilbert of Hoyland. *Sermon 30 on Canticle 4:9*. (Paris: Migne, 1854), PL 184:155, section 2.

Görres, Ida Fredericke. *The Hidden Face: A Study of St. Thérèse of Lisieux*. Translated by Richard Winston and Clara Winston. New York: Pantheon, 1959.

Green, Rowan A., trans. *Origen*. Preface by Hans Urs van Balthasar. New York: Paulist Press, 1979.

Greenhill, Eleanor Simmons. "The Child in the Tree: A Study of the Cosmological Tree in Christian Tradition," *Traditio* 10 (1954): 323–71.

Gregory the Great. *Morals on the Book of Job*. Translated by Members of the English Church. Library of Fathers of the Holy Catholic Church, vols. 18, 21, 23, 31. Oxford and London, 1838–61.

———. *Super Cantica Canticorum Expositio*. PL 79:471–548.

Grössler, Heinrich. *Die Blütezeit des Klosters Helfta bei Eisleben*. Jahres-Bericht über das Königliche Gymnasium zu Eisleben von Ostern 1886 bis Ostern 1887. Eisleben, 1887.

Guéranger, Prosper. Preface. In *The Exercises of Saint Gertrude*, translated by Thomas Alder Pope. London: Burns and Oates, 1863.

Halliwell-Phillips, James Orchard. *A Dictionary of Archaic and Provincial Words*. 7th ed. New York: Dutton, 1924.

Henryson, Robert. *Poems*. Selected and edited by Charles Elliott. Oxford: Clarendon Press, 1974.

Herrad of Hohenbourg. *Hortus Deliciarum*. Commentary by Rosalie Green, Michael Evans, Christine Bischoff, Michael Curschmann, T. Julian Brown, and Kenneth Levy, in 2 vols. Studies of the Warburg Institute, vol. 36, ed. J. B. Trapp. Leiden: E. J. Brill, 1979.

Hollander, Robert. *Allegory in Dante's Commedia*. Princeton: Princeton University Press, 1969.
Hopkins, Gerard Manley. *Poems*. Edited by W. H. Gardner and N. H. Mackenzie. 4th ed. London: Oxford University Press, 1967.
Howard, John. "The German Mystic: Mechthild of Magdeburg." In *Medieval Women Writers*, edited by Katherina M. Wilson, 153–85. Athens: University of Georgia Press, 1984.
Huysmans, J. K. *En Route*. Paris: P. V. Stock, 1907.
Ibañez, P. Pedro. "Statement of P. Pedro Ibañez on the Spirit of Saint Teresa." In *Santa Teresa de Jesús y la Orden de Predicatores*, by Felipe Martin, 660–65. Avila, 1909.
John of the Cross. *Complete Works*. Edited and translated by E. Allison Peers. 3 vols. Westminster, Md.: Newman, 1945.
Jordan of Saxony. "Prologue to History of the Beginnings of the Order of Preachers." In *Saint Dominic: Biographical Documents*, edited by Francis C. Lehner, 5–89. Washington: Thomist Press, 1964.
Jorgensen, Johannes. *Saint Bridget of Sweden*. Translated by Ingeborg Lund. 2 vols., in 1. London: Longmans Green, 1954.
Josephus. *Jewish Antiquities*. Translated by H. St. John Thackeray and Ralph Marcus. 9 vols. Cambridge: Harvard University Press, 1966.
Julian of Norwich. *A Book of Showings to the Anchoress Julian of Norwich*. Edited by Edmund Colledge and James Walsh. 2 vols. Toronto: Pontifical Institute of Medieval Studies, 1978.
———. *The Revelations of Divine Love*. Translated by James Walsh. New York: Harper and Brothers, 1961.
———. *Showings*. Translated by Edmund Colledge and James Walsh. New York: Paulist Press, 1978.
Katzenellenbogen, Adolf. *Allegories of the Virtues and Vices in Medieval Art*. Translated by A. J. P. Crick. New York: Norton, 1964.
Kempe, Margery. *The Book of Margery Kempe*. Edited by Sanford Brown Meech. EETS, o.s., 212. London: Oxford University Press, 1940.
Kirstein, Lincoln. *Dance: A Short History of Classical Theatrical Dancing*. New York: G. P. Putnam, 1935.
Knowles, David. *The Religious Orders in England*. Cambridge: Cambridge University Press, 1948.
Koenen, Ferdinand. "Matelda." *Deutsches Dante-Jahrbuch* 10 (1928): 155–72.
Krebs, Engelbert. "Gertrude v. Helfta." In *Die Deutsche Literatur des Mittelalters Verfasserlexikon*, edited by Wolfgang Stammler, vol. 2, cols. 43–44. Berlin: 1936.
Krühne, Max, ed. *Urkundenbuch der Kloster der Graftschaft Mansfeld*, Geschichtsquellen der Provinz Sachsen und angrenzender Gebiete 20, 129–92. Halle, 1888.
Langland, William. *The Vision of Piers Plowman*. Translated by Henry W. Wells. London: Sheed and Ward, 1938.
Leclercq, Jean. *Bernard of Clairvaux and the Cistercian Spirit*. Translated by Claire Lavoie. Kalamazoo: Cistercian Publications, 1976.
———. "Le genre épistolaire au moyen âge." *Revue du moyen âge latin* 2 (April 1946): 63–70.

———. *The Love of Learning and the Desire for God.* Translated by Catherine Misrahi. New York: Fordham University Press, 1960.
Ledos, Gabriel. *Sainte Gertrude.* Paris: Lecoffre, 1907.
Léonard, Augustin. "Studies in the Phenomena of Mystical Experience." In *Mystery and Mysticism: A Symposium,* 51–118. London: Blackfriars, 1956.
Lewis, Gertrud Jaron. *Gertrud the Great of Helfta: Spiritual Exercises.* Translation, notes, and indexes by Gertrud Jaron Lewis and Jack Lewis. Cistercian Fathers Series 49. Kalamazoo: Cistercian Publications, 1989.
———, trans. "The Mystical *Jubilus* by Gertrud of Helfta." *Vox Benedictina* 1, no. 4 (October 1984): 237–47.
———. "Studying Women Mystics: Some Methodological Concerns." *Mystics Quarterly* 10 (December 1984): 175–81.
Liguori, Alphonsus. *Glories of Mary.* New York: P. J. Kenedy, 1952.
Maritain, Jacques, and Raïssa Maritain. *Prayer and Intelligence.* Translated by Algar Thorold. New York: Sheed and Ward, 1943.
Marmion, Columba. *Sponsa Verbi.* Paris: Lethielleux, 1923.
Martin, Felipe. *Santa Teresa de Jesús y la Orden de predicadores.* Avila, 1909.
Mechtild of Hackeborn. *The Book of Gostlye Grace of Mechtild of Hackeborn.* Edited by Theresa A. Halligan. Toronto: Pontifical Institute of Medieval Studies, 1979. Microfiche.
———. *Liber specialis gratiae.* In *Revelationes Gertrudianae ac Mechtildianae,* vol. 2. Edited by monks of Solesmes [Louis Paquelin]. Poitiers-Paris, 1877.
———. *Le Livre de la Grâce Spéciale: Révélations de Sainte Mechtilde Vierge de l'Ordre de St. Benoit.* Translated by nuns of Wisques, from the Latin edition of Solesmes. Tours: Mame, 1928.
Mechtild of Magdeburg. *Das fliessende Licht der Gottheit.* Translated and edited by Margot Schmidt. Einsiedeln: Benziger, 1956.
———. *Offenbarungen der Schwester Mechthild von Magdeburg oder Das Fliessende Licht der Gottheit.* Edited by P. Gall Morel. Darmstadt: Wissenschaftliche Buchgesellschaft, 1963.
———. *The Revelations of Mechtild of Magdeburg (1210–1297), or The Flowing Light of the Godhead.* Translated by Lucy Menzies. New York: Longmans, Green, 1953.
Miller, William D. *Dorothy Day: A Biography.* San Francisco: Harper and Row, 1982.
Moell, C. J. "Devotion to the Sacred Heart." *NCE* 12:818–20.
Montalembert, Charles, comte de. *The Monks of the West.* Translated by Aurelien de Courson. 6 vols. London: Longmans, Green, 1896.
Neumann, Hans. "Mechthild von Magdeburg." In *Verfasserlexikon,* edited by Wolfgang Stammler, 6:260–70. Berlin, 1987.
New Catholic Encyclopedia. New York: McGraw-Hill, 1967.
Newman, Barbara. *Sister of Wisdom: St. Hildegarde's Theology of the Feminine.* Berkeley and Los Angeles: University of California Press, 1987.
Oehl, Wilhelm. *Mechtild von Magdeburg, Deutsche Mystiker.* 2 vols. Munich: Kosel, n.d.
O'Mahony, Christopher, ed. and trans. *St. Thérèse of Lisieux by Those Who Knew Her.* 1975. Reprint. Dublin: Veritas Publications, 1989.
Ong, Walter J. "Wit and Mystery: A Revaluation in Medieval Latin Hymnody." *Speculum* 22 (July 1947): 310–41.

Pastor, Ludwig von. *The History of the Popes*, translated by E. F. Peeler. St. Louis: Herder, 1949.
Patrologia cursus completus: series latina. Edited by J.-P. Migne. 221 vols. Paris, 1841–64.
Paulinus of Nola. *Letters of St. Paulinus of Nola.* Translated and annotated by P. G. Walsh. 2 vols. Ancient Christian Writers 35. Westminster, Md.: Newman, 1966.
Pius XII. "Haurietis Aquas." In *The Papal Encyclicals*, edited by Claudia Carlen, 4:291–313. Consortium Books. Wilmington, N.C.: McGrath, 1981.
Pourrat, Pierre. *Christian Spirituality in the Middle Ages.* Translated by S. P. Jacques. Westminster, Md.: Newman, 1953.
Power, Eileen. *Medieval People.* New York: Barnes and Noble, 1963.
Preger, Wilhelm. *Geschichte der deutschen Mystik.* 3 vols. Leipzig, 1874–93.
Putnam, George Haven. *Books and Their Makers during the Middle Ages.* 2 vols. 1896–97. Reprint. New York: Hilary House, 1962.
Raby, Frederick. *History of Secular Latin Poetry in the Middle Ages.* 2 vols. Oxford: Clarendon Press, 1934.
Rahner, Hugo. "The Beginnings of the Devotion in Patristic Times." In *Heart of the Savior: A Symposium.* Edited by Josef Stierli, translated by Paul Andrews. New York: Herder and Herder, 1958.
———. *Man at Play.* Translated by Brian Battershaw and Edward Quinn. New York: Herder and Herder, 1967.
Raymond of Capua. *Life of Catherine of Siena.* Translated by Conleth Kearns. Wilmington: Michael Glazier, 1980.
Richstaetter, Carl. *Christus Frömmigkeit in ihrer historischer Entfaltung.* Cologne: Bächem, 1949.
Rigby, Marjorie. Review of *The Booke of Gostlye Grace of Mechtild of Hackeborn*, edited by Theresa A. Halligan. *Review of English Studies*, n.s., 33 (1982): 194–95.
Rose, Martial, ed. *The Wakefield Mystery Plays.* Garden City: Doubleday, 1962.
Rudolf of Fulda. "The Life of St. Lioba." In *The Anglo-Saxon Missionaries in Germany*, by C. H. Talbot, 205–26. New York: Sheed and Ward, 1954.
Ruusbroec, John. *The Spiritual Espousals and Other Works.* Introduction and translation by James A. Wiseman. Classics of Western Spirituality. New York: Paulist Press, 1985.
Sarton, George. *Introduction to the History of Science.* 3 vols. Baltimore: Williams and Wilkins, 1931.
Sayers, Dorothy. *The Divine Comedy: Purgatory.* Baltimore: Penguin, 1955.
Schroeder-Sheker, Therese. "The Alchemical Harp of Mechtild of Hackeborn." *Vox Benedictina* 6 (January 1989): 49–55.
Sharp, Carola. "The Faith of Mechtild von Magdeburg and Her Life Under Cistercian Rule." Paper presented at the International Conference on Medieval Studies, Western Michigan University, Kalamazoo, Michigan, 11 May 1987.
Siwek, P. "Stigmatization." *NCE* 13:711–13.
Specht, Franz Anton. *Geschichte des Unterrichtswesen in Deutschland von den ältesten Zeiten bis zur Mitte des XIII Jahrhunderts.* Stuttgart, 1885.
Stagel, Elsbet. *Das Leben der Schwestern zu Töss.* Edited by Ferdinand Vetter. Deutsche Texte des Mittelalters 6. Berlin: Weidmannsche Buchandlung, 1906.

Stierli, Josef. *Heart of the Saviour: A Symposium on Devotion to the Sacred Heart*. Translated by Paul Andrews. New York: Herder and Herder, 1958.

Strauch, Philipp. "Kleine Beiträge zu Geschichte der Deutschen Mystik." *Zeitschrift für deutsches Altertum und deutsche Literatur* (Berlin) 27 (1883): 368–81.

———. "Mechthild von Hackeborn." *Allgemeine deutsche biographie* (Berlin) 21 (1970): 156.

[Suso, Henry]. *The Exemplar*. Edited by Nicholas Heller. Translated by M. Ann Edward. 2 vols. Dubuque: Priory Press, 1962.

Teresa of Jesus. *Complete Works*. Translated and edited by E. Allison Peers. 3 vols. New York: Sheed and Ward, 1946.

———. *The Letters of Saint Teresa of Jesus*. Translated and edited by E. Allison Peers. 2 vols. London: Burns, Oates, and Washbourne, 1951.

Thérèse of Lisieux. *Story of a Soul*. Translated by John Clarke. 2d ed. Washington, D.C.: ICS (Institute of Carmelite Studies) Publications, 1976.

Underhill, Evelyn. "Medieval Mysticism." In *Cambridge Medieval History*, 7:777–812. Cambridge: Cambridge University Press, 1932.

———. *Mysticism: A Study in the Nature and Development of Man's Spiritual Consciousness*. New York: New American Library, 1955.

Undset, Sigrid. *Catherine of Siena*. Translated by Kate Austin-Lund. New York: Sheed and Ward, 1954.

Vacandard, E. *Vie de Saint Bernard*. 2 vols. Paris, 1927.

Varagine, Jacobus de. *Legenda Aurea*. Edited by Th. Graesse. Vratislavia: Koerner, 1890.

Vernet, Felix. "Gertrude la Grande." *DTC* 6:1332–38.

———. *La Spiritualité Médiévale*. Bibliothèque Catholique des sciences religieuses 21. Paris: Bloud et Gay, 1929.

Vicaire, M. H. *St. Dominic and His Times*. Translated by Kathleen Pond. New York: McGraw-Hill, 1964.

Vossler, Karl. *Medieval Culture*, translated by William Cranston Lawton. 2 vols. New York: Harcourt, Brace, 1929.

Watson, Arthur. *The Early Iconography of the Tree of Jesse*. London: Oxford University Press, Humphrey Milford, 1934.

———. "The *Speculum Virginum* with Special Reference to the Tree of Jesse." *Speculum* 3 (1928): 445–69.

White, Terence Hanbury. *Bestiary*. New York: Putnam, 1954.

William of St. Thierry et al. *Vitae Sancti Bernardi Abbatis. Vita prima*. PL 185: 225–454.

Wyclif, John. *Select English Works of Wyclif*. Edited by T. Arnold. 3 vols. Oxford, 1869–71.

Index

Adolf of Nassau, 3–4, 16, 69
Albert of Austria, 69
Albert of Brunswick: attack on Helfta, 1, 4
Albert the Great, 7, 15

Baldwin of Magdeburg (brother of Mechtild), and Dominican Order, 15; letter of Mechtild to, 22
Benedictines, 113, 148–49
Bernard of Clairvaux: quoted, viii, 12, 114–32 passim; influence on Gertrude of Helfta, 113
Burchard, Count of Mansfeld, 1, 2
Burchard IV (father of Abbess Luitgard), 4–5

Carmelite Order, 112
Carthusians, 55
Catherine of Siena, 67, 118, 122, 126, 130, 141
Catherine of Watzdorff (abbess), 5, 112
Christ: sharing merits of, 53, 54; accessibility of, 110, 140. *See also* Face of Christ; Sacred Heart
Cistercians: General Chapter ruling forbidding new foundations, 6
Common life, 98
Cunegund of Halberstadt: transfer to Rodarsdorf, 2; first superior, 2, 13, 112

Dali, Salvador: "The Madonna of Port Lligat," 125
Dante, 40; and model for Matelda, 56–61

Death: contacts with the dead, 23–24, 32; at Helfta, 23–25
Debts, 106
Divine indwelling, 41–42
Divine Office. *See* Music
Dominic, 15, 43, 139
Dominican fathers and brothers, 15, 19, 55, 96, 102, 112

Eckhardt, Meister, 97
E. de Orlamunde: consecrated before birth, 45
Education of women in Germany, 9, 10
Eisleben, 4–5
Elisabeth of Schönau, 41
Elisabeth of Schwartzburg, 1–2
Esther, 115
Eucharist: frequent reception at Helfta, 117; opposition to by a confessor, 118; Gertrude's fervor, 119
Exercises, 106

Face of Christ: veneration of by Mechtild of Hackeborn, 30; by Gertrude of Helfta, 126–27
Fish: symbol of union with divinity, 135, 141
Florentina (nun who joined Luther), 5
Franciscans, 19, 96
Francis of Assisi, 114, 128, 133–34
Frederick II, 3

Gebhardt of Mansfeld, 3, 106
Gertrude of Hackeborn, virtues, 11–12, (abbess), 11–13; Hedersleben

169

Gertrude of Hackeborn (continued) foundation, 12; erroneous identification with Gertrude the Great of Helfta, 12, 69; illness and death, 13, 109; reward for care of community, 13; in writings of Gertrude of Helfta, 45; apparition of, 49; consultation with Gertrude of Helfta, 102

Gertrude of Helfta, viii, 1, 7, 10, 13; relationship with Mechtild of Hackeborn, 28, 36, 38–39, 41–42, 61, 127; compiler of *Liber specialis gratiae*, 44–61; origins, 62; joins community, 62; virtues and gifts, 62–63, 66, 69, 100–101, 104, 127; prayer life, 66–67, 105–6; *Exercitia*, 71–75; *Legatus divinae pietatis*, 75–80; style, 81–85 (*see also* Similitude); veneration of the Sacred Heart, 133–38, 141; and common life, 98–99; correction of faults in others, 103–5; death, 144–50

Great Interregnum, 3
Gregory the Great, 12, 108, 132

Hedersleben, 12
Helfta landscape, 2–3, 62
Henry Suso, 128
Henry of Halle, 15, 17, 20
Herman of Minden, 6–7
Herrad (abbess of Hohenbourg), 9
Hildegard of Bingen, 9
Hopkins, Gerard Manley, 77
Hrosvitha of Gandersheim, 9

Interdict, 4, 93, 119
Interregnum at Helfta, 4
Irmingard of Schwartzburg (widow of Gebhardt), 3

John the Evangelist, 145, 148
Jutta of Halberstadt (fourth abbess), 4

Kulturkampf, 5–6

Lambertini, Cardinal Prosper (Benedict XIV), 70
Lioba (abbess of Bischofsheim), 9
Louis and Albert of Hackeborn (brothers of Abbess Gertrude), 2, 12

Luitgard of Mansfeld (sixth abbess), 4
Luther, 5

Manual work: at Helfta, 7; praised in *Liber*, 7; in similitudes, 93; in *Exercises*, 106
Margaret Mary Alacoque, 133, 149–50
May Laws, 5–6
Mechtild of Hackeborn, 7, 8, 11, 13; origins, 26; joins community at Rodarsdorf, 26; virtues and gifts, 27, 28, 29; death, 28; common life, 29; counselor, 32; illness, mental anguish, temptations, 42–43; *Liber specialis gratiae*, 44–61; themes and style, 46–55 (*see also* Gertrude of Helfta: style and Similitude); *The Booke of Gostlye Grace*, 55; as model for Dante's Matelda, 56–61; relationship with Gertrude of Helfta, 71, 77, 89, 90, 94, 96–97, 109; veneration of the Sacred Heart, 133–38, 141
Mechtild of Magdeburg: origins, 13–14; arrival at Helfta, 14; writings, *Das fliessende Licht der Gottheit* (The Flowing Light of the Godhead), 14; encouragement by Henry of Halle, 17, 20; style, 20–22; letter to her brother Baldwin, 22
Music: importance at Helfta, 7–8; Great Psalter, recitation of, 8; Divine Office, 8, 34–35; Mechtild of Hackeborn, official chantress, 27; reparation for obscene songs, 36; musical images in *Exercises*, 73; Gertrude, second chantress, 93; alleluia in Christmas invitatory, 116
Mystical Body: the Church as, 121; as female figure, 121–22; as male figure, 122–24
Mystics: language of, 80, 83, 95–96

New Helfta, 5

Origen, 40–41
Otto (provost), 12

Peasants' Revolt, 75

Ribera, Francisco, 112
Ring: symbol of spiritual espousal, 111, 140–41, 147
Rodarsdorf, 2, 12, 26
Rudolph (emperor of the Romans), 69
Rupert, Archbishop of Mansfeld, 3

Sacred Heart, devotion: theology in patristic thought, 131; John the Evangelist as transitional figure, 131–32; Bernard's commentary on *Song of Songs*, 132; aspects of veneration, 132, 133; influence on Gertrude of Helfta, Mechtild of Hackeborn, and Mechtild of Magdeburg, 133–36; images of the Sacred Heart, 136, 138–40, 143
Samson, 40
Similitude: definition, 89; plants and animals, 89; parents and children, 90; family life, 90–91; friends, 91–92; professions, arts, and crafts, 92–93; singers and musical instruments, 93; household tasks, 93; gold, silver, and jewels, 94; perfumes and spices, 94
Solomon, 40

Song of Songs, 114, 132
Sophia of Mansfeld (third abbess), 3–4, 69
Sophia of Stolberg (abbess), 5
Stigmata, 63, 67
Symbolism, 46–48

Teresa of Avila, 39, 67, 100, 111–12, 121, 129–30
Theodore of Apoldia: approbation of writings of Gertrude of Helfta, 96
Thérèse of Lisieux, 39, 128, 150
Thomas Aquinas, 7, 15
Trajan, 40
Transverberation (the piercing of the heart): of Gertrude of Helfta, 68–69; of Teresa of Avila, 68–69; of Mechtild of Hackeborn, 135
Tree, symbolic, 46–47, 85–88
Trud Helfta, 5
Tutivillus (demon), 157–58 (n. 2)

Visitors: "tumult of," viii; "of great authority," 14
Vulrad, Archbishop of Halberstadt, 3

Wyclif, 52